PSYCHOLOGICAL CLASSIFICATION
of the
ADULT MALE
PRISON INMATE

SUNY Series in
New Direction in Crime and Justice Studies
Austin Turk, Editor

PSYCHOLOGICAL CLASSIFICATION
of the
ADULT MALE
PRISON INMATE

Patricia Van Voorhis

STATE UNIVERSITY
OF NEW YORK PRESS

Authors and/or publishers of work quoted or reprinted in this book have extended permission to do so. These works are as follows: Portion from "Current Explanations of Offender Behavior," by Marguerite Q. Warren and Michael J. Hindelang, reprinted from *Psychology and Criminal Justice*, edited by Hans Toch, with permission from Holt, Rinehart and Winston, Inc., ©1979. All rights reserved. Portion from "Prison Classification: The management and Psychological Perspectives" by Doris MacKenzie reprinted from *The American Prison: Issues in Research and Policy*, edited by Lynne Goodstein and Doris MacKenzie, with permission from Plenum Press and Doris MacKenzie, ©1989. All rights reserved. Figures reprinted from "Development in the Classification Process" by Robert Levinson, in *Criminal Justice and Behavior*, 1988, 15(1): 24–38, with permission from Sage Publications, Inc. Description of Megargee MMPI types from "MMPI-Based Criminal Classification System" by Lynn Zager, in *Criminal Justice and Behavior*, 1988, 15(1): 39–57, with permission from Sage Publications, Inc. Description of Interview I-level types and subtypes from "The Interpersonal Maturity Level Classification System: by Phillip Harris, in *Criminal Justice and Behavior*, 1988, 15(1): 58–77, with permission from Sage Publications, Inc. Description of Jesness Inventory types from "The Jesness Inventory Classification System: by Carl Jesness, in *Criminal Justice and Behavior*, 1988, 15(1): 78–91, with permission from Sage Publications, Inc. Portion from "Personality and Crime: Knowledge Destruction and Construction in Criminology" by Donald Andrews and J. S. Wormith in *Justice Quarterly*, 1989, 6(3): 289–310, with permission from *Justice Quarterly* and Donald Andrews. Portion from "Prediction and Classification in Criminal Justice Decision Making" by Don M. Gottfredson reprinted from *Prediction and Classification: Criminal Justice Decision Making*, edited by Don M. Gottfredson and Michael Tonry, with permission from The University of Chicago Press, ©1987. All rights reserved.

Published by
State University of New York Press, Albany

© 1994 State University of New York

All rights reserved

Printed in the United States of America

No part of this book may be used or reproduced
in any manner whatsoever without written permission
except in the case of brief quotations embodied in
critical articles and reviews.
For information, address the State University of New York Press,
State University Plaza, Albany, NY 12246

Production by Bernadine Dawes • Marketing by Bernadette LaManna

Library of Congress Cataloging-in-Publication Data

Van Voorhis, Patricia
     Psychological classification of the adult male prison inmate /
Patricia Van Voorhis.
     p.   cm. — (SUNY series in new dirrections in crime and justice studies)
     Includes bibliographical references (p.   ) and index.
     ISBN 0-7914-1793-X (hard : acid-free paper) : — ISBN
0-7914-1794-8 (pbk. : acid-free paper)
     1. Prisoners—Classification. 2. Prisoners—Psychology.
I. Title. II. Series
HV8763.v35   1993
356'.6—dc20   93-13292
                                                                    CIP

This book is dedicated to

Marguerite Q. Warren

TABLE OF CONTENTS

LIST OF FIGURES AND TABLES

ACKNOWLEDGMENTS

The author wishes to acknowledge numerous people for the help and expertise they offered to this research. They include on-site interviewers and research analysts Kathy Heffner-Grinley, John Simurdak, and Bruce Erdmann; University of Cincinnati graduate assistants Faith Lutze, Darlene Porter, Rene Kopache, Dorothy Crusham, and Slavitza Begovic; data consultants Nancy Wilson, Edwin Megargee, Marge Reitsma-Street, Stuart Alcock, Phil Harris, and Ted Palmer; copy consultant Karen Feinberg; and statistical consultants Zaid Ansari and Neil Ritchey.

My colleagues at the University of Cincinnati were helpful in the numerous ways that reflect the many hats worn by academics. Their assistance ranged from editorial comments (Francis Cullen) to assistance through the many bureaucratic nightmares of paying staff, setting up budgets, and scheduling conferences (Edward Latessa) to the constructive comments we exchange in passing as we discuss our work (Zaid Ansari, Joanne Belknap, Sandra Evans Skovron, James Frank, Robert Langworthy, Lawrence Travis, and John Wooldredge).

This endeavor was supported by a grant (#85-IJ-CX-0063) from the National Institute of Justice, and the findings reported in this book are essentially those for the NIJ-funded project.* A special note of appreciation is due Dr. Richard Laymon, Program Manager at NIJ, for his constructive assistance in monitoring this research and maintaining an exciting research agenda for the Program on Offender Classification and Prediction of Criminal

---

* This work is based on the findings and final report of a project by the same title, funded by the National Institute of Justice (#85-IJ-CX-0063). The content of this manuscript is attributable to the author, however, and does not necessarily reflect the official position or policies of the United States Department of Justice.

Behavior. The Federal Bureau of Prisons furnished a setting for conducting the research and funded a portion of the pilot study. We were assisted in our efforts by many staff members of the Bureau of Prisons, but I would especially like to thank Dr. John Ramer, our congenial and invaluable liaison between the project and the Federal Bureau of Prisons. I would also like to thank other members of the Psych ology department at the Federal Penitentiary in Terre Haute, Dr. William Elliot and Dr. Cindy Broshears. Other FBOP staff members who assisted us include FBOP Office of Research staff members Peter Nacci and Harriet Lebowitz and Terre Haute staff members Rick Veach, Gordon Pleus, Steve Heffner-Grinley, and the case managers, counselors, and work supervisors who assisted in completing the inmate assessment forms.

I would like to thank the first source of support for this project. The Graduate School at Indiana State University funded a pilot study that provided a valuable foundation for what ultimately became a large project.

Clearly, this project benefitted from the genius of the social scientists who created or contributed to the classification systems tested in this study. Moreover, these scholars were extremely generous with the time and consultation they offered to us. In this regard, I want to thank Stuart Alcock, Phil Harris, Carl Jesness, Edwin Megargee, Ted Palmer, Herbert Quay, Marge Reitsma-Street, Estelle Turner, Rita Warren, and Nancy Wilson.

Most notably, the overwhelming majority of the inmates who were asked to participate in this study consented; they willingly gave hours of their time to interviews, tests, and surveys. We were not able to offer compensation for their services, but could only suggest that their participation might improve our understanding of prison inmates and correctional classification. Their cooperation was both impressive and invaluable to the successful completion of this project.

A special thanks is also due to editor Rosalie Robertson at SUNY Press for her support during the initial phases of publication and to production editor Bernadine Dawes, who saw this manuscript through the myriad details of production, and indexer, Sandra Topping.

CHAPTER 1
INTRODUCTION

The failures of a century of correctional reforms, according to David Rothman (1980), occurred at the juxtaposition of "conscience and convenience." An abundance of new ideas and programs, supported enthusiastically by benevolent motives and moral ideologies ("conscience"), became failures as they deteriorated into political, economic, and administrative "conveniences."

Rothman spares neither the reformers nor the practitioners, but his admonitions to the reformers are particularly sobering. Their mistakes included a reluctance to question the adequacy of their designs and to modify them where warranted, as well as a failure to accommodate the social and political context of their changes. For these innovators, enthusiasm replaced rational planning and self-examination. As a result, we know remarkably little about the history and assumptions of the major practices and policies of social control and even less about why they failed.

Over a relatively short period spanning approximately thirty years, correctional classification is an important example of a practice that has been endorsed zealously and rapidly. At the same time, classification practices show serious signs of deteriorating into the disorganization and confusion that Rothman included under the rubric of "convenience."

It would indeed appear that correctional classification has been received enthusiastically. The research presented in this book, for example, was conducted largely in response to a growing demand for sound methods for classifying prison populations. At the outset, the rationale for this study was a recognition both of rapid increases in the size of these populations and of shifts in their composition (Bureau of Justice Statistics 1985). Adult male inmate populations seemed to have become more violent (Irwin 1980), and the increasing proportion of mentally ill or seriously troubled inmates was causing concern for policy makers and practitioners alike (Cohen 1985; McCarthy 1985). In addition, important court decisions had mandated improved, uniformly applied systems of classification as a means of reducing prison problems (e.g., Laaman v. Helgemoe, 347 F. Supp. 269, 275 [1977]; Palmagiano v. Garrahy, 443 F. Supp. 956 [1977]; Pugh v. Locke, 406 F. Supp. 318 [1977]).

At the same time, several classification systems had been developed for managing correctional facilities. Development was proceeding in two directions: (1) toward the construction of actuarial risk-assessment measures, which grouped inmates into categories relevant to security considerations (see Austin 1983; Kane and Saylor 1983; NIC 1982), and (2) toward the development of a second level of classification, psychological systems, which was advocated as a means of "internal classification." As the term implies, *internal classification* acts as a classification system within a classification system. The term includes a variety of systems that classify a correctional population which has already been assigned to a facility on the basis of security considerations (Levinson 1982, 1988).[1] As will be discussed shortly, internal classification systems (at least those that relied upon psychological characteristics) also had implications for treatment, adjustment to prison life, and etiological perspectives on crime causation (Levinson 1988; MacKenzie 1989; Megargee & Bohn 1979; Van Voorhis 1988).[2]

Acceptance of the internal classification systems became more obvious as several state systems began to adopt the practice of classifying inmates according to psychological criteria.[3] Meanwhile, the classification and prediction literature continued to proliferate.[4] Most importantly, empirical evaluations of the effect of internal classification in reducing dysfunctional inmate behaviors had shown favorable results (see Austin, Holien, Chan, and Baird, 1989; Bohn 1979, 1980; Levinson 1988; Quay 1984).

Simply put, the technology of correctional classification has seen greater and more rapid development in the last fifteen years than it has throughout the entire history of corrections. Indeed, the correctional historian will note that the first significant development beyond the notion of separating populations on the basis of age and gender occurred only during the last half of the nineteenth century, with the advent of the reformatory movement. At that time, progressive reformers put forward the notion of graduated release as a supplement to indeterminant sentencing and a treatment-based approach to corrections. The idea of matching inmates to specific institutions that reflected their security needs came even later. Finally, serious consideration of psychological needs and characteristics awaited the advent of the medical model during the 1930s (Clear and Cole 1986). These psychological tests, however, were for purposes of individual diagnosis, and were not generally administered in any systematic manner. The technology for a psychologically based classification system began in the late 1940s and 1950s for juveniles and during the mid-1970s for adults (Megargee and Bohn 1979), with most of the development occurring since 1978. Risk-assessment systems, for actuarial classification of inmates according to risk, developed during the 1970s (Gottfredson and Tonry 1987).

Notwithstanding these recent and rapid advances, concern for the destructive effects of "convenience" is clearly warranted. Despite obvious reasons for optimism, other sectors of correctional practice have virtually ignored the emerging technology of classification and differential treatment (Gendreau and Ross,1987; Palmer 1992; Van Voorhis 1987), thereby continuing the archaic practice of treating offenders as if they were all alike (Warren 1971, 1976). In addition, a growing body of evidence suggests that those agencies that *have* implemented classification may have done so carelessly. Too frequently, implementation consists of the premature adoption of one system, selected (quite understandably) on the basis of cost and ease of administration. Insufficient attention to matters of reliability and validity occurs as a matter of course. Some systems have not been matched appropriately to the organizational context for their use. Moreover, the practice of "norming" systems to specific populations, a commonplace practice in mental health and education, has been virtually ignored in corrections (Wright, Clear, and Dickson 1984). Finally, even systems that were selected for their efficiency appear to be experiencing unexpected problems in the form of staff error and noncompliance (Austin 1986; MacKenzie 1989; Schneider 1990). Thus, if these systems are examined closely, signs of "convenience" abound.

In response to these concerns, the research presented in this book was designed to support continued development of classification technology through a comparative assessment of the viability of five psychological systems for classifying offender populations: (1) Megargee's Minnesota Multiphasic Personality Inventory (MMPI)-Based Criminal Classification System (Megargee and Bohn 1979), (2) Interpersonal Maturity Level (I-level) (Sullivan, Grant, and Grant

1957; Warren and Staff of the Community Treatment Project 1966 [hereafter Warren et al.]); (3) Quay's Adult Internal Management System (AIMS) (Quay 1983, 1984); (4) the Jesness Inventory Classification System (Jesness and Wedge 1983); and (5) Conceptual Level (CL) (Hunt, Butler, Noy, and Rosser 1978). For now, it is sufficient to say that each of these systems is designed to classify correctional populations into either personality-based or developmental subgroups or both. The systems are described in greater detail below and in chapter 2.

This study endeavored to address certain shortcomings in the developing technology of correctional classification—specifically, that extant research has devoted insufficient attention to issues of reliability, validity, and utility. Indeed, three of the five systems— I-level, the Jesness Inventory, and Conceptual Level—were developed for juvenile correctional systems and have not been tested sufficiently with adult offenders. In addition, existing research has been confined to the refinement of single systems, and has neglected to make any comparison among similar systems. Lacking such a comparison, prior research has not established (*a*) which systems or combination of systems could be used most effectively with adult populations, (*b*) what procedures (e.g., interview, paper-and-pencil test, staff assessment, or combination) would assure maximum efficiency without compromising psychometric precision, (*c*) how the systems compared with one another or what their commonalities and differences could tell us about the specific systems and about general classification issues pertinent to this population, or (*d*) how the systems help us to better understand the prison experience. Questions remain regarding the number of personality or behavioral types that such a system should identify (Megargee and Bohn 1979), the specific dimensions that should be represented by each personality type, and the reliability and the predictive and construct validity of each system.

RESEARCH QUESTIONS

Expanding on the questions posed above, the empirical issues addressed by this study include both a series of tests of the single classification systems and a comparison among systems. The research questions directed to each system are as follows:

1. *Does the psychological typology divide the inmate population into a practical number of subgroups? Is there adequate variability in the distribution of inmates across these subgroups?* Presumably, correctional

practitioners must strike a balance between cost and the amount of descriptive information available for managing inmates. On the one hand, it makes little sense to divide a population into two groups. Although such a division is likely to be ideal cost-wise, the distinction is too crude to be useful. On the other hand, classifying a population into twenty groups certainly would allow for a precise delineation of differences between individuals. The cost, however, could be prohibitive because few facilities could offer so many unique living and programmatic options. A system with the greatest heuristic and pragmatic value lies somewhere between these extremes.

2. *Do the diagnostic categories identified by each system separate inmates into psychological types that predict meaningful behavioral distinctions?* Do they correlate with dysfunctional behaviors and adverse prison experiences?

3. *Is the classification system complete or able to classify all inmates, or does it result in a large proportion of inmates who do not fit into any of the diagnostic categories?*

4. *Are the psychometric qualities of the systems adequate?* Will results across raters be consistent?[5] Do the diagnostic categories identified by one system correlate with the same or similar categories identified by another system, thereby offering evidence of the construct validity of the system?[6]

5. *Can the types be described more adequately?* Do correlations between the system and other individual characteristics, as well as types identified by other systems, suggest ways in which the types can be redefined to reflect adult offenders more meaningfully?[7]

6. *Do the answers to the above questions hold true across types of institutions?* Are results for penitentiary inmates similar to those observed for minimum-security prison camp inmates?

The remaining questions address the comparison among the classification systems:

7. *How do the systems compare in efficiency, cost of administration, and psychometric precision?*

8. *Does the comparison of systems show instances in which a specific psychological type is identified more adequately by one system than by another?* Similarly, do any "unclassified" inmates represent an important psychological, personality, or behavioral dimension that is not identified by one system but appears to be identified by another?

9. *What does the comparison teach us about general classification and assessment issues for this population?* What are the most important

classification issues for this population? How many distinctive inmate types are needed to classify adult male inmates efficiently? What are they? What methods (e.g., interview, paper-and-pencil tests, or staff observation) will achieve the most satisfactory results?

These latter questions are answered in the course of reporting results of empirical tests, summarizing and comparing those results, and integrating the research findings with the research experience.[8] The empirical approach suggested by the questions posed above is an essential rejoinder to the naive dictates of convenience. Indeed, the crucial unanswered questions regarding the viability of correctional classification—the questions that appear as we witness the shift of classification into the realm of "convenience"—are primarily rational-empirical ones. For some readers, however, the chapters that follow may seem too close to the data or too empirical. In response, we offer numerous attempts to step back, summarize, and contextualize our many findings. Finally, in the concluding chapter and the discussions interspersed throughout the book, we endeavor to identify larger policy and theoretical implications in our research findings. Indeed, the study has much to say about how inmates do time.

Implications

Notwithstanding the empirical nature of this research, important policy, programmatic, and theoretical implications emerge from the questions posed above. All three types of implications are examined most effectively from the perspective of a typology. From this paradigm, all of the psychological systems serve not only the pragmatic purpose of classifying correctional inmates but also the broader function of dividing criminal populations into subcategories of individuals with relatively similar personality, behavioral, or developmental attributes. The resulting "types" furnish a new tool (perhaps even a new paradigm) for understanding these offenders in a richer sense than is often the case at present (MacKenzie 1989). In particular, the relationship between the classification types and various policies, programs, and theories becomes clearer, because in many instances our policies and our theories are differentially effective or applicable. In the paradigm of a typology, then, reasoning must shift from asking whether a given policy will be effective overall to asking for which type of inmate it will be effective.

Unquestionably, this paradigm shift has not been incorporated into the correctional policy debates of the last two decades. Though these debates have been vigorous, most have focused simplistically on the relative merits of punishment versus treatment (see Cullen and Gilbert 1982). Competing policies are broad. Treatment especially is conceptualized—and often applied—in a vague, unqualified way. The policy debate seldom centers on unique types of treatment unless a specific model is thrust into prominence in the media, where image and style surpass the importance of accumulated wisdom.[9]

It would seem even more unusual for policy makers and practitioners to plan for differences among offenders. Larger policy debates have pitted treatment against punishment, fueled by research suggesting that "treatment" has not worked. But other scholars and policy makers, including some who have criticized treatment in its broadest sense, maintain that some types of treatment indeed have been effective (Palmer 1992). More important, some types of treatment have been noted to be particularly effective when they target specific types of offenders (Andrews, Zinger, Hoge, Bonta, Gendreau, & Cullen 1990; Gendreau and Ross 1987; Palmer 1992; Warren 1983). These messages are typically ignored in policymaking and administrative circles.

Even though most researchers of classification confine applications to correctional treatment and management, the typologies have the clear potential to further our understanding of the prison experience and to contribute to the prisonization literature. In this paradigm, prison inmates make differential adjustments to prison and formulate differential perceptions of prison life. This message is not new. In his book *Living in Prison*, for example, Hans Toch (1977) shows convincingly that prisons affect inmates in dramatically individual ways. Toch's work focuses primarily on the different needs of prison inmates (e.g., safety, support, freedom, activity, privacy, structure, emotional feedback, and social stimulation).

One might argue that Sykes's (1958) *Society of Captives* and Irwin's (1980) *Prisons in Turmoil* also provide a differential approach because the authors identify different roles among prison inmates. Yet a psychological paradigm that qualifies those needs and roles according to personality, behavioral, and developmental factors can only enrich our understanding of prison adaptations. As the following chapters identify additional compelling differences among prison inmates, we contribute to a growing body of knowledge that continues to question the wisdom of undifferentiated approaches to correctional populations, whether they occur in policy, administrative, programmatic, or scholarly discourses.

Finally, psychological typologies offer crucial, though often overlooked, keys to the development of theoretical and empirical explanations of crime (MacKenzie 1989). In this vein, many theories of crime also ought to be viewed as applicable to some types of offenders and not to others (Warren and Hindelang 1979). Alternatively, typologies ought to suggest revisions and specifications to some theories (Clinard & Quinney 1986).

In a review of several sociological and psychological theories, Warren and Hindelang (1979) discuss the notion of matching theories to certain psychologically defined types of offenders (see also Warren 1976). They reach the following conclusions:

> It is important to emphasize that most etiological theories of criminal behavior are neither "right" nor "wrong." That is, many perspectives seem to explain the origins of illegal activities for some (but not all) offenders. Furthermore, there is nothing inherently incompatible between sociological and psychological theories; theories falling into each group may be useful for explaining the behavior patterns of some individuals. If our understanding of the complex processes which lead to law violation is to progress, it seems critical that we consider the likelihood that a range of theoretical approaches—sociological, psychological, and others—is required to explain the range of law-violating behavior. It seems reasonable, also, that future research on delinquents and criminals proceed, not so much with an eye toward falsifying various perspectives, but more toward ascertaining which perspectives seem best-suited to explain which patterns of illegal activities. (Warren and Hindelang 1979, 181)

In another sense, the classification systems address directly the causes and etiology of criminal behavior because the descriptions of types often link psychological factors to the dynamics of offending behavior (MacKenzie 1989). Yet, in recent decades, few studies have used classification models as measures of personality, developmental, or behavioral contributors to models of crime causation. In fact, although these inquires would appear to be inherently sensible, criminology has ignored, in a broader sense, the role of individual factors in formulating theoretical and empirical explanations of crime (Andrews and Wormith 1989).

Simply put, although the current study was conducted with applied, practical questions pertinent to the treatment and management of correctional populations, the broader implications for our understanding of crime etiology and prisonization are important benefits of improving the technology of psychological classification. As MacKenzie observes:

> The emphasis on rehabilitation seems important to most of us. However, the most important issue, and the reason we cannot drop the development of the psychological models, is that this perspective is directed to understanding criminal behavior and the etiology of such behavior. If we drop our interest in understanding and theory, where will we be 10 or 20 years from now? An even greater fear is that our work on theoretical issues will become separate from the prison environment. We will benefit most if we continue, as we have until recently, with our close interaction between practice and theory. (MacKenzie 1989, 186)

Because our research focuses on the reliability and the construct and predictive validity of psychological-classification systems, our immediate goal is to strengthen the methodology of differentiation. The results are clearly applicable to treatment and management of prison inmates. In a broader sense, we test the contributions of psychological factors to understanding the prison experience. Less directly, we strengthen the methodological tools for understanding the broader problem of criminal behavior.

RESEARCH SETTING AND DESIGN OVERVIEW

The study was conducted at the Federal Penitentiary and the Federal Prison Camp at Terre Haute, Indiana, between September 1986 and July 1988. The penitentiary is designated Level 4/5[10] on the Federal Bureau of Prisons (FBOP) security continuum; it also could be termed a low-maximum-security or high-medium-security facility. The prison camp is a minimum-security or Level 1 facility in the federal system.

Clearly, the penitentiary poses greater adjustment issues for the inmates incarcerated there. Although it fluctuates between Level 4 and Level 5, it evidenced the features commonly associated with a maximum-security institution. Perimeter security is a large wall with gun towers that were staffed twenty-four hours a day. The architectural style of this facility is described by Allen and Simonsen (1986) as a variation on the original Auburn model, consisting of wings containing tiers of cells (cell blocks). At the time of this study, almost all of the participants were required to live in two-man cells. A policy of controlled movement mandated that inmates could only move at the top of the hour unless they secured a written pass from a staff member.

In contrast, inmates at the Level 1 prison camp were free to move in an unrestricted manner. There were no gun towers or secure perimeters. The building itself was relatively new, and stood in bright contrast to the traditional architecture of the penitentiary.

A total of 190 camp inmates and 179 penitentiary inmates participated. At the time of the study, inmates were assigned to institutions according to security criteria provided by the FBOP Security Designation/Custody Classification System (Kane and Saylor 1983). They were not classified further within the institution according to any system for internal classification, nor did our research provide a means for doing so.

The study employed both a pre-post and a correlational design. At intake, project staff members collected classification/diagnostic information and social, demographic, and criminal-history background data. Inmates were tracked for six months or until their release date if they were required to serve less than six months. Follow-up data consisted of official reports of disciplinary infractions or victimizations, staff assessments of prison adjustment and work performance, and inmate self-report surveys of prison experiences.

DESCRIPTION OF THE FIVE CLASSIFICATION SYSTEMS

Chapter 2 reviews the five psychological classification systems examined in this research. At this point, it is useful to note that these systems can be subdivided into two categories: (1) typologies that are deduced from an underlying theoretical framework, or heuristic typologies, and (2) typologies that are derived from statistical observations of the data, or empirical typologies (Megargee and Bohn 1979). Megargee's MMPI-based taxonomy and Quay's AIMS typology exemplify the latter. Types emerged empirically as the result of factor or cluster analysis (e.g., Quay 1984) or as the product of sorting test results on the basis of MMPI profile configurations common to offenders (Megargee and Bohn 1979). Scales on the AIMS represent scores on personality/behavioral dimensions such as asocial aggressive, manipulative, dependent, neurotic anxious, and situational. The MMPI generates scores on such clinical dimensions as depression, hysteria, masculinity–femininity, paranoia, and psychopathic deviate, which later are organized into ten personality types based on various profile configurations. Both systems involve the administration of paper-and-pencil instruments. AIMS forms are completed by staff members, however, and the MMPI is completed by the inmates. Both may be scored mechanically.

Contrasting heuristic typologies differ from the MMPI or the AIMS both in their analytical procedures and in their underlying assumptions. The Interpersonal Maturity Level (Sullivan, Grant, and Grant 1957; Warren et al. 1966) and the Conceptual Level (Hunt, Butler, Noy, and Rosser 1978) represent measures that have some basis in cognitive developmental theory, ego psychology, cognitive complexity, social cognition, and other such constructs. These systems classify individuals according to the structural organization of their reasoning—how they think rather than what they think. Then they order the cognitive types on a developmental hierarchy ranging from least to most complex.

The two developmental systems share the following assumptions: (*a*) the underlying logic employed at a given stage or level of development appears to be consistent across situations; although the subject (content) of actual choices may differ, the structure of the reasoning is similar; (*b*) the stages described by the respective systems follow an invariant order; (*c*) no stage can be skipped in the course of development; (*d*) each stage is more complex than the preceding one; and (*e*) each stage is based on the preceding one and prepares for the succeeding one. Instead of the checklist or the objective format used by the AIMS and the MMPI systems, these developmental methods typically require the administration of open-ended questions either with paper and pencil or by interview. Because results are obtained by clinical assessments (sometimes assisted by scoring manuals) rather than by computer, the assessment process is sometimes time-consuming (Harris 1988).

In addition to the developmental stages, both the I-level interview method (Warren et al. 1966) and the Jesness Inventory method (Jesness and Wedge 1983) of assessing I-level classify according to personality subtypes within each I-level. The interview method employs a clinical assessment process. The Jesness Inventory Classification System might be described as a combination of the heuristic and the empirical methods; it is an actuarial method of assessing I-level. This is a paper-and-pencil test developed for use with delinquents, but more recent research has produced adult norms (Jesness 1988). The Jesness Inventory yields scores on eleven trait scales (e.g., social maladjustment, manifest aggression) and nine scales that correspond to the I-level subtype scales. Although the designer of this test claims to offer a more efficient and less costly method of assessing I-level (Jesness 1988), it is not clear that the Jesness I-level subtype definitions are entirely comparable to the interview subtype definitions, especially for adults. To name one difference, the Jesness I-level types do not incorporate the I_5 diagnosis, the highest level in the interview system.[11]

Figure 1-1 summarizes the differences among classification systems which have been discussed to this point. The systems differ as to: (*a*) whether they are derived empirically or theoretically and (*b*) whether they diagnose offenders according to personality, developmental criteria, or both. As will be seen in subsequent descriptions of each system (chapter 2), the systems identify somewhat comparable types (see Warren 1971). This overlap and similarity provides a rich opportunity for testing the construct validity of each system and for acquiring a more complete understanding of some of the types.

A final distinction between developmental and personality types is worth noting. Stage-based classification systems characterize individuals according to developmental characteristics, whereas personality-based typologies characterize them according to traits. The portrayal of characteristics in developmental terms implies expectations for changes in the individuals so classified. Measures of traits, although they should not be viewed strictly as static measures, give no indication of the point to which the subject already has progressed or what he or she has yet to experience (i.e., areas of underdevelopment) (Loevinger 1966).

The types identified by each system are described in greater detail in chapter 2. Further information on the administration of each system is offered in chapter 4.

THE ADMINISTRATIVE CONTEXT OF INTERNAL CLASSIFICATION SYSTEM

Internal classification, a fairly recent concept in corrections, is the product of a decision made within the four-tiered scheme illustrated in figure 1-2. According to this model, the first classification decision is predicated on security considerations. This decision is standard procedure for adult male inmates (Clements 1981; Levinson 1982, 1988), who are assigned to maximum-, medium-, or minimum-security facilities shortly after sentencing. This decision is increasingly facilitated by security-based or risk-assessment classification instruments that operationalize "risk" according to strong empirical predictors such as severity of offense, prior record, age at first arrest, drug and alcohol history, prior prison escapes or probation/parole revocations, and history of violent behavior (see

Figure 1-1: Overview of Classification Systems

| | Characteristic of the System | | | |
	Empirical	Theoretical	Developmental	Personality
Megargee MMPI	Yes	No	No	Yes
Quay AIMS	Yes	No	No	Yes
Conceptual Level	No	Yes	Yes	No
I-Level Interview	No	Yes	Yes	Yes
Jesness I-Level	Yes	Yes	Yes	Yes

Figure 1-2: Classification Flow Chart/Continuum

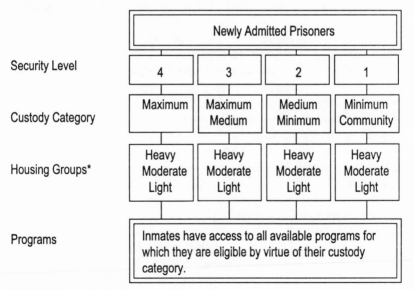

* Point of internal classification
Source: Levinson 1988

Andrews 1982; Bonta and Motiuk 1985; Gottfredson, Wilkins, and Hoffman 1978; Hoffman and Beck 1985; Hoffman and Stone-Meierhoefer 1979; Kane and Saylor 1983; NIC 1982).

Internal classification systems represent a second classification decision that endeavors to classify members of correctional populations after the security-based assignment to a given institution or community setting. Although this concept is new for adult corrections, it has long been common practice with juveniles. These systems classify according to either psychological criteria or needs-based criteria; it is the psychological systems that are of interest to this research. Numerous agencies throughout the United States and Canada have employed psychological systems such as I-level (Harris 1988), Conceptual Level (Reitsma-Street and Leschied 1988), Moral Development (Kohlberg, Colby, Gibbs, Speicher-Dubin, and Candee 1978), and Quay's Behavioral Classification System (Quay and Parsons 1972) in order to assign individuals to housing units or to match them to appropriate treatment options.

The rationale for such a process with adults is that correctional inmates, even after separation into different security levels, are not all alike. They can still be differentiated according to predatory versus dependent behaviors, differential levels of stress and adjustment, and other factors (Megargee and Bohn 1979; Quay 1984; Van Voorhis 1988). Furthermore, rates of serious incidents have decreased in institutions that separate inmates according to these criteria (see Austin, Holien, Chan, and Baird, 1989; Bohn 1979, 1980; Levinson 1988; Quay 1984). In addition, some sources have noted that internal classification systems could also be useful for treatment purposes (Megargee and Bohn 1979); among adults, however, these applications are underutilized, largely because treatment is underutilized. This latter point is unfortunate, because (as will be explained shortly) this research has uncovered numerous findings relevant to the issue of correctional treatment.

ORGANIZATION OF THE BOOK

The research goals outlined for this study are addressed in the eight chapters that follow. Chapter summaries are structured to review each chapter in the context of research goals pertinent to that chapter. The chapter on methodology, for example, describes standard research issues of measurement, analysis decisions, and design; but some of these concerns, such as the reliability of the classification measures, are also research goals.

Chapter 2 offers descriptions of each of the five classification systems and reviews the psychological attributes of each of the types identified by each system. Chapter 3 reviews previous research and further sets the context for the present study. Chapter 4 discusses the methodology of this study. The samples are described in chapter 5, along with a discussion of the distribution of subjects across each typology in each type of institution. Chapter 6 is devoted to the issue of construct validity; the types identified by one system are compared to similarly identified types on the other systems. This chapter reports results of bivariate and clustering analyses of the data.

Chapter 7 correlates the classification types with official and self-report measures of institutional disciplinary infractions and reports of victimizations. Chapter 8 explores relationships between the types and treatment-related measures of adjustment to prison, such as stress, coping, treatment utilization, fear of prison life, and staff assessments of adjustment to prison. Bivariate and multivariate procedures of analysis are conducted in chapters 6, 7, and 8. Chapter 9 summarizes the research issues as they address each of the research questions posed earlier in this chapter. Chapter 9 also provides a review of each system and a profile of each type, which incorporates our findings. In this chapter we also integrate field experiences with research findings and offer recommendations to practitioners. Policy and research implications are offered in Chapter 10.

CHAPTER 2

DESCRIPTIONS OF THE FIVE CLASSIFICATION SYSTEMS

The classification systems are described in this chapter along with brief overviews of the psychological characteristics of each of the types identified by each system. In compiling these descriptions, we borrow from the work of the system's author or other widely recognized authorities on the system. It is important to point out that descriptions for the I-level and Conceptual Level systems are those that were developed for juvenile populations, because, as indicated earlier, the systems have not been widely studied among adults. Thus, this chapter contains only the accounts available at the outset of this research and none of the descriptors and modifications that resulted from the study. As we report the applicability of the systems to two separate populations of adult male prison inmates, we ultimately suggest additional characteristics (see chapter 9 for a summary).

EMPIRICAL TYPOLOGIES

Megargee's MMPI-Based Typology

The Megargee MMPI-Based typology was designed for use with youthful and adult offenders (Megargee and Bohn 1979). The original construction and validation samples were selected at the Federal Correctional Institution in Tallahassee, Florida. As the title implies, the classifications are obtained from results of the Minnesota Multiphasic Personality Inventory (MMPI), one of the most widely used psychodiagnostic instruments in the field of mental health.

The classification system was constructed by Edwin Megargee and his associates through a process of separating MMPI profiles into ten categories on the basis of common profile configurations (e.g., slopes, shapes, and elevations). The scoring rules for doing this are available in a book titled *Classifying Criminal Offenders* (Megargee and Bohn 1979). Computer scoring programs and scoring services are also available.

Most agencies can classify roughly 67% of the profiles by computer. The remaining 33% of the cases must be classified clinically in order to break tied diagnoses and to assign diagnoses to profiles that the computer designates as "unclassified" (Zager 1988).

The ten types are described below along with a brief description of the MMPI profile associated with the type. Megargee gave each type a nondescript name (e.g., Able, Baker, Charlie) in order to allow an empirical process of identifying the behavioral characteristics of each type, thereby discouraging any biasing effects from preconceived labels. Zager's (1988) description of each of the types, in order from least to most disturbed, follows:

> *Item:* The MMPI profile lacks elevation with scales generally under 70. Items are described as a generally stable, well-adjusted group with minimal problems or conflicts with authorities.
>
> *Easy:* The profile has low elevations with the top scale below 80 and often below 70. Scales that often are elevated are 4 and 3, and the profile slopes down to the right. Easys are described as bright and stable, with good adjustment, personal resources, and interpersonal relationships. Many are underachievers.
>
> *Baker:* The profile has moderate elevations, with typical elevations on scales 4 and 2 and sloping down to the right. Bakers are described as inadequate, anxious, constricted, and dogmatic, with a tendency to abuse alcohol.
>
> *Able:* The profile has moderate elevations, typically on scales 4 and 9. Ables are described as charming, impulsive, and manipulative. They are achievement-oriented and often adjust well to incarceration.
>
> *George:* The profile has moderate elevations similar to Baker, but scales 1, 2, and 3 are more elevated. Georges are described as hardworking, submissive, and anxious, with learned criminal values. They often take advantage of educational and vocational programs.
>
> *Delta:* The profile has moderate to high elevation on scale 4, with other scales below 70. Deltas are described as amoral, hedonistic,

egocentric, manipulative, and bright. They are impulsive sensation seekers who have poor relations with peers and authorities.

Jupiter: The profile has moderate to high elevations sloping up to the right, with elevations typically on scales 8, 9, and 7. Jupiters are described as overcoming deprived backgrounds to do better than expected in prison and upon release.

Foxtrot: The profile has high elevations with the top scale over 80 and others over 70. It slopes up to the right with scales 8, 9, and 4, the top three scales. Foxtrots are described as tough, streetwise, cynical, and antisocial. They have deficits in most areas, extensive criminal histories, and poor prison adjustment.

Charlie: The profile has high elevations with the highest scale above 80 and several scales above 70, typically peaking on scales 8, 6, 4, and sloping to the right. Charlies are described as hostile, misanthropic, alienated, aggressive, and antisocial. They have extensive histories of poor adjustment, criminal convictions, and mixed substance abuse.

How: The profile has very high elevations with at least three scales above a T-score of 70, and is characterized by multiple elevations rather than individual scale elevations. Hows are described as unstable, agitated, and disturbed, mental health cases. They have extensive needs and function ineffectively in major areas (pp. 42-43).

Since the development of this system, a second version of the MMPI, the MMPI2, has been released by the University of Minnesota Press. MMPI2 endeavored to eliminate sexist language and other outmoded content and to improve the test norms. Even though the original MMPI remains widely used, Megargee and his associates are currently adapting the ten prison types to MMPI2.

Quay's Adult Internal Management System (AIMS)[1]

This is the only one of the five systems that does not require an inmate's written or verbal response. Two objective instruments are used: one is completed by a correctional staff person who has knowledge of the inmate's behavior; the other is completed by a staff member upon examining the inmate's background reports and conducting a general intake or presentence interview that need not be structured according to the test format. Scores on five dimensions result: Asocial Aggressive, Immature Dependent, Manipulative, Neurotic Anxious, and Situational (Quay 1983, 1984).

This system was developed in the Federal Bureau of Prisons with support from the National Institute of Corrections. An earlier version was constructed and applied in juvenile correctional settings (Quay and Parsons 1972). The system for juveniles utilizes similar procedures of administration, and the type descriptions are somewhat comparable but not identical.

The characteristics of each of the adult types are as follows. [Descriptions are taken from items found on the behavioral checklists (Quay 1983, 1984)].

Asocial Aggressive: Gets along with "hoods," uses leisure time to cause trouble, frequent use of profane language, cannot be trusted, victimizes weaker inmates, impulsive, unpredictable, seeks excitement, talks aggressively, blameless, quick-tempered, holds grudges, seeks to get even, tries to form cliques, openly defies rules and regulations, stirs up trouble among inmates, aids or abets in breaking rules, uncontrollable as a child, antisocial values supporting criminal behavior, irregular work history, tough, defiant, physically aggressive, guiltless, braggart, lack of concern for others.

Immature Dependent: Tries to but can't follow directions, socially withdrawn, takes little pleasure in anything, sluggish, drowsy, moody, brooding, seems dull and unintelligent, never seems happy, passive, easily led, daydreams, seems mentally off in space, inattentive, reluctant to participate, has few (if any) friends, difficulty managing everyday problems in living, depressed.

Situational: Has expressed guilt, expresses a need to improve, supported wife and children, claims offense was motivated by family problems, single marriage, suffered financial reverses.

Manipulative: Continually tries to con staff, doesn't trust staff, complains of unfairness, feels unjustly confined, plays one staff member against another.

Neurotic Anxious: Worried, anxious, tense, unable to relax, continually asks for help, seems afraid, easily upset, afraid of other inmates, often sad and depressed.

THEORETICAL TYPOLOGIES

Interpersonal Maturity (I-level)

I-level (Warren et al. 1966) is a classification system and treatment model that focuses on the ways in which people make sense of themselves and others as well as the ways in which they interact. The classification scheme consists of five levels that characterize individuals on a cognitive developmental scheme pertaining to self and interpersonal perspectives. This system began with the theoretical work of Sullivan, Grant, and Grant (1957) and developed into a classification system for use with juvenile offenders in the California Youth Authority during the 1960s and 1970s (Warren et al. 1966; Warren 1983). In addition to the five levels, the offender classification system also provides personality subtypes for three of the levels.

As indicated in chapter 1, this developmental scheme (the levels) shares assumptions held by other cognitive-development theories (e.g., Harvey, Hunt, and Schroder 1961; Kohlberg 1958; Loevinger 1966; Sullivan, Grant, and Grant 1957): (*a*) the underlying logic employed at a given stage or level of development appears to be consistent across situations, and although the subject (content) of actual choices may differ, the structure of the reasoning is similar; (*b*) the stages described by the respective systems follow an invariant order; (*c*) no stage can be skipped in the course of development; (*d*) each stage is more complex than the preceding one; and (*e*) each stage is based on the preceding one and prepares for the succeeding one.

The levels of interpersonal development range from the least mature stage of the newborn infant to an ideal stage of interpersonal maturity which exists in theory but in actuality is seldom reached in our culture. A description of the social frame of reference that characterizes each level shows how individual perceptions of and reactions to others and the environment change with development of interpersonal maturity. Warren et al. (1966) refer to the frame of reference embodied in each level as a relatively consistent set of expectations and attitudes, a kind of interpreting and working philosophy of life. This way of making sense of one's environment, then, is relatively consistent across situations until the individual matures into the next level, where a new frame of reference is integrated with previous experiences and perspectives.

Although seven levels have been set forth in the theoretical work of Sullivan, Grant, and Grant (1957), only four levels have applicability to delinquent and offender populations. Harris's (1988) abbreviated description of levels 2 (I_2), 3 (I_3), 4 (I_4), and 5 (I_5) follows. [More detailed accounts are available in Marguerite Q. Warren's writings (1969, 1971, and 1983)].

I_2 is a stage typical of very young children. Major concerns center on differentiating persons from objects. Other persons are viewed solely as sources of gratification (e.g., as "givers" and "takers," evidencing no understanding of, or ability to predict or influence, the behavior of others).

I_3 youths have learned that they have power; their behaviors affect the responses they receive from others. Much of their activity centers on learning how power is structured. They tend to apply stereotyped rules and simple formulas when interacting with others.

I_4 youths operate from a set of internalized values. They are aware of feelings and motives in themselves and in others and the relevance of these motives and feelings to communication and relationships with others. They tend to be rigid in their application of rules and to be concerned with their own uniqueness.

I_5 individuals are considerably less rigid in their application of rules than are persons at Stage 4; they tend to see grey areas in situations and are tolerant of viewpoints different from their own. Role conflict is a major concern of such individuals. The most distinguishing characteristic of this stage is empathy,—the capacity to experience the world from the perspective of another person (pp.64).

The personality subtypes for each level are neither theoretically derived nor developmental: rather, they are empirically identified personality-based subtypes of the four levels described above. They might also be considered the personality-based adaptations found to be evidenced at each of these levels. Harris's (1988) descriptions are as follows:

I_2:   *Asocial Passive:* Responds to unmet demand by withdrawing, whining, or complaining.

Asocial Aggressive: Responds to unmet needs with open aggression

I_3:   *Immature Conformist:* Conforms to whoever has the power at the moment and sees self as less powerful than others.

Cultural Conformist: Conforms exclusively to a specific group of peers.

Manipulator: Counteractive to any source of power, adult or peer. Extremely distrustful of others.

I_4 and I_5:   *Neurotic Acting-out:* Internally conflicted due to negative self-image. Responds to internal conflict by putting up a facade of superadequacy and maintaining a high level of activity. Attempts to keep others at a distance through distracting behavior or verbal attack, even though he or she may be very sociable.

Neurotic Anxious: Also internally conflicted due to a negative self-image. Responds to internal conflict with guilt, anxiety, or depression. Tends to be introspective and frequently attempts to engage others in gaining self-understanding. Self-analysis is not genuine; it is an attempt to reduce anxiety while preserving both positive and negative parts of self-identity.

Cultural Identifier: As part of his or her socialization process, certain values were internalized that permit a range of delinquent acts.

Situational-emotional Reaction: Responds to a current crisis situation, or an emotional change that is recent in origin (pp. 65–66).

The Jesness Inventory (I-level) System

The Jesness Inventory Classification System (Jesness and Wedge 1983) might be described as a combination of the heuristic and the empirical methods because it has been portrayed as an actuarial method of assessing I-level. This system also had its origins in the California Youth Authority. It is a paper-and-pencil test developed for use with delinquents, but more recent research has produced adult norms (Jesness 1988). The Jesness Inventory yields scores on eleven trait scales (e.g., social maladjustment, manifest aggression) and nine scales that correspond to the I-level subtype scales.

Although Jesness claims to offer a more efficient and less costly method of assessing I-level (Jesness 1988), it is not clear that the Jesness I-level subtype definitions are entirely comparable to the interview subtype definitions, especially for adults. One difference is evident in the fact that the Jesness I-level diagnosis does not incorporate the I_5 type. Another distinction between the two systems occurs in Jesness's description of the Cultural Identifier (Ci) as highly motivated and possessing a nondelinquent orientation. In contrast, Cis, as diagnosed by the interview method, evidence an asocial value system typically learned in an offender subculture. Thus, Jesness type descriptions, below, identify similar but not identical traits (Jesness 1988):

I_2Aa *(Asocial Aggressive):* From deprived background; negative attitudes toward authority, family, and school; unpredictable, nonconforming, aggressive, and obtrusive behavior; delinquent orientation; and high self-reported delinquency.

I_2Ap *(Asocial Passive):* From deprived home background; negative attitudes toward family and school; low verbal aptitude; nonconforming, inappropriate behavior; poor peer relations; and negative self-concept.

I_3Cfm *(Immature Conformist):* Positive attitudes toward home, school, and authority; conforming behavior; often dependent (follower); positive, uncritical self-concept, and low self-reported delinquency.

I_3Cfc *(Cultural Conformist):* From deprived background; low motivation, poor achievement, and negative attitudes toward school; alienated, distrustful, and hostile toward adults and authority; delinquently oriented friends; delinquent self-concept; and high self-reported delinquency.

I_3Mp *(Manipulator):* Generally positive attitudes toward school; positive self-concept; manipulative, sometimes obtrusive behavior; and inconsistency between self-evaluations and objective measures (e.g., official versus self-reported delinquency).

I_4Na *(Neurotic Acting-Out):* Above-average verbal aptitude; behavior problems in school; negative attitudes toward authority; family conflicts; self-presentation as adequate and independent, but somewhat cynical and disenchanted; often provocative, outspoken, and nonconforming; and high self-reported delinquency.

I_4Nx *(Neurotic Anxious):* Mostly positive attitudes toward school; conforming; somewhat perturbable, dependent, anxious, and insecure; nondelinquent orientation; family and interpersonal conflicts; and low official delinquency.

I_4Se *(Situational):* Above-average socioeconomic background; positive attitudes toward school and family; positive nondelinquent self-concept; confident; naive; conforming; good interpersonal relationships; and low self-reported and official delinquency.

I_4Ci *(Cultural Identifier):* High verbal aptitude; highly motivated for school; positive attitudes toward authority, school, parents, and self; confident; good interpersonal relationships; nondelinquent orientation; and low self-reported and official delinquency (pp. 80–82).

Conceptual Level

This system builds on Conceptual Systems Theory (Harvey, Hunt, and Schroder 1961), which was first put forth as a general theory of personality development. The theory positions individuals on a developmental hierarchy of increasing conceptual complexity, social maturity, self-responsibility and independence. Conceptual development progresses through a maximum of four conceptual levels. Thus, the system is a cognitive-developmental model and is the only one of the five to omit reference to personality characteristics.

Conceptual Level was designed first for educational purposes, and later it was applied to juvenile correctional populations, mostly throughout Canada. Most applications occur in conjuction with the Conceptual Level Matching Model (Hunt 1971), a procedure that uses the Conceptual Level diagnosis to determine the level of environmental structure needed by a program client.

Descriptions of the scores assigned to responses to the Paragraph Completion Method (PCM) (Hunt, Butler, Noy, and Rosser 1978) are as follows:

Score 0: These individuals are characterized as self-centered and unaware of the thoughts and needs of others. When they fail to achieve their wants, they react either in an unsocialized, hostile, and impulsive manner or in a passive pattern of withdrawal.

Score 1: These individuals are concerned with social acceptance. They apply stereotypes, formulas, and dichotomous thinking to decision making. Decisions and evaluations are typically predicated on concerns for social acceptance and the expectations of authority figures.

Score 2: Independence is a primary concern. Persons diagnosed at this score consider alternatives and other viewpoints, but focus on an independent resolution. They reveal some tolerance for ambiguity and diverse opinions.

Score 3: Like Score 2 individuals, persons diagnosed at this stage are open to a variety of viewpoints. Their decision-making, however, shows a greater ability to compromise and to integrate the viewpoints of others. They are secure in their independence but do not compromise values to please others. They are willing to accept full responsibility for the consequences of their behavior.

Scores for the responses to the sentence stems of the PCM are averaged. While CL is viewed as a continuum, applications of the system require the formulations of types. The types developed for use with delinquents are: (*a*) Stage A, a person who is characteristically egocentric and cognitively concrete; (*b*) Stage B, the individual who shows an intermediate degree of cognitive complexity and norm orientation; (c) Stage C, independent and internally motivated; and (d) Stage D, one who evidences an interdependent orientation, who looks at situations from all angles (Reitsma-Street and Leschied 1988).

DISCUSSION

In sum, the five classification systems studied in this research identify forty-one psychological types assumed to make useful distinctions among correctional clients. The systems differ according to whether they were developed for adult offenders (Megargee MMPI and Quay AIMS) or juvenile offenders (I-level Interview, Jesness I-level, and Conceptual Level) and by whether they identify personality or developmental constructs or both. It may be apparent, however, that there are also some similarities across systems. All four of the personality-based systems, for example, provide for a neurotic or high-anxiety diagnosis. All of the personality-based systems also identify a type of correctional client who seems more entrenched in a criminal value system than others. The cognitive-developmental types, I-level and Conceptual Level, also identify comparable developmental constructs. Similar commonalities were discussed in Warren's (1971) identification of "bands" of comparison among several classification systems. Her work showed that the classification systems had independently identified six types common to juvenile correctional populations: asocial, conformist, antisocial-manipulator, neurotic, subcultural identifier, and situational.

These "bands," or areas of agreement, are important both because they further our understanding of criminal behavior and, in a technical sense, because they provide the means for testing the construct validity of similarly identified types. Thus, construct validity can be tested by examining correlations between similarly defined types. The empirical relationships also help to further refine type descriptions, as will be shown in chapter 6.

CHAPTER 3

PREVIOUS RESEARCH

The context for the present study was influenced both by research on the classification systems that we examine here and by a rapidly emerging literature on the methodology of classification and prediction. Several comprehensive reviews of the systems and of classification methodology have been published in recent years. This section does not attempt to repeat that work, but instead surveys the literature narrowly confined to the issues of the present study.[1] We begin with a brief discussion of some of the methodological themes in the literature and then move to a more specific focus on the psychological systems used in this research.

METHODOLOGY OF CLASSIFICATION
AND PREDICTION

An overview of this type must include a discussion of the emerging literature of both classification and prediction. Much of this work has paralleled the development of the specific psychological systems, while another body of research speaks more precisely to prediction and risk-assessment systems.[2] Although these two areas of study tend to inform each other, prediction and classification are not necessarily synonymous (MacKenzie, Posey, and Rapaport 1988; MacKenzie,1989; Van Voorhis 1987; Wright 1988). For our purposes, classification typically involves an assignment of individuals to groups considered relatively homogeneous on characteristics relevant to their adjustment to the prison experience; prediction and risk-assessment systems, commonly used in pretrial, probation, and parole agencies, operate like insurance actuarial tables, predicting an offender's probability of absconding, rearrest, or technical violation. In contrast, proponents of psychological classification are sometimes cautious in approaching hypotheses of a relationship between the classification types and future offense behaviors (Jesness 1988; Megargee and Bohn 1979).[3] Thus, the methodological and statistical issues relevant to prediction cannot always be applied to classification, but often they offer suggestive guidance.

Generally, this broad array of technical literature has devoted considerable attention to the reliability and validity of the prediction and classification instruments. The more general issues pertaining to reliability and validity are discussed in this section; in a later section, we discuss them as they pertain to specific systems. Researchers also have addressed topics such as base rate and selection ratio problems, criterion variable considerations, and issues of data analysis.

Collectively, the research literature suggests that statistical procedures for constructing and testing prediction and classification instruments have improved greatly in recent years but that these techniques can be only as good as the data they analyze (Gottfredson 1987a). Sources fault both the criterion and the predictor variables in this regard.

Occasionally the predictor variables—for our purposes, the classification "types"—are adopted prematurely, with insufficient attention to reliability or predictive accuracy. For some systems, virtually no published accounts of interrater reliability are available. In such cases, correctional personnel may find it difficult to apply the diagnostic system, because the types often overlap or because the diagnostic process is vulnerable to the diagnostician's subjective discretion and biased perceptions (Brennan 1987; Gibbons 1975). On a related issue, little has been done to compare the systems in an attempt to identify commonalities that validate or refine type descriptions (Brennan 1987; Gottfredson 1987a; Megargee and Bohn 1979).

Some investigators have taken this discussion so far as to oppose the use of psychological classification altogether when instead they might have advocated further development of the technology (Brennan 1987). Opposition, however, may not be completely attributable to concerns for measurement limitations. Indeed, many readers will recognize what Andrews and Wormith (1989) recently described as "antipersonality themes in mainstream criminology [which] have been fueled for years by highly suspect moral, professional, and ideological concerns and by something less than a rational empirical approach" (289).[4]

Despite the critics' concerns, interrater reliability figures—measures of the extent to which the type constructs can be recognized and applied consistently—vary considerably. In some cases they are unreported. Elsewhere, percent interrater agreement ranges from low (e.g., 55%) to moderate (85%) among trained researchers and assessment personnel and to good (90% and higher) among professionals who specialize in the administration of a specific system. Clearly, however, improvements are required for measurements that generate less-than-ideal reliability values; this point will be a theme throughout this book.

Prediction and classification researchers do not always limit their attention to prediction or classification measures. Criterion variables also warrant some concern. Indeed, sources caution that flawed criterion measures will also mar the accuracy of predictor or classification measures. Most often these concerns are directed toward measures of recidivism. In the worst-case scenario, classification systems are devised through analyses of relationships between the predictor variables and a dichotomized recidivism measure, characterized crudely as success or failure (Gottfredson 1987b; Maltz 1984). Such measures ignore factors such as the behavior of the decision maker in arrest (Gottfredson 1987a) or in our case, in citation for a prison infraction (Light 1990); favorable changes in reoffending patterns, such as decreased severity or frequency and increased time to failure (Maltz 1984; Palmer 1978); or other desirable treatment outcomes such as educational attainments or employment (Palmer 1978). Recidivism measures are also affected by the nature of the follow-up time intervals (Maltz 1984).

One response to these matters would be to utilize multiple criteria of success. This approach is advocated, not only as a means of improving the reliability and validity of the criterion measure (Dunford and Elliot 1984; Farrington 1987) by assessing recidivism through the use of self-report and official measures, but also as a means of conceptualizing desired outcomes and descriptions more clearly (Gibbons 1975; Light 1990; Poole and Regoli 1980). Indeed, recidivism is not the only relevant outcome or correlate of correctional classification (Megargee and Bohn 1979) or of correctional interventions (Palmer 1978); failures to recognize this fact have hindered the advancement of both correctional treatment (Palmer 1978) and criminology (Gibbons 1975).

With regard to the psychological classification systems, recidivism is a related outcome factor but a more distal outcome than for a risk-assessment prediction model. Classification experts remind us increasingly that these systems are designed for a variety of purposes. Since predicting recidivism is only one purpose, failure to consider the other purposes of a system threatens optimal use and development of classification technology (Brennan 1987; Gottfredson 1987a; MacKenzie 1989; MacKenzie, Posey, and Rapaport 1988). Alternative purposes incorporate treatment, evaluation, and case management considerations such as (*a*) providing nonclinically trained human-service workers with a coherent scheme for differential programming and processing; (*b*) uniform application of criteria for differentiation; (*c*) qualifying the treatment results according to types of correctional clients and thus avoiding the problem of "masking" (Palmer 1978; Warren 1971), (*d*) case management, or assisting correctional efforts to match a client to appropriate treatment; (*e*) alerting correctional personnel to potential prison-adjustment problems (Megargee and Bohn 1979); and (*f*) advancing etiological perspectives on criminal behavior (MacKenzie 1989). These intents may be more relevant to the notion of internal classification than to the risk/security classifications. Although psychological typologies *may* identify some types as more prone to recidivism than others, the institutional adjustment and crime dynamics factors are the more proximate measures.

The use of multiple-outcome criteria also improves our understanding of the types identified by each system. Thus, it answers some of the earlier critics who observed that some systems are based quite simplistically on the cross-classification of a few poorly measured variables (Brennan 1987).

Another methodological issue relevant to criterion measures concerns the base rate problem, or the statistical difficulty in predicting extremely common or uncommon behaviors (Gottfredson 1987b; Monahan 1981). Here, dependent variables with poor variability (high or low base rates) produce unstable correlates or uncertain predictor weights. In addition, it is difficult to improve upon the validity of predicting the most common outcome—the outcome that might occur, for example, among 80% of the sample. Of what utility is a prediction instrument that predicts an outcome accurately 78% of the time if the modal outcome occurs 80% of the time (Gottfredson 1987b)?[5] This problem can be alleviated somewhat through the use of continuous rather than dichotomous outcome measures (Gottfredson 1987a), through a process of "statistical bootstrapping," or through the construction of prediction models for homogeneous groups of offenders rather than for a larger, nondifferentiated sample (Gottfredson 1987b). Other suggestions include measures that are affected less strongly by the base rate problem, such as "mean cost rating" (MCR) (Berkson 1947) or "relative improvement over chance" (RIOC) (Loeber and Dishion 1983), in order to determine the extent to which a system is more valuable than chance predictions.

Both the prediction and the classification literature have reviewed recent improvements in statistical techniques for developing prediction models (Gottfredson 1987b) or classification systems (Brennan 1987). Yet their applicability to the task of testing existing psychological typologies seems to be limited to multivariate analysis of the incremental contribution of psychological variables as compared to social, demographic, offense-related, or environmental predictors. Indeed, few researchers have incorporated psychological classification factors into prediction models for ongoing use in applied settings.[6]

PSYCHOLOGICAL CLASSIFICATION IN CORRECTIONS

Turning to the literature on the diagnostic systems encompassed by this research, three important observations emerge: (1) The classification systems have generally not been tested across a variety of populations; (2) most research has endeavored to refine single systems; and (3) issues of reliability and validity either are not clear or await further refinements. These correctional assessment methods, in other words, often have not been normed to populations other than those for which they were developed.[7]

Comparisons of the applicability or cross-classifications among systems are almost nonexistent (Brennan 1987; Gottfredson 1987a). Generally, researchers have not compared systems within a given population in order to determine which system or combination of systems is most predictive. In addition, researchers have not validated sufficiently the constructs, or types, identified by each system through empirical examination of the relationships between these constructs and other measures of the same or similar dimensions.

Reliability

Repeated sources have faulted psychological classification as unreliable (e.g., see Beker and Hyman 1972, Brennan 1987; Gibbons 1975); these discussions are correct, as far as they go. Typically, however, they fall far short of a full and fair assessment of the matter. Most of the criticisms have been directed at I-level assessments. Indeed, across existing studies, interrater reliability for the clinical I-level diagnoses range from 37% to 74% for sub-type and from 67% to 86% for level. Test-retest reliability ranges from 84% to 96% for level and from 75% to 80% for subtype (see Harris 1988). Test-retest reliability for the Jesness Inventory measure of I-level has been reported at 48% for subtype and 68% for level (Jesness 1988).

Interrater reliability for the Paragraph Completion Method of assessing Conceptual Level usually is reported as a reliability coefficient, in which the relationship between the assessments is measured rather than the extent of absolute agreement. The originators of the system report a range from .74 to .91 across 26 studies (Hunt, Butler, Noy, and Rosser 1978). Reitsma-Street (1984) reports an average interrater coefficient of .85 resulting from her ongoing checks with raters working with offender populations.

Similar figures do not appear to be available for the AIMS (Quay 1983). Interrater reliability for the MMPI-based system, when agreement into the ten Megargee types is considered, ranges from a low of 68% (Carey, Garske, and Ginsberg 1986) to a high of 90% (Dahlstrom, Panton, Bain, and Dahlstrom 1986; see Zager 1988). Most agreement rates are in the 80% range (Zager 1988). Attempts to assess the test-retest reliability of the Megargee MMPI system have been reported as low (e.g., Johnson, Simmons, and Gordon 1983), but these tests have been confounded methodologically by differing sample compositions and test conditions (Zager 1988).

On the basis of these observations, the critics' concerns seem to warrant continued investment in the technical improvement of the systems. In another sense, however, the criticisms seem to be over-simplified, for whenever reliability problems occur, three explanations are plausible. First, one may fault the measurement process; but, to be accurate, one must also consider the construct being measured (Babbie 1986; Isaac and Michael 1990). Clearly, measuring the dynamics of the human personality is quite different from measuring a more stable construct such as height. With this point in mind, perhaps we should view the above figures more favorably. In fact, although the reliability figures for these systems require some degree of clinical judgment, they are considerably higher than those observed for clinically derived diagnoses of psychological disorders (Meehl 1954; Monahan 1981).

Second, the reliability arguments also may be ignoring some of the validity findings. As noted in many studies conducted to date and in the findings reported in subsequent chapters of this book, the systems differentiate offenders in theoretically expected ways.

That is, reliability problems are not so great as to produce unexpected, nonsensical correlations between the types and the criterion behaviors.

Finally, reliability problems should not be separated from organizationally generated process problems. If an overcrowded correctional facility lacks the resources to use an instrument according to its prescribed design (Clements 1982; Toch 1981), one can hardly expect reliable results. Moreover, if staff members are resistant or careless (Austin 1986), or seek to alter the assumptions of the system without revalidation and reliability checks, accuracy problems can be expected (Austin 1986; Van Voorhis 1987; Wright, Clear, and Dickson 1984). In fact, it appears that problems are occurring in this way, even with systems that were designed to be "simple" (Austin 1986; MacKenzie 1989; Schnieder 1990).

Notwithstanding these concerns, research conducted to date on the psychological systems reveals some promising directions for refinement. First, systems that have moved from a totally open-ended clinical process to some degree of structure show noted improvements in reliability. The experience with Kohlberg's Moral Development system is an instructive example. During the late 1970s, Lawrence Kohlberg and his associates refined the scoring system of Moral Development to include a manual of prototypical stage responses to the moral dilemmas posed during their standard interview. Raters also were provided with more scoring rules for resolving ties, discrepancies, and transitional statements. The added structure greatly improved the reliability of their moral-judgment diagnoses (Kohlberg, Colby, Gibbs, Speicher-Dubin, and Candee 1978). In a less elaborate sense, a similar development is evident in the latest method for assessing Conceptual Level, the Paragraph Completion Method (Hunt, Butler, Noy, and Rosser 1978).

It is also important to note that most of the systems studied in this research were not designed to be learned in a single training session, so that the diagnostician could administer the system thereafter without any refresher courses or checks for reliability. Across systems, the highest reliability figures have been reported for professionals who work with the system continuously, in established training or assessment centers. In fact, assessment techniques have been noted to "drift" over time if diagnosticians (or indeed, agencies) do not update their skills periodically or conduct ongoing checks of reliability (Harris 1988). Authorities now suggest that the classification process must be solidly entrenched in the organizational and treatment procedures of a facility.

Construct Validity

Do commonalities exist among various offender typologies? Sources disagree, but the value of identifying some elements in common has been maintained since at least 1966, when the National Institute of Mental Health (NIMH) convened a conference on offender typologies. One of the objectives of the session was to determine areas of agreement between the typologies current at that time (Warren 1971). The importance of identifying such commonalities is supported by the following points:

1. The construct validity of the types delineated by one system is strengthened by a significant correlation with types identified similarly by other systems.

2. Moderate or high correlations between types defined by one system with less similar types or traits defined by another system further refine the descriptions of the types delineated by both (Megargee and Bohn 1979, 265; Warren 1971, 255). In the case of the MMPI-based systems and other inductive, empirically based systems, such findings may also help to add a theoretical framework to the typology (Megargee and Bohn 1979, 266).

3. Flaws inherent in one system may become apparent upon comparison with other systems used to classify the same population. Examples of such flaws include but are not limited to (a) failure to identify mutually exclusive types, (b) failure to exhaust all types potential in the sample, (c) identification of too many types, and (d) identification of too few types.

4. One of the initially proposed reasons for conducting several cross-classification studies was the hope of promoting a single agreed-upon system for use across similar facilities. Greater consistency in classification was suggested as a means of assessing the comparative efficacy of treatment and management strategies across different agencies and target populations (Warren 1971, 255).

Sources disagree about the extent to which any such identification of commonalities has been conducted to date. Some maintain that criminal typologies in general "lack consensus and stability" or suggest too much "overlap and ambiguity and lack of integration" (Brennan [1987] citing Gibbons [1975] and Solomon [1977]). Nevertheless, some work has been done in this area. Theoretical commonalities have been proposed (Van Voorhis 1984; Warren 1971) and some empirical validation of those commonalities has been attained (e.g., see Van Voorhis 1988). For example, the pilot study for this research, which involved 52 federal inmates, provided limited empirical support for (1) stage development constructs through empirical relationships among I-level, Moral Judgment, and Conceptual Level: (2) a neurotic construct through a relationship between the Quay and the I-level diagnosis; and (3) agreement among Quay, MMPI, and I-level assessments regarding the diagnosis of a "committed criminal type"[8] (Van Voorhis 1988). Agreements among situational[9] and immature-dependent types were not noted, but cell sizes were insufficient for tests conducted of these relationships.

Jesness also noted the construct validity of the stage-based measures in a comparison of Loevinger's measures of ego development (r = .47, or .33, controlling for age, race, and verbal IQ; Harris 1988). Limited support for the construct validity of I-level again was found in Werner's assessment of California Personality Inventory (CPI) clusters (Werner 1975). In addition, Jesness has reported numerous expected correlations between subtype and relevant differences in attitudes, self-concept, influence of delinquent peers, responsibility, and confidence (Jesness 1988). Agreements between the Jesness Inventory and clinical assessments of I-level are 67% for level and 47% for subtype (Jesness and Wedge 1983).

Zager (1988) reports that some of the characteristics of the MMPI types (Easy, Able, Charlie, Item, Jupiter, Foxtrot, and How) are supported by correlations with relevant psychological instruments and self-report data, but not with similar types as identified by another classification system. Groups Delta, Baker, and George, however, have not been validated in ways consistent with the original type descriptions, either in the pilot study for this research or in other studies.

Additional studies include Keck's (1978) comparison of I-level with Quay classifications among juveniles, and Carbonnel's (1983) cross-validation of I-level (Jesness Inventory) and the MMPI-based types at the Federal Correctional Institution in Tallahassee. Keck found expected relationships between the I-level Neurotic Anxious diagnosis and the Neurotic type on the Quay typology (57% agreement). Youths diagnosed as Neurotic Acting-out (Nas) were most likely to be diagnosed as BC III (Psychopathic/Unsocialized) on the Quay system (80% agreement). I_3 Cultural Conformists (Cfcs) typically were classified either as BC I (Inadequate/Immature; 45.5% agreement) or as BC IV (Subcultural Identification). Theoretically, one would expect other areas of agreement (e.g., I_4Ci and

BC IV), but such agreements are not reported. Carbonnel's study did not report substantial agreements.

Predictive Validity and Institutional Adjustment

As noted above, discussions of the predictive validity of criminal-prediction and offender classification systems often become focused somewhat narrowly on the criterion measures of recidivism. Clearly, psychological classification systems have been held to this standard as well, somewhat to the discomfort of their originators, most of whom presented these systems as treatment, case management, and administrative tools. It is to their credit and to the ultimate benefit of correctional practitioners that the various psychological types often *do* correlate with disciplinary infractions and offending behaviors, but such findings warrant qualification. As noted above, disciplinary offenses are indirect or distal outcomes, which perhaps are mediated by more proximate attitudinal and adjustment measures. Similarly, the use of psychological classification systems for internal classification is supposed to result—and typically does result—in reduced incidences of disciplinary behaviors; but this may be attributable as much to the differential treatment of offenders as to their psychological differences. Thus, evidence of predictive validity is found in a variety of correlates, including correctional adjustment and attitudes and both prosocial and antisocial behaviors.

Of the five systems examined in this research, only two—AIMS and the MMPI-based system—were developed for use with adult correctional populations. I-level has been applied almost exclusively in private and public juvenile settings throughout the United States and Canada (Warren 1983). Applications of the interview method to adult populations appear to be confined to early studies of military prisoners in a Navy Retraining Command during the late 1950s and early 1960s (Grant and Grant 1959),[10] to a small sample of adult offenders ordered to pay financial restitution and/or to perform community service (Heide 1982), and to the pilot study for the present research (Van Voorhis 1988).

Heide's research suggested a relationship between I-level and offenders' compliance with the terms of restitution. The pilot study for this research observed no relationship between I-level and disciplinary infractions, but noted that the few inmates diagnosed at I_2 and I_3 were more likely to be victimized than offenders diagnosed at I_4 and I_5 (Van Voorhis 1988). Limited cell sizes, however, place obvious limitations on these conclusions. Jesness (1988) maintains that the norms obtained for 18-year-olds are applicable to adults, but published accounts do not exist.[11]

Conceptual Level (CL) has been used most widely in educational and juvenile correctional settings. Little is known about its applicability to adults (Reitsma-Street 1984; Reitsma-Street and Leschied 1988). The pilot study found, however, that lower-CL males were more likely to be victimized than males diagnosed at higher levels (Van Voorhis 1988).

Despite the lack of research among adults, these three systems have been tested extensively among juveniles; results have been reviewed in depth elsewhere (see Harris 1983, 1988; Jesness 1988; Reitsma-Street 1984; Reitsma-Street and Leschied 1988; Warren 1983).

Predictive validity of the I-level clinical method is seen in the differential adjustments to the treatment options offered by the Community Treatment Project of the California Youth Authority (Palmer 1974). Other tests assess primarily the construct validity of I-level (Harris 1988).[12] Over several tests of the validity of the Jesness Inventory I-level subtypes, Jesness reports that subtype differentiates youths consistently on such factors as observers' ratings of institutional behavior, self-reported delinquency, disciplinary referrals, classroom disturbances, and subsequent offenses and probation referrals (Jesness 1988).

In Reitsma-Street and Leschied's (1988) review of seven studies of Conceptual Level among male adolescent samples, the authors conclude that lower-CL offenders consistently displayed more asocial, impulsive, aggressive behaviors and fewer, problem-solving types of behaviors, while higher-CL offenders use more socialized, complex, and independent approaches to interpersonal situations and difficulties.

The MMPI-based classification system was developed and validated on large samples of youthful offenders at the Federal Correctional Institution (FCI) in Tallahassee (Megargee and Bohn 1979). Several validation studies have been conducted, but the results conflict. Some investigators reported expected correlations with disciplinary infractions and other measures of institutional adjustment (e.g., Booth and Howell 1980; Edinger 1979; Edinger and Auerbach 1978; Louscher, Hosford, and Moss 1983; Megargee and Bohn 1979; Megargee and Carbonell 1986; Van Voorhis 1988; Walters, Scapansky, and Marlow 1986; Wright 1988; Wrobel, Wrobel, and McIntosh 1988). Others report unfavorable results (e.g., Baum, Hosford and Moss 1983; Dahlstrom, Panton, Bain, and Dahlstrom 1986; Hanson, Moss, Hosford, and Johnson 1983; Moss,

Johnson, and Hosford 1984). Three of the latter studies were conducted at FCI Lompoc and have been since faulted in rejoinders by Zager (1983, 1988). The studies show evidence of sampling bias and improper classification procedures; actually they were efforts to postdict violent tendencies (a phenomenon with an extremely low base rate) in a group of inmates who may not have been representative of the Lompoc population. In addition, Motiuk, Bonta, and Andrews (1986) report that the MMPI system was not successful in predicting program success and reincarceration. Zager (1988), however, criticizes these authors' strategy of regrouping cases. Specifically, inmates classified as How on the system were grouped among the nonproblematic inmates, when in fact they are noted for making the worst adjustments to correctional settings.

The validation research for Quay AIMS Adult Internal Management System spanned one open institution, four Federal Correctional Institutions, and five Federal Penitentiaries. Although these data show relationships between the Quay categories and institutional behavior, the Quay system has not been tested as widely as the MMPI-based system. The pilot study observed expected relationships between the classification system types and disciplinary dispositions. Asocial aggressive and Manipulative inmates were significantly more likely to incur disciplinary infractions than were offenders designated as less aggressive (e.g., Neurotic Anxious, Immature Dependents, and Situational) (Van Voorhis 1988).

Two types of studies have direct implications for applied operational use while at the same time showing evidence of validity. The first group includes evaluation studies of the effects of internal classification on institutional behavioral patterns, whereby inmates are assigned to housing units on the basis of a classification process and are tracked for several months.[13] This group of studies also might be described as taking a "longitudinal" validation approach (Gottfredson 1987b). The second group includes comparative studies of the predictive merits of two or more systems.

Adult correctional facilities have been slow to implement internal psychological classification, but a limited number of studies show favorable results. They include Quay's (1984) study of the applicability of AIMS, Levinson's application of AIMS and of the Federal Prison Systems' Unit Management process, Bohn's (1979, 1980) evaluation study of a program that assigned inmates to living units on the basis of the MMPI, and a study of a facility in the state of Washington which classified inmates according to the Prisoner Case Management System (PCM) (Austin Holien, Chan, and Baird 1989). All of these studies showed favorable reductions in the proportion of disciplinary infractions committed during the follow-up periods.

The second type of research seeks to identify optimum methods of internal classification by comparing the predictive validity of the psychological system with that of another internal classification process. One such study compared the efficacy of the MMPI typology to the Federal Bureau of Prisons's Custody Level Designation System (Hanson, Moss, Hosford, and Johnson 1983), and noted that the Custody Level Designation score was much more predictive of prison adjustment than were the Megargee types. In all likelihood, however, this result was obtained primarily because the custody scores are not always independent of the disciplinary data.

This problem occurs in a number of systems designed as second-level or internal-classification systems to supplement risk-assessment systems. By design or by staff error, depending on the system, they are tautological (Van Voorhis 1987). Because scores on these systems depend on clients' behaviors, the effectiveness of the systems cannot be measured by how well the scores correlate with disciplinary infractions, probation violations, and other events. Prediction and predictive validity assume that "whatever the criterion (the event or state to be predicted), this assessment must be made independently of any steps used in arriving at the prediction. Prediction requires two independent assessments separated over time" (Gottfredson 1987a, 2). Thus, systems that consider correctional behaviors *after* the point of intake may serve as effective monitoring vehicles for making uniform case management decisions, but they are not prediction systems. From an applied standpoint, their most crucial flaw is in predicting initial events, because apparently it takes a problem to predict one.

The comparison of systems contains an additional, conceptual flaw: The research questions fail to recognize that the risk and psychological systems are designed to serve different rather than competing purposes (MacKenzie 1989; MacKenzie, Posey, and Rapaport 1988). In fact, a recent comparison among the Megargee MMPI typology, Toch's Prison Preference Inventory (Toch 1977), and a risk-assessment model developed by the State of New York showed that no single system was superior to another; there were advantages and disadvantages to each (Wright 1988). The risk measures were related to disciplinary infractions, whereas the psychological systems were related to prison adjustment. Thus, the question is not which system predicts adjustment most accurately (as many of these comparison studies set out to determine) but rather which systems predict which outcomes most accurately.

Regardless of predictive efficacy, most psychological systems are expensive to implement and should not be undertaken without clear commitments from administrative and treatment staff. Accordingly, Gendreau, Andrews, and others have recommended attention to alternative predictors before widespread implementation of the more expensive classification process (e.g., Andrews, Bonta, and Hoge 1990; Gendreau, Madden, and Leipciger 1980). For example, if self-report indicators of amenability to treatment or potential for violence are correlated highly with institutional infractions, Gendreau asserts that it makes little sense to adopt the more expensive procedures. Although his argument is more relevant to security concerns than to treatment, it would be important to explore the position of psychological predictors relative to other factors.

DISCUSSION

A decade or more ago, amidst concerns about ineffectiveness of treatment (Martinson 1974) and adverse effects of labeling (Schur 1971), and in the face of criticism of the earlier approaches to differential treatment (Beker and Hyman 1972; Lerman 1975), one might have predicted the demise of correctional classification and notions of differential placement and treatment. Yet the outcome has been quite different. Classification continues to represent a major area of research and practice (Brennan 1987, Gottfredson 1987a). In many instances, however, systems may have been applied without appropriate knowledge of reliability and validity considerations or without even a close fit between the system's purpose and the consumer's intent.

A number of issues emerge from the preceding review in the form of rather conspicuous gaps in our knowledge. Certainly the psychological classification of adult inmates is in a developmental stage. It is fairly clear that classified institutions are safer places than unclassified. Yet little research has been conducted on the effects of classification for treatment, even though most of these systems have fairly clear treatment implications. In light of the nature of the personality constructs that form the basis of the system, reliability should be an ongoing consideration, not simply a question for preliminary studies. A sense of where reliability problems are likely to occur and how to remedy them is also needed.

Predictive validity is perhaps an overstated concern, insofar as it pertains to the relationship between psychological types and recidivism. Certainly most of the systems correlate to some degree with institutional behaviors, but they may differentiate inmates more clearly on other important factors such as vulnerability, stress, amenability to treatment, and self-esteem. These outcome factors have not received much attention, although in fact they are relevant (proximate) to the psychological-classification systems.

Finally, a number of sources have pointed to the need for comparative assessment of the systems (Brennan 1987; Gottfredson 1987a; Megargee and Bohn 1979; Warren 1971). Such a comparison would not simply assess comparative predictive validities, but would offer important knowledge about certain questions regarding classification. Which systems seem to work best for which issues? How does administration process translate into assessment outcomes? Which administration procedures work best for which types of settings? What does a comparison of types tell us about the construct validity of the types identified by the respective systems?

CHAPTER 4

METHODOLOGY

Details of the research design for this study are set forth below. The intent of this chapter, however, goes beyond a technical overview of the project: Some of the measurement issues relate to both the research questions and the tasks of executing the study. In particular, we devote considerable attention to examining the reliability of two of the classification variables, the I-level interview method and Quay's Adult Internal Management System (AIMS). We also furnish reports of the research experience, assuming that, for some readers, discussions of test administration procedures and accounts of some of the organizational considerations in administering these systems may be as valuable as the more technical details of the research.

SAMPLE SELECTION

The sample pool consisted of inmates serving their first institutional placement after sentencing or revocation of probation. In order to examine the viability of the classification systems across distinct types of institutions and inmates, we sampled from two institutional populations, which were described in chapter 1.

Transferring inmates or inmates who already had served a portion of their sentence were ineligible. The rationale for limiting the sample to newly admitted inmates in this way reflects concern for empirically well-established changes in inmates' psychological states across phases of the incarceration experience (see Bukstel & Kilmann 1980). In addition to controlling for the amount of time served, selection criteria also excluded non-English-speaking inmates, inmates who could not read, and (where possible) inmates who were expecting release or transfer within four months of their admission.

Participation in the study was voluntary.[1] Thus, in addition to the above considerations, inmates were excluded from the sample for (a) refusal to participate, (b) repeated failure to respond to "call-outs," (c) being unavailable during the first month of their sentence (e.g., out on writ, in lock-up), and (d) not being contacted by the research staff. The last situation occurred when the number of intakes for a given month surpassed the time available to interview all potential participants. This happened primarily during transitions in project staff, when an interviewer was either beginning or terminating employment with the project, or during months when training clinics were scheduled.[2] Less frequently, there were a few months during which the prison facilities received an excessive number of admissions. In both situations, staff members were instructed to select inmates at random in order to avoid biasing the selection process.

Table 4-1 shows the size of the sampling pool and the distribution of cases across participation categories. The totals for the two institutions represent the total number of intakes designated as first placements from sentencing or probation violators respectively. Not all of these inmates, however, fit all of the selection criteria. When factors of eligibility and availability are considered, the penitentiary pool consists of 346 inmates and the camp pool consists of 300. Computation of the response rate, however, was based on the ratio of inmates interviewed to inmates asked to participate. Because we saw no indication of any systematic reason why an inmate would be in the "not contacted" category, or no way to contact the unavailable inmates,[3] consideration of these inmates in computation of the response rate would have created a misleading view of the representativeness of the research sample. Thus the response rates for the penitentiary and the camp were 76% and 83%, respectively.[4]

DATA COLLECTION PROCESS

This research has produced data pertaining to (a) diagnostic assessments on the five classification systems, (b) interview rating items on numerous content dimensions, (c) social, demographic, and criminal record background data, (d) six-month official follow-up measures of prison disciplinary infractions, (e) staff ratings of prison adjustment and work performance, and (f) self-report

Table 4-1: Frequency Distribution of Inmates in the Sample Pool across Participation Categories

Participation Category	Penitentiary	Prison Camp
Interviewed	179	190
Refusals	57	40
Ineligible: Non-English-Speaking	68	12
Ineligible for Other Reasons[a]	8	18
Not Contacted[b]	98	70
No Shows	12	0
Unavailable[c]	13	0
	---	---
Total Sampling Pool	435	330

[a] Includes inmates who could not read or those serving less than four months before release or transfer.

[b] Represents a random selection of eligible inmates who were not contacted because of time constraints.

[c] This category consists of inmates who were out on writ or in lock-up during the first month of incarceration.

measures of prison adjustment. The procedures for collecting these data are shown in figure 4-1.

As is apparent from figure 4-1, data-collection procedures varied greatly across the various data sources. Inmates participated in one long interview, two testing sessions, and, at least four months later, a session to complete a follow-up survey. The prison staff completed the Quay Correctional Adjustment Checklist (CAC) and two follow-up instruments, the Megargee Prison Adjustment Rating Form and the Megargee Work Performance Rating Form. The project research staff completed the remaining data-collection activities, including record checks, ratings of interview data, and the Quay Correctional Analysis of Life Histories Checklist (CALH). More specific details about the collection process are reserved for the section below on measurement.

AVAILABILITY OF DATA

It was not always possible to obtain a complete set of intake and follow-up data for each inmate interviewed. Attrition of data occurred for a number of reasons, including (*a*) inmates' withdrawing from the study after participating in the interview, (*b*) staff members' reluctance to complete the Quay Correctional Adjustment Checklist and the Megargee Work Performance and Adjustment Rating Forms, and (*c*) unanticipated releases or transfers. The reasons are specific to each measure; they are discussed in further detail in the section below on measurement.

Data availability for each data source is shown in table 4-2. In most instances, we were able to obtain data on at least 85% of the inmates participating in the study. With the exception of the Quay CAC, the follow-up survey, and the Megargee Prison Adjustment Rating Form (at the prison camp), we obtained the minimum sample size proposed for this research (N = 150 at each site). It should be noted that the follow-up survey was not built into the original design of the study[5] and was not implemented until nine months after the project began. As a result we could not always secure the inmate's compliance or locate the inmate. In fact, many of the camp inmates had been released before the first set of follow-up surveys was administered.

To address concerns related to data attrition, we conducted tests of comparison between the surveyed and the nonsurveyed participants to determine areas of over- or underrepresentation. Tests for difference of proportions (chi-square) and difference of means (t-tests), however, revealed that the surveyed groups were not signifi-

Figure 4-1: Data Sources and Collection Procedures

Data	Time of Administration	Administration
Intake Classification Data		
1. I-Level interview	1 month after commitment	Research analyst
2. MMPI	2 months after commitment	Research analyst
3. Conceptual level	2 months after commitment	Research analyst
4. Jesness Inventory	2 months after commitment	Research analyst
5. AIMS classification		
CAC	3 months after commitment	Prison staff
CALH	Upon receipt of interview and PSR data at University of Cincinnati	Graduate assistant
Intake Background Data		
1. Shipley	2 months after commitment	Research analyst
2. Presentence report	By 4 months after commitment	Research analyst
Institutional Adjustment Data		
1. Megargee Prison Adjustment Form	4, 5, & 6 months after commitment	Counselor/case manager
2. Megargee Work Performance Form	4, 5, & 6 months after commitment	Work Supervisor
3. Official disciplinary reports	6 months after commitment	Research analyst/graduate assistant
4. Self-report inmate survey	4 months after commitment	Research analyst

Table 4-2: Data Availability and Percentages of Sample Represented for Intake and Follow-up Data

Data Source	Penitentiary		Prison Camp	
	N	Percent	N	Percent
Intake Background Data				
Presentence Report	177	99	190	100
Shipley-Hartford	154	86	176	93
Interview Content Items	167	93	187	98
Classification Data				
I-level	177	99	188	99
Quay AIMS	150	84	122	64
Megargee MMPI	164	91	171	90
Jesness I-level	153	85	173	91
Conceptual Level	150	84	176	93
Follow-up Data				
Megargee Work Adjustment	177	99	167	88
Megargee Prison Adjustment	177	99	135	71
Disciplinary Data	167	93	180	95
Follow-up Survey	111	62	114	69

cantly different from the nonsurveyed groups on background factors of age, race, education, urban environment, employment status
at arrest, prior record, and WAISR-IQ (Shipley 1940). Nevertheless,
the difference between the survey sample and the full sample
amounts to approximately sixty cases, depending upon the institution and the test. This could still produce a situation where a finding
for the surveyed cases would have been different for the larger sample. This issue becomes particularly crucial as we compare findings
across official, self-report, and staff criterion measures. To make the
tests comparable, however, would have seriously compromised the
degrees of freedom for all of the tests. We chose in this study to maximize the degrees of freedom. A different examination of the comparison across follow-up measures, using only those cases which
had data on all follow-up measures, is available elsewhere (Van
Voorhis, forthcoming).

MEASUREMENT OF RESEARCH VARIABLES

Social, Demographic, and Criminal History Variables

In-depth presentence investigations (PSIs) are conducted routinely
for federal prisoners and probationers, and were available for nearly all of the penitentiary inmates (N = 177, 99%) and all of the
prison camp inmates. The PSIs consistently furnished data pertaining to age, race, marital status, number of dependents, last grade in
school completed, primary occupation, employment status at the
time of arrest, and military service. In addition, the PSIs provided
rap sheet summaries that furnished data on the extent and nature
of prior criminal activity and types of sanctions served and their
outcomes. Finally, detailed accounts of the incident(s) leading to
each inmate's arrest furnished information for measures such as
weapons possession, co-offender involvement, victim–offender
relationship, evidence of victim precipitation, evidence of professional criminal activity, and nature of the conviction charge. The
project staff also coded such system processing variables as date of
arrest, date of conviction, type of plea, and length of sentence.
Finally, IQ data was obtained by the staff's administration of the
Shipley Institute of Living Scale (Shipley 1940).[6] The data collection
form for these variables is shown in Appendix A.[7]

Interview Background (Content) Items

In addition to furnishing the material needed to formulate an I-
level diagnosis, interviews with the inmate subjects produced a

great amount of data directly relevant to the content of the interview. In a semistructured manner, the I-level interview (Appendix B) spans the inmate's perceptions relevant to the following: expectations of the prison sentence and institutional patterns, details of the conviction offense, perceptions of the victim(s), prior criminal involvements, marital stability, childhood and family history, affectivity, coping, alcohol and drug use, friends, military history, work history, school history, future orientation, and self-concept. In addition, raters characterized the subjects on several clinical items according to each rater's global assessment of the interview. These characteristics included concern for others, role-taking abilities, assertiveness, locus of control, and others.

We obtained a total of 244 variables from the rather lengthy interview (averaging 2.5 hours). Collection of these data involved five research assistants in a process of rating 354 interviews. Of the 244 variables, 192 attained an interrater agreement of 70% or higher. Since we used only three of these variables in the present study, the reader is referred elsewhere for details of the content analysis and reliability assessments (see Van Voorhis 1991). The three variables used in analyses reported in chapter 8 are (*a*) Does the inmate see others as willing to help? (*b*) Is the inmate "institutionalized" (penitentiary only)? and (*c*) Is the inmate oriented to the notion of rehabilitation? The percent interrater agreement for each of these items was 73%, 92%, and 72%, respectively.

Classification Variables

It is, of course, standard research practice to establish the reliability and validity of key variables at the beginning of the research report, but in this study, reliability and validity are also primary research questions. One of the goals of this research was to examine the reliability of systems that had not been tested previously for reliability in similar prison settings. The latter concerns were most pertinent to the Quay and the I-level systems.

Project interviewers conducted I-level assessments after extensive training. Their ratings were monitored throughout the project by periodically obtaining second ratings from experienced I-level trainers and practitioners. The reliability of the Quay AIMS diagnoses was assessed by second rating a subset of cases. This too was conducted by the project staff. Results of other tests—the MMPI, Conceptual Level, and Jesness Inventory—were sent to the most experienced assessment resources available for scoring/rating.

In most cases, it was our practice (albeit an expensive one) to repeat work that had been discovered to be flawed or to make revisions in administration or collection procedures when we thought the changes might reduce the likelihood of error. In the following sections, we offer additional details of these administration and assessment procedures. We also describe the procedure for monitoring the soundness of the data collection and assessment process for each of the classification systems studied in this research.

I-level classifications (interview method) were obtained through the administration of the semistructured interview described in the previous section on content analysis. The rating/ assessment of I-level is essentially a clinical process in which raters compare interview material to rather lengthy prototypical descriptions of each type and select the most appropriate diagnoses. Questions are open-ended, and the interview process is flexible in order to encourage maximum input from the subject. In this regard, I-level, like other clinical assessments, requires a certain degree of caution (Meehl 1954). In fact, in recent years, practitioners and researchers have expressed concern about the interrater reliability of I-level. Because no clear rules for decision-making have been developed, sources fear that agencies may be using different classification criteria (Harris 1988).

As indicated in chapter 3, interrater reliability has ranged from 67% to 86% for I-level and from 37% to 74% for subtype (see Harris 1983, 1988; Jesness 1988; Palmer and Werner 1972). Some observers would argue that these figures are not as bad as other clinically obtained diagnoses (see Meehl 1954; Sawyer 1966), but even these somewhat low figures are maintained at a high cost of training, second rating, and monitoring. Three weeks of training in the use of I-level is recommended. In addition, routine or frequent second ratings are necessary (Harris 1988).

The present study was not immune to these costs. Interviewers were trained initially by the project director and in a week-long intensive session conducted by a highly experienced I-level trainer. Interviews were rated by the interviewers and often were second-rated by either another interviewer, the project director, or one of three consultants in I-level assessment who worked contractually for the project. The second ratings were conducted in order to assess and monitor the reliability of the ratings.

Two types of second ratings were obtained. *Consensus ratings* involved joint ratings and a team approach to rating and discussing a case. This approach was used extensively during the training of each interviewer/rater and periodically throughout the project in an attempt to identify common sources of disagreement and to prevent a process whereby raters could "drift" into selective hearing and differential information-processing techniques in formulating their diagnoses. *Blind ratings* were conducted on 106 interviews; these resulted in 138 rater pairs, which formed the basis for computing the final reliability of the I-level classifications obtained in this research. These interviews were rated independently. Results typically were shared with other raters to obtain feedback, but the reliability computations are taken from the assessment formulated before any discussions were held.

The results are low but fall within the ranges established by previous research (see chapter 3). In the present study, the interrater reliability was 74% for level and 51% for subtype. These figures are lower than those obtained in the pilot study (82% for level and 65% for subtype) (Van Voorhis 1988), but the pilot study data were rated by only two raters, whereas the present study employed seven raters throughout the course of the research. In comparison to another study involving adults—a group of New Mexico probationers (Heide 1982)—our reliability results are higher for level and similar for subtype. In the New Mexico study, Heide reported an interrater reliability of 63% for level and 51% for subtype.

We attempted to identify common areas of disagreement or to determine whether some types identified by the system were more difficult to arrive at than others. Concordance rates, however, were similar across subtypes—(*a*) Se = 50%, (*b*) Ci = 45%, (*c*) Na = 55%, and (*d*) Nx = 44%—and there were numerous areas of disagreement. The following problems were most common: (*a*) It was difficult to differentiate Nas from Nxs, (*b*) Se ratings often were linked to an Na or Nx diagnosis, and (*c*) Cis were paired somewhat less frequently with an Na diagnosis.

In a number of instances, raters concurred in their areas of disagreement; they disagreed not about what they heard but rather about how to weight various pieces of information or how to diagnose transitional or potentially multiply classifiable offenders in order to arrive at a final diagnosis. Because the system does not provide for these situations in a structured manner, scholars have called for a revision in the system which would furnish decision-making rules for such cases (Harris 1988).

In order to explore this matter further, we assessed reliability a second time to incorporate cases in which raters were having difficulty in deciding between two or possibly three different ratings.

In order to do this, we examined raters' notes for all of the discordant diagnoses for instances in which one rater might have entertained a second diagnosis that agreed with the other rater's first diagnosis. Notes were not always complete enough to answer this question, but those that were available revealed that raters at least heard the same level in 88% of the cases and the same subtype in 66% of the cases. This finding tends to support the need for a more finely structured process.

Conceptual Level was measured by the Paragraph Completion Method (Hunt, Butler, Noy, and Rosser 1978), a semiprojective test consisting of six incomplete sentence stems: (*a*) What I think about rules . . . ; (*b*) When I am criticized . . . ; (*c*) What I think about parents . . . ; (*d*) When someone does not agree with me . . . ; (*e*) When I am not sure . . . ; and (*f*) When I am told what to do . . . . Subjects are asked to complete the thoughts with at least three sentences per stem.

Each of the six responses receives a score ranging from 0 to 3. The final score may be an average of the subject's three highest sentence-stem scores or the average of five sentence-stem scores.[8] Responses are scored by raters who assess the material for degree of cognitive complexity and degree of differentiation and integration (Reitsma-Street and Leschied 1988). The process is guided by a self-teaching manual that offers prototypical responses for each level of integration.

Results of the tests administered in this research were scored by an experienced researcher and trainer of Conceptual Level. Interrater reliability coefficients among offender populations are typically above .85 (Reitsma-Street 1984; Reitsma-Street and Leschied 1988). Test-retest coefficients range from .45 to .56 among nonoffender populations, but test-retest data are not available for offender populations (Reitsma-Street and Leschied 1988).

The Jesness Inventory I-level Classification System is portrayed as an actuarial method of assessing I-level. The I-level classifications are obtained through a paper-and-pencil test, the Jesness Inventory which contains 155 true–false items that yield scores on eleven personality-attitudinal scales and nine I-level subtype scales. The I-level subtype scales form the basis of the classification system (Jesness and Wedge 1983). Although the system was established for delinquents, adult norms are available. The latter are essentially norms for an 18-year-old population, but the authors assert that several studies have found them adequate for adult populations (Jesness 1988).

In the present study, test results were sent to Consulting Psychologists Press in Palo Alto, California, for computerized scoring. Sources report somewhat low test-retest reliability figures for this method, 48% for subtype and 68% for I-level. The test-retest correlation was .65 (Jesness 1988).

Megargee MMPI-Based Offender Classification System results were obtained from the widely used 566-item Minnesota Multiphasic Personality Inventory (MMPI). Test results were sent to the Criminal Justice Assessment Services at Florida State University, a scoring center established by the system's originator, Edwin Megargee. This computerized process classified 149 (89%) of the penitentiary tests and 157 (86%) of the prison camp tests into single- or multiple-classification types. *Unclassified*, in this sense, meant that the computer issued a statement that none of the scoring criteria had been met. Further, 115 (69%) of the penitentiary tests and 113 (62%) of the prison camp tests were classified uniquely, each into a single type. This outcome is consistent with other research which has shown repeatedly that the computerized system uniquely classifies approximately two-thirds of the correctional populations (Megargee and Bohn 1979; Zager 1988).

Since sources on the MMPI system maintain that the remaining 33% of the MMPI protocols usually can be scored clinically, we returned all "tied" or "unclassified" protocols to Megargee, who agreed to assess the results. We also sent results that suggested validity problems back to the center for review. Typically, MMPI results are brought into question when the validity scales indicate a problem, but this is not a straightforward process with offender populations because it is not unusual for offenders to "fake good" or "fake bad." In addition, some of the types identified by the system (e.g., Hows) may find it difficult to complete the test because of the pathology that they evidence (see Megargee and Bohn 1979). Ultimately, 164 (98%) of the penitentiary and 171 (94%) of the camp protocols were classified uniquely either by computer or clinically. In comparison to other studies, these proportions are somewhat high. Zager (1988) notes that "in most settings, 80 percent to 96 percent of the cases are ultimately uniquely classified." Our procedure, however, required the use of somewhat liberal criteria. We excluded from further analysis the cases in which the raw L (lie) score was 10 or more (six penitentiary and nine prison camp cases). As shown in table 4-3, however, several additional validity problems were apparent. As a check against this liberal application of the criteria, the subsequent MMPI analyses were conducted a second time; at that point,

Table 4-3: Validity Scores for MMPI Profiles

Validity Criteria	Penitentiary		Prison Camp	
	N	Percent[a]	N	Percent[a]
Valid profile	90	54	105	58
F-K > 13	35	21	45	25
F > 79 T	11	7	7	4
Qu > 50	1	1	1	1
F > 99 T	4	2	0	0
L > 7 < 10	20	12	15	8
L ≥ 10[b]	6	4	9	5
Total	167	100	182	100

[a] Percentages may not add to 100 due to rounding.
[b] Discarded from the analysis.

only the most valid cases were used in order to assure that this decision regarding inclusion had not affected the results.

Even though the **Quay Adult Internal Management System** was the easiest instrument to complete, it proved the most difficult of the five systems to administer. The system requires completion of two behavioral checklists, the 63-item Correctional Adjustment Checklist (CAC) and the 50-item Checklist for the Analysis of Life History (CALH). The CAC was designed to be completed by the prison staff after observing the inmate for a brief period of time. The fact that this design typically involved a counselor or case manager posed a number of difficulties. First, counselors and case managers reported large caseloads and excessive paperwork. As a result, they sometimes objected to any additional expectations. This situation was most obvious shortly after data collection began, when the research staff observed that approximately four staff members were completing the CACs by responding positively to every item on every form. In addition, some prison staff members felt that, because of large caseloads, they did not always know the inmates well enough to complete the CAC.

We took a number of steps to address these problems. First, the project director attended a prison staff meeting to discuss the problems connected with the CAC. Second, a prison case manager, who was also well versed in research methodology, was hired contractually to coordinate collection of the CAC data at the penitentiary during off hours and to serve as a liaison between case managers and the project staff. Third, CACs were given to a work supervisor if the counselors or case managers felt they did not know the inmate well enough.[9] Fourth, we readministered the CACs that we found had been completed inadequately and stopped approaching staff members who, we found, were submitting flawed data.

Despite these efforts, data attrition was a problem. As stated earlier, CACs were available for only 150 (84%) of the penitentiary inmates and 122 (64%) of the camp inmates. This problem was most apparent for the camp sample, but comparison tests (chi-square) between the tested group and the group not tested revealed no significant differences on factors pertaining to race, age, education, length of sentence, and prior record.

Table 4-4 portrays these issues in greater detail. The finding that most of these problems occurred at the camp may be attributable to the fact that the longer sentences at the penitentiary gave the research staff more time either to obtain the first CAC or to submit a second CAC if the results on the first were found to be flawed. These problems were more difficult to correct at the camp

Table 4-4: Details of Quay AIMS Data Collection

Collection Issue	Penitentiary		Prison Camp	
	N	Percent[a]	N	Percent[a]
Level of Difficulty				
Not difficult (knows inmate)	51	44	46	87
Difficult	64	55	7	13
N of Months (Intake to CAC)				
3 or less	97	72	46	39
4 to 8	31	23	50	42
9 or more	6	4	23	19
Role of Person Completing CAC				
Counselor	3	2	18	15
Case manager	136	95	44	36
Work supervisor	4	3	44	36
Interviewer	0	0	15	12
Inaccurate CAC				
Yes, redone	2	1	30	21
No, accurate CAC	148	91	92	63
Yes, discarded	13	8	23	16

[a] Percentages may not add to 100 due to rounding.

because some of the inmates were released early.[10] Although a strong effort was made to obtain the CACs according to our original plan of collecting them within three months of intake, we decided to continue attempting to obtain the data even if we could not do so within that period. As table 4-4 shows, some of the cases were obtained after the three-month deadline.

CALHs were completed by the research staff after they listened to the interview and reviewed the background data collection form containing PSI information. Generally, no problems arose during this part of the data collection.[11]

In order to assess reliability, we obtained a second set of Quay AIMS assessments, consisting of both the CAC and the CALH, on a random selection of 38 inmate subjects. The reliability sample consisted of 18 penitentiary inmates and 20 camp inmates. As shown in table 4-5, reliability was examined in several ways. Generally, overall interrater reliability was low: 55% interrater agreement and an interrater reliability coefficient (Cramer's V) of .41 (p ≤ .10). It was particulary low in the penitentiary (50%) and somewhat higher at the prison camp. The higher·reliability figures for the camp, however, may be attributable to the limited variability across diagnostic categories in that setting. Most of the camp inmates who were classified on this system were either Manipulators (18%) or Situationals (67%).[12] Reliability figures generally improve as the number of classification categories decreases and lessens the number of potential sources for disagreement.

As will be apparent in later chapters, we collapsed the AIMS classifications for some analyses, combining Neurotic Anxious and Immature inmates into one category and Asocial Aggressive and Manipulative inmates into another. We did this in order to consider the possibility that if disagreements in judgment involved disagreements between similar classifications, the errors might be less serious than the disagreements between dissimilar types. Moreover, a portion of the analysis of the AIMS data conducted for chapters 7 and 8 uses the collapsed categories in order to improve cell frequencies and degrees of freedom. Results show that rater agreement within recoded categories is somewhat higher: 63% overall, 56% for the penitentiary, and 70% for the prison camp (Cramer's V = .59, p ≤.05).

We obtained the highest reliability figures by omitting any data known to have been obtained by a few case managers who were suspected of filling out forms inaccurately. As shown in table 4-5, omission of this material raises reliability figures to 67% overall, 56% for the penitentiary, and 82% for the prison camp

Table 4-5: Percent Interrater Agreement and Interrater Reliability Coefficients for Quay AIMS

Test	Percent Agreement		Coefficient Cramers's V
	N	Percent	
Interrater			
All cases	38	55	.41 *
Penitentiary	18	50	
Prison Camp	20	65	
Recoded			
All cases	38	63	
Penitentiary	18	56	
Prison Camp	20	70	
Test Retest			
All cases	21	67	.59 **
Penitentiary	10	50	
Prison Camp	11	82	
Omitting Potential Rater Problems			
All cases	27	67	.57 **
Penitentiary	16	56	
Prison Camp	11	82	
Recoded			
All cases	27	74	
Penitentiary	16	62	
Prison Camp	11	91	
Least Difficult Cases			
All cases	23	56	.50 *
Penitentiary	14	50	
Prison Camp	9	78	
Recoded			
All cases	23	65	
Penitentiary	14	57	
Prison Camp	9	78	

* $p \leq .10$

** $p \leq .05$

(Cramer's V = .57, p ≤ .05). Within the recoded categories, these figures rise to 74% overall, 62% for the penitentiary, and 91% for the prison camp. The latter were in the range of results considered acceptable for further analysis. Because we either readministered or excluded AIMS data known to be inaccurate, these final reliability figures should be considered to represent most accurately the data sets that were used in this research.

In assessing test-retest reliability, we analyzed only those cases in which both sets of diagnoses were completed within the first three months of intake. This procedure was intended to test the stability of the assessment process; however, results also may have been attenuated by the staff's increased familiarity with the inmates' behavior.

Although we had also considered the possibility of controlling for raters' level of difficulty in completing the CAC, preliminary analyses suggested that such additional precautions were unnecessary. As table 4-5 shows, the least difficult cases were no more likely to be agreed upon than others. This also was the case in a similar analysis of the I-level diagnoses. In both cases, it is likely that the assessment of "certainty" was merely another judgment call; that is, raters were no more likely to agree on the level of certainty than on the final AIMS diagnosis.

Follow-Up Variables

The literature on prediction and classification faults much of the existing research for overreliance on official record data rather than depending on optimally relevant theoretical variables (Farrington 1987). The problem is manifested in a number of ways, but in the most common practice, outcomes are limited to officially recorded recidivism measures.

Closely paralleling this practice in prison settings is the common use of officially noted disciplinary infractions as criterion variables. The results are obvious: Not all institutional problems are recorded officially or recorded in sufficient detail (Light 1990). Further, disciplinary infractions are only one of many outcomes of interest to correctional scholars and practitioners. Most important, they are not the outcomes with the greatest theoretical relevance to the psychological classification measures—measures pertinent to treatment amenability, stress, coping, fear, aggressive behaviors, suicide prognosis, and other elements make far more sense. Added to this are many problems associated with the use of single- rather than multiple-outcome measures; reliability and validity are easier to establish by obtaining more than one measure of a given construct (Farrington and Tarling 1985). Finally, the practice of comparing systems on only one criterion ignores the possibility that the systems serve different purposes (MacKenzie 1989), as shown by the likely observation that some systems will correlate more strongly on some criterion measures than on others.

For these reasons, we tracked the inmate subjects of this research on multiple criteria: self-report measures obtained from surveys of the inmates, prison-record data of disciplinary infractions and victimizations, and staff ratings of institutional adjustment and work performance.

Follow-up surveys were administered to inmates at least four months after intake or before release if they were serving less than four months.[13] Because the survey was not implemented until nine months after the beginning of the project, and because we attempted to obtain data on as many cases as possible, the follow-up period was often longer than four months. In the penitentiary, for example, time intervening between intake and the administration of the survey ranged from three to thirty-six months ($\bar{X}$ = 7.2 mo., median = 6.0 mo.). At the prison camp, follow-up ranged from 2 to 12 months, with an average of 5.5 months.

The content of the survey spanned such topics as inmates' perceptions of the availability of help in the institution; participation in treatment and educational programs; work absenteeism; health; victimization experiences and threats; awards; participation in aggressive, threatening, or other illegal activity; contact with family and friends; communication strategies; stress; sources of stress; coping strategies; and attitudes and beliefs about crime and imprisonment. One of the stress measures consisted of a five-category measure of the extent to which the inmate was experiencing stress: (1) "I have not experienced stress. I usually do not worry about things"; (2) "I sometimes worry about things, but I feel that I can keep it under control"; (3) "I worry a lot about things, but usually I can find some way to feel better after a while"; (4) "I worry a lot and have difficulty finding something that will help me feel better"; and (5) I worry so much that I sometimes feel sick." The other stress measure consisted of the Center for Epidemiological Studies Depression (CESD) Scale, which measures a generalized, pervasive form of psychological distress (Radloff 1977). A copy of the 175-item survey is appended (Appendix C).

Other items consisted of Likert-type scales depicting the extent to which an inmate engaged in a specified activity. For example, several items designed to identify coping strategies offered responses such as (1) "I do not do this activity"; (2) "I do this but it is not at all helpful"; (3) "Somewhat helpful"; (4) "Very helpful"; (5) "Extremely helpful." Items tapping specific sources of inmates' stress were four-item Likert-type scales ranging from "not at all stressful" to "extremely stressful." Finally, some items asked respondents to indicate the number of times they had experienced a given event or engaged in a particular behavior. The options were (1) "never," (2) "once," or (3) "more than once."

The analysis described in this report focuses on the following self-reported behaviors and experiences: aggressive and threatening behaviors, nonviolent violations of prison rules, fear of prison life, victimizations or threats of victimizations, stress, treatment utilization, activity as a coping strategy, perceived help from others, formation of friendships with other inmates, and communication with staff. The final measures consisted of cumulative indexes combining two to seven variables into composite measures. This data reduction strategy involved a two-step process of first selecting items on the basis of face validity and then conducting an item analysis that refined the scale further in order to maximize internal consistency.

The scales for the two settings were not identical and should not be used to compare the results across samples. Our attempts to make the scales identical revealed clear differences, particularly concerning the respondents' perceptions of the aversiveness of the environments, their fear, and their aggressiveness toward others. Items constituting each index were selected to reflect the most salient features of each setting; as a result, they could differ from setting to setting. Moreover, in order to improve internal consistency (alpha) coefficients, item analysis occasionally resulted in the deletion of an item from the scale for one institution but not from the corresponding scale for the other institution.

Indexes for the penitentiary are shown in table 4-6. A list of the items comprising each index is shown in Appendix D. Similar information for the prison camp appears in table 4-7 and Appendix E, respectively. The distributions were skewed for some scales, particularly the victimization and the disciplinary scales. Yet, although the majority of inmates reported not being engaged in aggressive, threatening behaviors, violating prison rules, or experiencing threats and attacks from other inmates, there were enough such inmates to permit further analysis. Moreover, the indexes evidenced much greater variability than some of the single items would have displayed. Nevertheless, as a correction for the remaining irregular distributions, we ran all analyses of

Table 4-6: Survey Follow-up Scales, Penitentiary

Scale	Range of Scores	Mean	Standardized Alpha	N
Victimization Scales				
Victimization	1.0–3.5	1.3	.75	111
Fear	1.0–4.0	1.5	.80	111
Support Networks				
Perceives help	1.0–3.7	1.9	.70	107
Has friends /support	1.0–5.0	2.8	.73	109
Communication	1.0–4.3	2.4	.67	108
Program Utilization				
Participation	1.0–4.0	2.2	.65	107
High activity	1.0–5.0	3.1	.64	110
Stress				
Extent[a]				
CESD scale	5–85	36.9	.78	111
Self-Report Disciplinary				
Self-report aggression	1.0–2.7	1.2	.71	110
Nonviolent	1.0–3.5	1.3	.58	110

[a] This is a single variable rather than a cumulative index.

Table 4-7: Survey Follow-up Scales, Prison Camp

Scale	Range of Scores	Mean	Standardized Alpha	N
Victimization Scales				
Victimization	1.0–3.0	1.5	.70	111
Fear	1.0–2.3	1.2	.58	113
Support Networks				
Perceives help	1.0–3.4	2.1	.57	111
Has friends/support	1.0–5.0	3.1	.71	113
Communication	1.0–5.0	2.5	.62	113
Program Utilization				
Participation	1.0–4.0	2.2	.63	109
High activity	1.0–4.2	2.5	.68	108
Stress				
Extent[a]				
CESD scale	5.0–75.0	34.1	.76	111
Self-Report Disciplinary				
Self-report aggression	1.0–3.0	1.3	.63	114
Nonviolent	1.0–2.3	1.0	.68	113

[a] This is a single variable rather than a cumulative index.

skewed data a second time using log transformations of each scale.

As noted above, the amount of time from prison intake to survey administration fluctuated among respondents. Therefore, as a final step in the construction of the self-report measures, we determined whether the results could have been biased by our inability to administer all surveys at the same phase of incarceration. We did this by correlating a measure of the number of months intervening between an inmate's admission and his completion of the survey with the survey indexes. None of the tests conducted for the penitentiary data proved significant. Two tests of the prison camp data, however, showed a significant relationship between the amount of time served and the self-report measures. The first test revealed a significant relationship between time and the fear index (Pearson's $r = -.19$, $p \leq .05$), an indication that inmates were likely to evidence fear of other inmates earlier in the sentence than later. The second test revealed a correlation between time and the indicator of one's tendency to form supportive friendships ($r = -.26$, $p \leq .003$), and showed a greater tendency to form supportive friendships early in one's term rather than later. To correct for these observations, we control for the time variable in the analysis of the prison camp self-report data shown in chapter 8.

Follow-up measures of officially recorded disciplinary infractions and victimizations were obtained by examining the inmate's central file six months after prison admission. We noted the inmate's disciplinary log, disciplinary reports, and records of protective and administrative custody. Although the six-month follow-up singly censored time frame was the basis for the original design, follow-up periods sometimes were less than six months if the inmate was released early. This happened more frequently, however, in the prison camp ($N = 59$, or 33%) than in the penitentiary ($N = 5$, or 3%). Follow-up periods in the prison camp ranged from one month to six months and averaged 5.3 months.

As shown in table 4-2, these data were available for most of the inmate participants. Relatively few inmates (11 prison camp inmates and 12 penitentiary inmates) were transferred to other facilities. We tracked these cases to those facilities by letter, requesting the follow-up information.[14]

The disciplinary data were coded as follows: (*a*) number of disciplinary infractions over the entire follow-up period; (*b*) number of follow-up months available; (*c*) total number of violent infractions; (*d*) total number of incidents involving insubordination or disobeying prison rules; (*e*) total number of drug- or alcohol-related incidents; (*f*) total number of incidents involving theft or destruction of property; (*g*) total number of infractions involving threatening staff or inmates with bodily harm; (*h*) total number of incidents involving possession of a weapon; (*i*) total number of gambling incidents; (*j*) whether a transfer occurred; (*k*) number of infractions in each of the six months of follow-up in addition to the nature of the infraction.[15]

Many of the measures identified above were found to represent relatively rare events; therefore, limited variability precluded their being used in the analyses. Three variables were selected for the penitentiary follow-up: (1) drug and alcohol infractions, (2) all disciplinary infractions, and (3) insubordination. Only two variables could be used from the prison camp data: all disciplinary infractions and citations for insubordination. For the final measures, we calculated a rate per month times 100. We also computed log transformations for second analyses of these data in order to determine whether corrections for the distribution limitations affected the results.

Staff ratings of institutional adjustment and work performance were obtained from the Megargee Prison Adjustment Rating Form and the Megargee Work Performance Rating Form (Megargee 1972). Where possible, each instrument was administered three times to each inmate (during the fourth, fifth, and sixth month following admission). Occasionally it was not possible to obtain all three evaluations for each inmate, but we had three Megargee Prison Adjustment Forms for 172 (97%) of the penitentiary inmates and for 69 (41%) of the prison camp inmates. Three Megargee Work Performance Rating Forms were available for 172 (97%) of the penitentiary inmates and 95 (70%) of the prison camp inmates.[16] As might be expected, it was more difficult to obtain all three in the prison camp than at the penitentiary because of early releases.

Generally, case managers and counselors completed the Prison Adjustment Rating Forms and the work supervisors completed the Work Performance Rating Forms. If necessary, work supervisors also completed the Prison Adjustment Rating Forms. Because both facilities required the Megargee Work Performance Rating Form, these documents often could be obtained from an inmate's central file. With the Prison Adjustment Rating Form, however, we experienced some of the same difficulties as when we collected the Quay CAC. They were resolved in the course of resolving the problems with the Quay AIMS data.

Despite these problems, the staff ratings proved to be very sensitive criterion measures. Early in the analysis, however, we discovered that some of the adjustment forms had been completed by the same staff member who completed the Quay CAC. This occurred for 72 (41%) of the penitentiary cases and for 20 (15%) of the prison camp cases. Some aspects of the research design may have corrected for this potential lack of independence. First, correctional staff had no knowledge of the actual Quay AIMS classification. Second, their assessments on the prison adjustment measures were not completed at the same time as the Quay CAC measures. Third, the final Quay classification represented the synthesis of the staff member's completion of the CAC and the interviewer's rating of the CALH. As a precaution, analyses of the relationship between the Quay AIMS classification and the staff ratings were conducted twice, once with all of the data and again without the cases that might have been contaminated.

Rating forms offered primarily five-point Likert-scale responses to the questions asked. Typically the items ranged from a poor assessment (1) to average (3) to excellent (5). Staff rating measures for each of these items consisted of an average of the number of ratings available for each subject. The items selected for inclusion in the study are shown in table 4-8. The Megargee Prison Adjustment Rating Form also contains a checklist at the end, where staff are asked to indicate whether the characteristic pertained to the inmate (yes or no). Final measures for these items were nominal indicators of whether the inmate had received a rating of "yes" on any of the three (or fewer) evaluations. "Loner," shown on table 4-8, is such an item. A code of "yes" means that on one or more of the adjustment forms a staff member had checked the item, an indication that the staff member considered the inmate to be a loner.

DATA ANALYSIS PLAN

Most details of the data analysis are provided at the beginning of each chapter or as they pertain to specific research questions. Generally, we achieved the aims of this research through a variety of strategies including cross-tabular analysis for bivariate questions and multivariate analysis using multiple regression (OLS), probit analysis, and common factor analysis.

Table 4-8: Megargee Prison Adjustment and Work Performance Scales

Scale	Penitentiary			Prison Camp		
	$\overline{X}$	Range	s.d.	$\overline{X}$	Range	s.d.
	Disciplinary Measures					
Relations with other men[a]	3.09	1.3–5.0	.47	3.56	1.7–5.0	.72
Relations with authorities[a]	3.24	1.3–5.0	.54	3.60	1.7–5.0	.65
Verbal/physical aggressiveness[b]	3.23	1.0–4.7	.54	3.53	2.0–5.0	.66
Cooperativeness[a]	3.12	1.0–5.0	.56	3.56	2.0–5.0	.61
Need for supervision[a]	3.04	1.0–4.3	.52	3.50	1.3–5.0	.68
Response to supervision[a]	3.21	1.0–4.7	.54	3.57	1.7–5.0	.68
	Treatment Measures					
Emotional Control[c]	3.06	1.7–4.0	.41	3.37	1.0–5.0	.34
Maturity[a]	3.09	1.0–4.7	.55	3.55	1.7–5.0	.70
Motivation[a]	3.50	1.0–5.0	.71	3.91	1.5–5.0	.69
Learning Ability[a]	3.57	1.3–5.0	.69	3.94	2.0–5.0	.68
Loner	mode (no) = 92%					
Follows Crowd	mode (no) = 89%					

[a] Scale ranges from poor (1) to average/satisfactory (3) to excellent (5).
[b] Scale ranges from extremely hostile (1) to generally doesn't carry a chip on his shoulders (3) to very passive (5).
[c] Scale ranges from very emotional (1) to average (3) to super-controlled (5).

CHAPTER 5

DESCRIPTIONS OF
THE SAMPLES

This chapter describes the social, demographic, and offense characteristics of the penitentiary and the prison camp samples. The distributions of offenders in the five correctional classification systems are also presented as one of the research goals of this study.

SOCIAL AND DEMOGRAPHIC
BACKGROUND CHARACTERISTICS

The background characteristics of the two offender groups are shown in table 5-1. With the exception of the WAIS-R scores, which were obtained from the Shipley Institute of Living Scale, these data were extracted from presentence reports. The two samples differ substantially in these and in the offense-related characteristics, which will be reported later in this chapter.

In profiling the two groups, the prison camp inmates can be characterized as slightly older than the penitentiary inmates, predominantly white, and more likely to have families. The average age of the penitentiary inmates was 33 (median = 32), whereas the average age of the camp inmates was 37 (median = 36).

The educational, employment, and economic histories of the two groups differ dramatically. At the time of their arrests, the penitentiary inmates were far more likely to be unemployed and to report either no occupation or a criminal occupation. Most of the camp inmates (75%) had at least a high school education or a GED, whereas only 53% of the penitentiary inmates had completed high school requirements.[1]

Table 5-1: Frequency and Percent Distribution of Inmates across Social and Demographic Variables

Variable	Penitentiary N	Penitentiary Percent[a]	Prison Camp N	Prison Camp Percent[a]
Age at admission				
19 to 29	64	37	47	25
30 to 45	97	56	101	53
46 and older	12	7	42	22
	173	100	190	100
Race				
White	89	50	151	80
Black	74	41	31	16
American Indian	5	3	1	1
Hispanic	8	5	5	3
Asian	1	1	2	1
	177	100	190	100
Marital status				
married	57	33	88	47
never married	47	27	38	20
divorced	39	22	41	22
separated	13	7	8	4
widowed	2	1	2	1
common-law married	14	8	11	6
other	1	1	0	0
	173	100	188	100
Number of dependents (exclusive of the inmate)				
none	80	47	56	30
one	27	16	51	27
two	23	13	29	15
three	25	15	32	17
four or more	16	10	21	11
	171	100	189	100
Education (last grade completed)				
6 to 11 years	81	47	47	25
high school	34	20	74	39
GED	35	20	17	9
some post-high school	19	10	24	13
college graduate	2	1	24	13
some post-college work	2	1	4	2
	173	100	190	100
Evidence of school failure				
yes	110	66	55	29
no	57	34	132	71
	167	100	187	100

Table 5-1 *(continued)*

Variable	Penitentiary N	Penitentiary Percent[a]	Prison Camp N	Prison Camp Percent[a]
WAIS-R (Shipley)				
less than 95	82	53	57	32
96 to 105	42	27	60	35
106 and above	30	20	59	33
	154	100	176	100
Primary occupation				
no occupation	34	20	9	5
professional	8	5	22	12
manager/administrator	8	5	31	16
sales	6	3	12	6
clerical	1	1	3	2
craftsman	10	6	27	14
transport/equipment operator	6	3	6	3
laborer	61	36	66	35
farmer	1	1	5	3
service worker	3	2	1	1
armed services	2	1	1	1
student	1	1	1	1
househusband	0	0	2	1
criminal occupation	28	16	3	2
	169	100	189	100
Employment status (at arrest)				
not working	117	70	53	28
working, full time	29	17	104	55
working, occasionally	12	7	28	15
working, status unknown	9	5	4	2
	167	100	189	100
Military service				
yes	40	23	73	39
no	133	77	115	61
	173	100	188	100
Cited for problems while in the military				
yes	27	67	16	22
no	13	33	57	78
	40	100	73	100

[a]Percentages may not sum to 100 because of rounding.

It would be difficult, however, to characterize the prison camp inmates as "mainstream." Indeed, despite their relative differences from the penitentiary inmates, a substantial proportion of the camp inmates' records showed evidence of school failure (29%), below-average IQ (32%), and employment difficulties (43%). Of those who served in the military (73 or 39% of the entire camp sample), 16 were reported to have been cited for problems. As will be seen in the next section, approximately one-third of the camp inmates had current or prior records indicating serious drug or alcohol involvement. The differences between these two groups nevertheless offer a rich opportunity to compare classification systems in two settings that differ in important ways.

PRIOR RECORD BACKGROUND CHARACTERISTICS

As shown in table 5-2, most of the offenders in both samples had records of prior criminal involvement. The most distinguishing difference between the two groups concerned their prior prison experience: The majority of penitentiary inmates (72%) had served a prior prison term, whereas only 18% of the camp inmates had done so. In addition, a substantial proportion of the penitentiary inmates who had prior records also had records of violations of the conditions of prior sanctions, such as escapes (20%), probation revocations (45%), and parole revocations (43%).

The length and the seriousness of the prior criminal records are much greater for the penitentiary inmates than for the prison camp inmates.[2] Sixty-five percent of the penitentiary inmates, but only 15% of the prison camp inmates, evidenced prior records of violent behavior. Records of drug-related involvements, shown in table 5-2, are somewhat higher for the penitentiary inmates than for the camp inmates if current involvements are included, but are substantially higher for the penitentiary inmates when current offenses are not considered.

CHARACTERISTICS OF THE CONVICTION OFFENSE

Table 5-3 presents the frequency and percentage distribution of inmates across their most serious conviction charges. Conviction on a drug-related charge—particularly possession with intent to distribute—characterizes a major portion of the offenses. Among prison camp inmates, drug offenses represent the modal offense category. For penitentiary inmates, the proportion of drug convictions (26%) is surpassed only by the proportion of offenders convicted of bank crimes (27%), specifically armed and unarmed bank robbery. As

Table 5-2: Frequency and Percent Distribution of Inmates across Offense History Variables

Variable	Penitentiary		Prison Camp	
	N	Percent[a]	N	Percent[a]
Prior adult or juvenile record				
yes	171	97	140	74
no	6	3	50	26
	177	100	190	100
Prior adult arrests				
yes	169	96	140	74
no	8	4	50	26
	177	100	190	100
Prior adult convictions				
yes	161	92	119	63
no	15	8	71	37
	176	100	190	100
Prior prison sentence				
yes	121	72	25	18
no	47	28	115	82
	168	100	140	100
Amount of prior time served (includes jail time)[b]				
two years or less	30	21	22	56
25 mos. to 5 years	39	28	3	8
61 mos. to 10 years	22	16	1	2
more than 10 years	10	7	0	0
time served unknown	39	28	13	33
	140	100	39	100
Record of prior arrests for dealing in drugs[b]				
yes	45	27	41	29
no	122	73	99	71
	167	100	140	100
Record of prior professional criminal activity[b]				
yes	66	39	19	14
no	102	61	119	86
	168	100	138	100
Record of prior violence[b]				
yes	109	65	21	15
no	59	35	115	85
	168	100	136	100

Table 5-2 *(continued)*

Variable	Penitentiary		Prison Camp	
	N	Percent[a]	N	Percent[a]
Record of prior sex offenses[b]				
yes	15	9	1	1
no	152	91	140	99
	167	100	141	100
Prior arrest for the same offense as present offense[b]				
yes	44	26	33	23
no	124	74	108	77
	168	100	141	100
Record of drug-related offenses (current or prior)				
yes, prior record	19	11	12	6
yes, current offense	28	16	26	14
yes, both	39	23	22	12
no	86	50	124	67
	172	100	184	100
Record of alcohol-related offenses (current or prior)				
yes, prior record	26	15	41	22
yes, current offense	11	7	3	2
yes, both	23	13	7	4
no	110	65	138	73
	170	100	189	100
Prior prison escapes[c]				
yes	28	20	2	5
no	112	80	37	95
	140	100	39	100
Prior probation revocations[d]				
yes	49	45	16	24
no	61	55	51	76
	110	100	67	100
Prior parole revocations[e]				
yes	41	43	5	29
no	54	57	12	70
	115	100	17	100
Prior record as a juvenile				
yes	78	47	23	13
no	87	53	157	87
	165	100	180	100

Table 5-2 *(continued)*

Variable	Penitentiary N	Penitentiary Percent[a]	Prison Camp N	Prison Camp Percent[a]
Prior incarceration as a juvenile[f]				
yes	47	66	8	36
no	<u>24</u>	<u>34</u>	<u>14</u>	<u>64</u>
	71	100	22	100
Record of violent behavior as a juvenile[f]				
yes	26	37	2	10
no	<u>45</u>	<u>63</u>	<u>19</u>	<u>90</u>
	71	100	21	100

[a] Percentages may not sum to 100 because of rounding.
[b] Includes only offenders with prior arrests.
[c] Includes only offenders who have served prior prison or jail terms.
[d] Includes only offenders who have had prior terms of probation.
[e] Includes only offenders who have had prior terms of parole.
[f] Includes only offenders with prior juvenile records.

Table 5-3: Frequency and Percent Distribution of Inmates across Most Serious Current Offense Charge

Variable	Penitentiary		Prison Camp	
	N	Percent[a]	N	Percent[a]
Drug charges				
sale of controlled substance	0	0	7	4
possession with intent to distribute	29	16	54	28
possession	1	1	1	1
manufacturing controlled substance	1	1	0	0
importation of controlled substance	0	0	2	1
theft of controlled substance				
involving murder	1	1	0	0
conspiracy to distribute	14	8	30	16
Subtotal	46	26	94	49
Violent offenses				
felony murder/homicide	5	3	0	0
voluntary manslaughter	1	1	0	0
murder for hire (interstate)	2	1	0	0
arson	2	1	0	0
conspiracy to commit arson	1	1	0	0
kidnapping	2	1	0	0
robbery (unarmed)	1	1	0	0
robbery (armed)	2	1	0	0
conspiracy to kill a government				
official	4	2	0	0
threatening the President	3	2	0	0
aiding and abetting to threaten				
the President	1	1	0	0
rape	2	1	0	0
sexual molestation	1	1	0	0
mailing a threat	1	1	0	0
Subtotal	28	16	0	0
Charges of illegal operations				
(other than drugs)				
counterfeit	0	0	4	2
conspiracy to commit counterfeit	0	0	2	1
transporting stolen autos (interstate)	3	2	2	1
conspiracy to transport stolen property	1	1	2	1
racketeering (RICO)	3	2	1	1
aiding and abetting (auto theft)	0	0	3	2
FDA - selling adulterated food	0	0	1	1
unlawful activity (interstate)	0	0	1	1

Table 5-3 *(continued)*

Variable	Penitentiary N	Penitentiary Percent[a]	Prison Camp N	Prison Camp Percent[a]
conducting illegal business	1	1	1	1
infringement of a copyright	0	0	1	1
theft/possession/conversion of				
U.S. Treasury checks	0	0	4	2
transportation of person under 18				
interstate to engage in prostitution	1	1	0	0
unauthorized sale of stolen miliary				
equipment	0	0	1	1
Subtotal	9	5	23	12
Bank crimes				
bank larceny	2	1	0	0
bank robbery (unarmed)	13	7	1	1
aiding and abetting unarmed bank				
robbery	1	1	0	0
bank robbery (armed)	28	16	0	0
aiding and abetting armed bank				
robbery	2	1	1	1
theft of bank funds	0	0	1	1
misapplication of bank funds	0	0	3	2
bank fraud	2	1	2	1
Subtotal	48	27	8	4
Postal crimes				
mail fraud	2	1	13	7
possession of stolen mail	1	1	4	2
Subtotal	3	2	17	9
Fraud (other)				
bribery	0	0	1	1
embezzlement	0	0	3	2
forgery	2	1	0	0
credit card fraud	2	1	12	6
wire fraud	0	0	1	1
extortion	1	1	1	1
false claim on income tax	2	1	4	2
forged securities (interstate transfer)	1	1	2	1
failure to file income tax	0	0	4	2
Subtotal	8	5	28	15

Table 5-3 *(continued)*

	Penitentiary		Prison Camp	
Variable	N	Percent[a]	N	Percent[a]
Theft				
burglary	2	1	0	0
theft	0	0	3	2
possession/sale of stolen property	0	0	1	1
interstate transfer of stolen property	0	0	4	2
Subtotal	2	1	8	4
CJ system violations				
probation violation	0	0	1	1
Other				
mutiny	1	1	0	0
malicious destruction	0	0	1	1
enticing a minor	1	1	0	0
aiding and abetting	0	0	2	1
Subtotal	2	1	3	2
Customs immigration violations				
illegal alien	1	1	0	0
Firearms and weapons charges				
unregistered firearm (possession)	7	4	1	1
possession of weapon (as a convicted felon)	17	10	3	2
prohibited weapon (possession)	4	2	1	1
unlawful dealing in weapons	1	1	0	0
carrying firrearm during commission of a felony	0	0	1	1
receipt of explosives	1	1	0	0
Subtotal	30	18	6	5
Total	176	100	190	100

[a] Percentages may not sum to 100 because of rounding.

would be expected, some of the penitentiary inmates (16%) were convicted for violent offenses, whereas none of the camp inmates had such a conviction. Firearms and weapons charges[3] also characterized a larger proportion of the penitentiary inmates (17%) than of the camp inmates (3%). Offenses committed by the camp inmates were more likely to involve illegal operations (12%) and other forms of fraud (15%).

Table 5-4 shows other characteristics of the criminal incidents and the types of criminal behaviors committed by these inmates. The penitentiary inmates were more likely than the camp inmates to use a weapon, usually a gun, and to commit an offense against a victim. In other ways, however, the groups were quite similar. The proportions of inmates across characteristics were similar for both groups in regard to the nature of co-offender involvement, type of victim, evidence of victim precipitation, and engagement in professional and skilled criminal activity.

As to the generalizability of these findings, federal inmates are not typically viewed as comparable to inmates serving time in state facilities. In large part, this observation considers the types of offenses committed by federal inmates rather than the nature of their criminal careers. The reasoning holds that federal crimes are much more likely to involve fraudulent practices, which fall within federal jurisdiction under various provisions of the interstate commerce clause, than to be violent crimes or "street crimes," which would involve state and local jurisdictions. Consideration of these inmates' prior records, however, casts doubt on this line of reasoning in regard to the penitentiary inmates. Indeed, the great majority of the penitentiary inmates have careers involving numerous instances of violent and property-offending behaviors that received state sanctions. Moreover, the advent of a pervasive problem with drugs, which involves both state and federal criminal justice systems, has resulted in a growing proportion of inmates serving time for drug-related crimes in all types of facilities, and thus may have eroded traditional distinctions between the two. If concerns for generalizability of the samples can be raised, they are directed most appropriately to the prison camp inmates, who constitute a more heterogeneous group of offenders with limited careers.

DIAGNOSTIC AND CLASSIFICATION DISTRIBUTIONS

Table 5-5 shows the distributions of inmates across the classification and diagnostic types that represent the focus of this study. One of the questions asked at the outset of this research concerned

Table 5-4: Frequency and Percent Distribution of Inmates across Characteristics of the Conviction Offense

Variable	Penitentiary N	Penitentiary Percent[a]	Prison Camp N	Prison Camp Percent[a]
Type of weapon carried				
none	88	51	170	90
knife/sharp instrument	5	3	0	0
gun	73	42	14	7
bomb	2	1	1	1
other	6	3	4	2
	174	100	189	100
Co-offender involvement				
yes, not organized	32	18	32	17
yes, organized	75	43	96	51
none	67	39	61	32
	174	100	189	100
Offense involved a victim				
no	60	34	118	62
yes	114	66	71	39
	174	100	189	100
Victim–offender relationship				
acquaintance	18	16	3	4
business known to offender	29	25	20	28
stranger—personal	16	14	9	13
organizational or governmental	49	43	38	54
unknown	2	2	1	1
	114	100	71	100
Evidence of victim precipitation				
yes	9	8	8	11
no	98	90	64	89
unknown	2	2	0	0
	109	100	72	100
Evidence of professional criminal activity				
yes	62	36	50	27
no	109	64	137	73
	171	100	187	100
Evidence of criminal activity requiring complex skills				
yes	25	15	53	28
no	145	85	134	72
	170	100	187	100

[a] Percentages may not sum to 100 because of rounding.

Table 5-5: Frequency and Percent Distribution
      of Classification Types

Typology	Penitentiary		Prison Camp	
	N	Percent[a]	N	Percent[a]
Jesness Inventory I-level				
I2-Aa	5	3	2	1
I2-Ap	3	2	5	3
I3-Cfm	20	13	28	16
I3-Mp	32	21	37	21
I3-Cfc	43	24	33	19
I4-Se	21	14	29	17
I4-Na	19	12	17	10
I4-Nx	7	5	16	9
I-4-Ci	3	2	6	3
	153	100	173	100
I-level (Interview Method)				
I4-Na	38	22	48	26
I4-Nx	30	17	19	10
I4-Se	16	9	36	19
I4-Ci	17	10	21	11
I4-N	2	1	0	0
I5-Na	18	10	11	6
I5-Nx	23	13	24	13
I5-Se	11	6	26	14
I5-Ci	21	12	2	1
I5-N	1	1	1	1
	177	100	188	100
Conceptual Level-CL3				
.5–.9	10	7	5	3
1.0–1.4	81	54	72	41
1.5–1.9	48	32	74	42
2.0+	11	7	25	14
	150	100	176	100
Conceptual Level-CL5				
.5–.9	27	18	17	10
1.0–1.4	94	62	88	50
1.5–1.9	25	17	59	34
2.0+	4	3	11	6
	150	100	175	100
Quay AIMS				
Asocial Aggressive	21	14	9	7
Immature Dependent	10	7	6	5
Neurotic Anxious	23	15	3	3
Manipulator	42	28	22	18
Situational	54	36	82	67
	150	100	122	100

Table 5-5: *(continued)*

Typology	Penitentiary		Prison Camp	
	N	Percent[a]	N	Percent[a]
Megargee MMPI-Based System				
Able	32	20	27	16
Baker	6	4	6	4
Charlie	13	8	7	4
Delta	23	13	8	5
Easy	11	7	17	10
Foxtrot	11	7	4	2
George	14	8	18	10
How	23	14	16	9
Item	27	16	65	38
Jupiter	5	2	3	2
	164	100	171	100

[a] Percentages may not sum to 100 because of rounding.

the management implications of the observed distributions—that is, whether or not each system divided the inmate sample into administratively feasible subgroups. Upon examining these data, we might question the distribution found for the Quay AIMS typology in the prison camp, because the greatest proportion of inmates (67%) were diagnosed as situational. We may make an observation similar to that observed in the pilot study with respect to Kohlberg's Stages of Moral Judgment. Here, almost all of the inmates were diagnosed at Stage 3 or at transitional points between Stages 3 and 4 or 2 and 3 (Van Voorhis 1988). Thus, it is reasonable to question the administrative value of the information offered by the moral judgment diagnosis, because that diagnosis formulated a classification which typified most of the inmates in the sample and did not divide the population into meaningful subgroups. Both the treatment and the management implications of the system for settings such as this are questionable.[4]

To a lesser extent, distributional questions might also be raised for the Conceptual Level (CL) typologies, because most inmates were diagnosed with a CL between 1.0 and 1.9. This issue, however, is resolved more easily by collapsing the two highest types. The resulting type would represent a combination of individuals with more similar characteristics than that resulting from the combination of aggressive, neurotic anxious, and immature dependent types, as needed for collapsing the Quay AIMS typology in the camp setting.

We should note that this concern for an adequate distribution of inmates across all categories of the system may be overstated; it assumes that administrators and practitioners are not likely to welcome implications that suggest day-to-day provisions for a minority of inmates who nevertheless are important by virtue of their exceptionality. It thereby ignores relevant case management implications for identifying an inmate who needs special attention or services *whether or not* many other inmates are like him. For example, although some types pertain to exceptional inmates, they also identify inmates who are more likely to be victimized (e.g., CL < .9) (Van Voorhis, 1988); who need mental health services (e.g., How) (Megargee and Bohn 1979); or who are potentially violent (Foxtrot) (Megargee and Bohn 1979).

How do these distributions compare to those observed in other studies? To answer this question, we compared the distributions reported in table 5-5 with (*a*) those distributions reported in the pilot study for the Megargee MMPI-based system, the AIMS, the I-level, and the CL systems (Van Voorhis 1988); (*b*) the Megargee MMPI-based system as reported in previous research (Megargee and Bohn 1979); (c) Heide's (1981) study of I-level among adult probationers (subtypes only); (d) Carbonnel's (1983) study of the Jesness Inventory I-level among federal prisoners (levels only); and (e) Quay's validation samples for the AIMS (1983). Not all of the comparison samples enumerated above are ideally comparable to the samples studied in this research. Most notably, the pilot study was conducted on a small sample (N = 42), which may have yielded unstable distributions; in addition, Heide's research was conducted on a sample of New Mexico probationers which contained an atypically high proportion of Hispanics. As a result, these comparisons must be viewed with caution.

One of the more obvious conclusions to be drawn from these comparisons concerns the remarkable stability of the Megargee system across studies involving similar types of institutions. A one-sample chi-square test of the differences between our penitentiary distribution and the distributions observed in Megargee's original study, for example, revealed that the distribution of the Megargee types across the two samples did not differ significantly. Although we did not conduct statistical comparisons with other reports of the Megargee distributions, visual comparisons revealed considerable similarity across comparable settings.

The comparisons for the other systems, however, showed significant differences between these data and those observed in earlier studies including our own. At both sites we observed (a) fewer Asocial Aggressives and Immature Dependents and more Neurotic Anxious, Manipulative, and Situational inmates than were observed by Quay (1983); (b) a higher distribution of inmates on the I-level developmental continuum than reported by Heide (1981);[5] (c) more Situational and Cultural Identifier types than observed by Heide; and (d) fewer I_2 and I_4 and more I_3 inmates than observed by Carbonnel (1983).

In comparison to the pilot-study distributions, again we find far more penitentiary and camp inmates diagnosed at I_5 and fewer classified at I_3 and I_4. This may be attributable to the use of somewhat different I-level rating criteria from one study to the next.[6] Distributions for the Quay AIMS results also differ: The pilot study reports proportionately more Asocial Aggressive and Immature Dependent inmates and fewer Neurotic Anxious and Manipulative inmates. The pilot-study distribution for the Megargee MMPI types appeared to be similar to the penitentiary distribution, but one-sample chi-square tests failed to confirm that similarity. Distributions on CL3 and CL5 measures also were similar in the two studies. The CL3 measures in these studies were not significantly different at $p \leq .05$.

The comparisons between the camp and the penitentiary samples reveal expected differences. Generally, the camp distributions evidenced a higher proportion of situational or benign types and fewer committed criminal types than at the penitentiary. With the I-level interviews, for example, we observed (as with the AIMS diagnoses) far more Situational inmates (33%) at the camp than at the penitentiary (15%). Similarly, there were proportionately more Cultural Identifiers (22%) at the penitentiary than at the camp (12%). Asocial Aggressive (AIMS) inmates accounted for 14% of the penitentiary inmates and 7% of the camp inmates. The penitentiary sample was also characterized by a higher proportion of Manipulative inmates according to the Quay system. MMPI comparisons for the two samples also support the pattern of fewer committed criminal types and more benign types at the prison camp as compared to the penitentiary.

Conceptual Level scores were somewhat higher for the camp inmates than for the penitentiary inmates. For example, only 20% of the penitentiary inmates received CL5 scores greater than 1.5, whereas 40% of the camp inmates received scores above that level. Surprisingly, we did not observe a similar pattern for the I-level interview ratings of level, where slightly fewer inmates were diagnosed I_5 at the camp (35%) than at the penitentiary (42%). The Jesness Inventory classifications for level also cast doubt on the camp interview ratings because a higher proportion of camp inmates than of penitentiary inmates were classified at I_4, the highest level on the Jesness Inventory continuum.

SUMMARY

Only two of the five systems—the Megargee MMPI system and the Conceptual Level—appear to be reasonably stable across similar research settings. The Jesness Inventory has not been studied sufficiently among adult inmates to be evaluated in this manner. The comparative instability of the I-level interview system and the Quay AIMS may underscore the limited reliability figures reported in chapter 4. In the case of the AIMS instruments, however, the instruments also may be somewhat sensitive to caseload sizes and raters' roles. Most of the ratings for the pilot study were conducted by work supervisors, whereas the ratings for the present study were made by case managers and counselors. Work supervisors completed the Quay observation forms (CAC) only when the counselors or case managers indicated that they were unable or unwilling to do so. We might argue that the work supervisors were in a better position to know the inmates' behavioral patterns, but their bases for behavioral judgments also might differ substantially from those of the treatment staff. It seems highly likely that the results for the Quay form may vary according to the staff member's knowledge of the inmate and his or her own role.

Despite these considerations, differences across the two sample distributions were in the expected directions. Fewer committed-criminal and manipulative types and more benign types were observed at the prison camp than at the penitentiary.

CHAPTER 6

CONSTRUCT VALIDITY

This chapter is concerned with two issues: (1) the construct validity of the classification types and (2) further refinement and definition of the types. In discussing the former point, we present an empirical analysis of the correlation of each type with similarly defined (convergent) types in the other systems; in addressing the latter, we examine convergent and divergent correlations for patterns that may either define the type further or, alternatively, call its validity into question. In a more general sense, this analysis seeks to learn more about the classification needs of prison inmates, such as how many types are needed to classify these populations and what types are the most common to specific settings.

The existing literature suggests that the construct validity of these systems needs further research and development. Most research has involved an analysis of the relationship between the types and institutional behaviors or background factors; very little attention has been given to validating the integral psychological constructs. The few exceptions include Quay's report of a relationship between the Quay Asocial Aggressive type and the Pd scale of the MMPI (Quay 1983) and Jesness's comparison of the Jesness Inventory with self-appraisal behavioral scales measuring obtrusiveness, responsibility, and confidence (Jesness 1988). The most comprehensive and most successful validation research appears to be Megargee's validation of the MMPI-based system, which uses scales of the California Personality Inventory, psychologists' observations, several attitudinal scales, and an earlier version of the Quay system (Megargee and Bohn 1979). These exceptions notwithstanding, we know very little about the construct validity of these systems, especially I-level and Conceptual Level, which were developed for youthful offender populations. The need for further validation is clear.

In addressing the second task of this analysis—an exploration of observed divergent correlations—this chapter deals with the following issues: (1) Are some types defined further by secondary characteristics? (2) How many types optimally characterize this population? (3) Do the types perform differently in each setting, such that these systems should be validated for types of settings rather than for adult male prisoners as a whole?

TEST PROCEDURES

The analysis began with a theoretical discussion of the hypothesized commonalities among systems. This step involved a "bootstrap" approach which initially hypothesized several theoretical matches among the types (Van Voorhis 1984; Warren 1971) and then tested those hypotheses in the pilot phase of this research (Van Voorhis 1988). The original hypotheses are shown in table 6-1. Upon testing them with the 52 inmates who constituted the pilot-study sample, we reached the following conclusions (Van Voorhis, 1988):

1. The construct validity of the cognitive developmental measures is supported strongly. The developmental measures used in the pilot study consisted of Kohlberg's Stages of Moral Judgment, I-level (interview method), and Conceptual Level.

2. Strong agreement exists among several types characterizing a committed criminal dimension (e.g., Megargee's Charlie and Foxtrot, I-level Cis and Cfcs, and Quay's Asocial Aggressive types). Although the original hypotheses directed us more definitively, it was not possible to delineate these agreements more finely into such types of criminal psychopathology as subcultural, aggressive, psychopathic, violent, or power-oriented.

3. The construct validity of the Quay and the I-level neurotic types is supported. This validity was stronger when the I-level Neurotic Acting-out types were excluded from the analysis. This finding is not surprising because the Na's acting-out pattern usually evidences little verbal anxiety and may appear to some observers to be closer to the committed criminal types.

4. No agreement exists among situational types in any of the systems. We speculated that this finding may have been due to a tendency to use situational categories as "catchalls" in which to place inmates who could not be diagnosed as belonging to any of

Table 6-1: Hypothesized Commonalities among Systems

Construct	Hypothesized Similarities
Cognitive Development	I-level (interview), Conceptual Level, Moral Judgment
Neurotic	I-level: I_4Na, I_4Nx, I_4N, I_5Na, I_5Nx, I_5N Quay: Na Megargee: Baker, George
Situational	I-level: I_4Se, I_5Se Quay: Si Megargee: Item, Easy
Immature Dependent	I-level: I_2Ap, I_3Cfm Quay: Id Megargee: How, Baker
Character Disorder, Psychopathy	I-level: I_3Mp Quay: Mp, Aa Megargee: Delta, Able
Subcultural	I-level: I_3Cfc, I_4Ci, I_5Ci Quay: Aa Megargee: unmatched
Power-oriented	I-level: I_3Cfc, I_4Ci, I_5Ci Quay: Aa, Mp
Manipulative	I-level: I_3Mp Quay: Mp Megargee: Able, Delta

the other types. Cell sizes for testing these relationships were somewhat limited, however, in part because of the small sample size.

5. No agreement exists among immature dependent types. This construct in fact may be more meaningful, more definable, and more identifiable among youths than among adults. The fact that the construct was developed for use with juveniles lends obvious support to this speculation.

6. Too few inmates were diagnosed as manipulative on each system to allow us to conduct the various tests adequately.

On the basis of these findings, we revised the first set of hypotheses into those shown in table 6-2. This table also depicts hypothesized relationships for the Jesness Inventory I-level types, which were not a part of the pilot study but are tested in this research. Situational, manipulative, and dependent constructs, although unsupported by the pilot study tests, are tested again in this research in the event that sample-size limitations may have attenuated findings of the pilot study. In contrast to the earlier hypotheses, we now hypothesize one committed criminal type rather than three. We conducted the analyses on all types and did not collapse types in order to improve cell sizes for the statistical tests. Nevertheless, some types characterized so few subjects that computed statistics may be somewhat unstable. These types are noted in tables 6-3 through 6-13.

One of the Megargee types, How, is not included in any of the hypotheses, because no similar types exist in the other systems. Hows are described in terms of psychopathology, as "unstable, agitated, and disturbed mental health cases," whereas types in the other systems are described according to global personality characteristics. We would expect to see type How correlate with several types, particularly neurotic or immature types in the systems that do not incorporate psychological disturbance into type descriptions. These statistical relationships, however, offer misleading support for construct validity.

We performed two types of statistical analyses. The first consisted of bivariate correlations (phi) among the types. The second used common factor analysis (principal axis) to determine whether the developmental and the personality measures converged in theoretically meaningful or valid ways (Carmines and Zeller 1985). On the basis of the classification theories and type descriptions, we hypothesized that the developmental measures would form a unifactorial structure and that the personality measures would con-

Table 6-2: Revised Hypothesized Commonalities among Systems

Construct	Hypothesized Similarities
Cognitive Development	I-level (interview), Conceptual Level, Jesness Inventory I-level
Neurotic	I-level: I_4Na, I_4Nx, I_4N, I_5Na, I_5Nx, I_5N Quay: Na Megargee: Baker, George, Jupiter Jesness: Na, Nx
Situational	I-level: I_4Se, I_5Se Quay: Si Megargee: Item, Easy Jesness: Se, Ci
Immature Dependent	I-level: I_2Ap, I_3Cfm Quay: Id Megargee: Baker Jesness: Aa, Ap, Cfm
Manipulative	I-level: I_3Mp Quay: Mp Megargee: Able, Delta Jesness: Mp
Committed Criminal	I-level: I_3Cfc, I_4Ci, I_5Ci Quay: Aa Megargee: Charlie, Foxtrot Jesness: Aa, Cfc

verge into the five personality factors listed in table 6-2.
RESULTS OF BIVARIATE ANALYSES

Results of the bivariate analyses appear in tables 6-3 through 6-13 and are organized according to hypothesis. Construct validity is supported not only by whether a measure converges with a theoretically similar measure but also by whether it diverges from a theoretically dissimilar measure (Campbell and Fiske 1959); therefore, discussions include two tables for each hypothesized construct. The first table presents the results of tests for convergence, or the relationships between types hypothesized to be similar and expected to be significant. This table also identifies as "anomalies" any significant and convergent relationships that were hypothesized to be divergent.[1]

The second table shows significant divergent correlations. For parsimonious reasons, we chose only those divergent relationships that are related significantly to the construct being tested.

Simply put, a valid measure will converge with the hypothesized matches and will diverge (denoting a negative[2] or an insignificant correlation) from all measures that are not theoretically relevant. But there are other useful ways to interpret these findings. Because significant divergent relationships, especially strong relationships, are also valuable indicators of what personality dynamics are most *unlike* the type being tested, they can help us to further define the type. Anomalies, types that converge with theoretically dissimilar types, pose questions about the construct validity of the measure being tested, because they show that the measure positively correlates with an unrelated type. As explained earlier, however, sometimes the anomalies show patterns that are informative in themselves and suggest important secondary characteristics of the type being analyzed.

Situational

Table 6-3 shows that all of the situational measures were related significantly to at least one other situational measure. Most were related to at least two types. Quay's Si type, for example, correlated with situational types in all of the other systems and diverged from all other possible measures; these findings strongly support the validity of that type. Similar results occur for the Jesness Se type and the Megargee Easy type, although in these instances, anomalies are observed.

Further inspection of table 6-3 suggests that the construct may not be unidimensional. This concern arises when we observe mea-

Table 6-3: Correlation Matrix for Construct Validity Tests, Situational Measures

| | | Hypothesized Convergent[a] | | | | | | | Anomalies[b] |
| | | Quay | Megargee | | Jesness | | I-level | | |
Classification Type		Si	Easy	Item	Se	Ci	I_4Se	I_5Se	
Quay: Situational	pen	1.00	.23***	.06	.18**	.10	.16**	.04	none
	camp	1.00	.13*	.07	.04	.11	.21***	.03	none
Megargee: Easy	pen		1.00		.20***	.15**	.08	.12**	Jesness Cfm .14*
	camp		1.00		.12*	.04	.12*	.15**	Jesness Cfm .14**
Megargee: Item	pen			1.00	.09	.20***	.03	.15*	none
	camp			1.00	.10*	.12*	.14**	.12*	Jesness Mp .10*, Jesness Cfc .16**, I_4Na .18***
Jesness: Se	pen				1.00		.00	.20***	Megargee Delta .12*
	camp				1.00		.03	.12**	Quay Mp .12*
Jesness: Ci[c]	pen					1.00	.05	.15**	none
	camp					1.00	.08	.10*	none
I-level: I_4Se	pen						1.00		Jesness Cfm .21***
	camp						1.00		Jesness Cfm .17***, Megargee Baker .16*
I-level: I_5Se	pen							1.00	Jesness Nx .19**, Megargee Foxtrot .12**
	camp							1.00	Jesness Mp .12*

[a] Significant relationships (agreement) predicted.
[b] Convergent items predicted to be divergent.
[c] Cell frequencies on this variable were limited to 5 or fewer cases in both samples.
 * $p \leq .10$
 ** $p \leq .05$
 *** $p \leq .01$

sures correlating with one situational type in another system but not with the other. The Quay Si, for example, correlates with Easy but not with Item on the Megargee system, with the Jesness Se but not with the Jesness Ci,[3] and with the I_4Se but not with the I_5Se. Our explanations are speculative, but in each instance the Quay Si type appears to have correlated with the lower-functioning situational type on the other systems.

Other correlations—the relationship between Easy and Jesness Se, Item and Jesness Ci, Item and I_5Se, and again between Jesness Ci and I_5Se—also appear to divide the situational construct into higher- and lower-functioning types. Thus, if there are two situational types, we may describe one as an underachieving, perhaps naive, individual who becomes involved in criminal activity during periods of adversity or perhaps through attempts to catch up with a perceived notion of where one should be in life (an I_4 notion). Classifications of this type include Easy, Quay Si, Jesness Se, and I_4Se. The other type might pertain to an individual who is functioning and achieving at a higher, perhaps brighter, level (Item, Jesness Ci, and I_5Se), albeit occasionally in a criminal or unethical fashion. Further, raters may tend to place benign individuals, particularly those who conform to the middle-class notion of "normal," into this latter type when no other classification is available to them.

We found several significant convergent relationships between the situational measures and those types hypothesized to be divergent. Two of these relationships, correlations with the Jesness Cfm, appear to make sense in light of the above discussion. The Cfm, dependent and somewhat immature, is observed to correlate with the lower-functioning situational types (Easy and I_4Se). Another type of anomaly shows relationships between neurotic types and situational types (e.g., with Jesness Nx and I_5Se at the penitentiary and with Baker and I_4Se at the prison camp). It is somewhat surprising, however, that additional correlations between situational and neurotic items were not observed with the I-level situational classification resulting from the interview method, because interviewers occasionally reported difficulties distinguishing the I-level Situational individuals from neurotic-anxious individuals who also evidence a noncriminal value system. In addition, situational individuals often demonstrate a great deal of stress and guilt regarding their criminal activity. This affect tends to be especially apparent early in their prison terms. Sometimes this temporary situational anxiety may be mistaken for the longer-term and more global trait anxiety and the low self-esteem of the neurotic offender.

Another set of anomalies shows correlations between situational types and criminal, manipulative, or acting-out types. The important observation here is that they occur primarily at the prison camp, as in the relationships between Jesness Mp and Item, between Jesness Cfc and Item, between I_4Na and Item, and between Jesness Mp and I_5Se. The findings may question the validity of the situational types in the prison camp, suggesting that the designation as situational fails to fully characterize these inmates. This suggestion is further supported by the classification distributions in this setting; most (perhaps too many) minimum-security inmates are diagnosed as situational. Furthermore, while the situational classification may characterize primary components of their personality, it may fail to identify important secondary characteristics.

The final two anomalies—relationships with between Jesness Se and Delta and between I_5Se and Baker—are less amenable to explanation. They also cause less concern, because they are weak relations and significant at a probability level of only .10.

The final observation concerns the differences between the two samples. In some cases, convergent correlations observed in the penitentiary did not hold for the prison camp sample. More often, however, convergent relationships occurring in the penitentiary were observed to be weaker in the prison camp rather than differing in direction or not existing at all. Again the camp sample includes a higher proportion of situational inmates, but minimum-security federal inmates may also make up such an atypical criminal sample that the usual criminal classification types may be less relevant to this population.

Divergent correlations are listed in table 6-4 and show the types of personality dynamics most unlike these situational inmates. With the exception of the anomalies noted above, the findings indicate that situational types diverge from committed criminal, acting-out, and manipulative-personality dynamics. This observation is clearest and strongest for the penitentiary data.

Immature Dependent

The patterns shown in table 6-5 suggest that the immature types do not converge well in these populations. It is also evident that the tests were constrained by inadequate cell sizes. The only convergent relationships noted among the dependent types are between Quay Id and Jesness Aa and between Baker and Jesness Cfm. Further, it is quite difficult to generalize from these findings, because so few offenders were classified as Aa or Baker.

Table 6-4: Significant Divergent Relationships, Situational Measures

Classification Type		Divergent Correlates
Quay: Situational	pen	Jesness Mp = .15** I_4Ci = .18**
	camp	none
Megargee: Easy	pen	Quay Mp = .17** Quay Na = .11* Jesness Mp = .14*
	camp	I_4Ci = .11* I_4Nx = .11* I_5Nx = .13** Jesness Cfc = .12* Jesness Na = .11*
Megargee: Item	pen	Quay Aa = .17**
	camp	none
Jesness: Ci[a]	pen	Quay Mp = .21** Megargee Delta = .12*
	camp	I_4Na = .11*
Jesness: Se	pen	Quay Aa = .16* Megargee Able = .11* Megargee Charlie = .12* Megargee Foxtrot = .11* I_4Na = .14**
	camp	Quay Aa = .13* Megargee How = .15** I_4Na = .11*
I_4Se	pen	Quay Aa = .13* Quay Na = .13** Megargee Able = .16** Jesness Na = .12*
	camp	Quay Aa = .15** Quay Id = .12* Megargee Able = .12* Megargee Delta = .10* Megargee Foxtrot = .13** Megargee George = .11* Jesness Cfc = .11* Jesness Na = .16**

Table 6-4: *(continued)*

Classification Type		Divergent Correlates
I_5Se	pen	Megargee Able = .13**
		Jesness Cfm = .10*
		Jesness Cfc = .17*
	camp	Jesness Cfc = .11*

^a Cell frequencies on this variable were limited to 5 or fewer cases.

  * $p \leq .10$

 ** $p \leq .05$

*** $p \leq .01$

Table 6-5: Correlation Matrix for Construct Validity Tests, Immature Dependent Measures

		Hypothesized Convergent[a]					Anomalies[b]
		Quay	Megargee	Jesness			
Classification Type		Id	Baker	Aa	Ap	Cfm	
Quay: Id	pen	1.00	.05	.26***	.04	.01	George .23***, Jupiter .12*, I_4Nx .13**, I_4Ci .11*
	camp	1.00	.05	NC	.04	.00	Foxtrot .19**, How .25***, Jesness Cfc .13* I_5Na .14*, I_5Nx .15*
Megargee: Baker[c]	pen		1.00	.03	.03	.04	Quay Na .14*, I_4Ci .16**
	camp		1.00	.03	.03	.13**	I_4Se .16**
Jesness: Aa[c]	pen			1.00			How .15*, I_4Nx .19***
	camp			1.00			How .15*, I_4Nx .13*, I_4Ci .14**, Able .10*
Jesness: Ap[c]	pen				1.00		Charlie .13*
	camp				1.00		How .18**
Jesness: Cfm	pen					1.00	Easy .14**, How .26***, I_4Se .21***
	camp					1.00	Easy .14**, Quay Na .33***, I_4Se .17***

[a] Significant relationships (agreement) predicted.
[b] Convergent items predicted to be divergent.
[c] Cell frequencies on this variable were limited to 5 or fewer cases in both samples.
NC: Not computed.

* $p \leq .10$

** $p \leq .05$

*** $p \leq .01$

We observed far more anomalies. The most evident occurs in the relationship between the Megargee How measures and the other dependent types. Because How is described as psychologically disturbed, such an inmate often may appear immature and dependent. Immaturity and dependency needs, however, are secondary to the overall disturbance pattern evidenced by Hows.

Another pattern observable among the anomalous correlations consists of four correlations between the immature types and a neurotic type (e.g., Jesness Cfm x Quay Na, Megargee Baker x Quay Na, Quay Id x Megargee George, Jesness Aa x I_4Nx, and others). For many of these tests, however, we encountered problems with cell sizes, so our conclusions are conservative. Yet, as in the correlations with How, discussed above, immature dependent patterns may be secondary to the neurotic anxious traits evidenced by the neurotic inmates. Some inmates may be diagnosed as immature, inadequate, or dependent instead of neurotic. These anomalous findings are not surprising; in fact, Megargee notes this possibility when he describes type Baker as incorporating both the inadequate and the neurotic traits.

These findings suggest that it may not be useful to attempt to isolate an immature type among adult inmates. Although immaturity may appear in connection with other traits, such as psychological disturbance, high anxiety, and low self-esteem, it is likely to be secondary to those traits. It may make sense to characterize juveniles as immature and dependent, and this may be the most salient and observable feature of their personality. Adults, however, may evidence such a personality trait not as a global characteristic but rather as one that is complicated by more important psychological factors.

Three anomalies occurred with the I_4Ci: one with Megargee Baker, another with Jesness Aa, and a third with Quay Id. Two involved unstable tests, because few Bakers or Aas were present in either sample. A similar finding occurs in the relationship between Foxtrot and Quay Id inmates at the prison camp and with Charlie and Jesness Ap at the prison camp. These findings are anomalies, not readily explainable by anything other than the instability of the tests involved. Admittedly, it is difficult to support an assertion that the immature dependent type of inmate has anything in common with the streetwise committed criminal. A correlation with I_4Se and Baker and with Quay Id and Megargee Foxtrot among prison camp inmates may occur for a similar reason.

A final anomaly, however—a correlation between Jesness Cfm and I_4Se—is stable. Moreover, we observed it in both the penitentiary and the prison camp data sets. It may be that the Jesness Cfm type, among adults, shares some of the traits of the I_4Se. In fact, Jesness (1988) describes Cfm offenders as evidencing "positive attitudes toward home, school, and authority; conforming behavior; often dependent; positive, uncritical self-concept, and low self-reported delinquency (p 80–81)." The description is not unlike that offered for the less developed situational type discussed above. Another explanation notes that several of the anomalous correlations involve weak correlations with I_4 types obtained through the interview method.

Since rating these interviews, and upon presenting these results to sources familiar with the I-level research, we have considered the possibility that perhaps some of the I_4 inmates should have been classified I_3. Indeed, one of the explanations for the distribution differences between the pilot sample and the present sample may be found in the training differences between the pilot study and the larger study. We believe that the most recent trainers established less conservative criteria for classifying an inmate I_4 rather than I_3. This difference may explain why no I_3 inmates appear in the present sample, although there were 4 (8% of the sample) in the pilot study.[4]

Divergent correlations shown in table 6-6 evidence only one pattern, a tendency for immature types, Jesness Cfm, and Quay Id to be most unlike Megargee Ables. These findings emerged from stable tests.

With few exceptions, results for the prison camp sample differ markedly from those observed for the penitentiary. The findings presented for the immature type, suggest that (1) this type characterizes an extreme minority of inmates in both samples, (2) it is a type that is not stable across samples, and (3) it shares characteristics with so many other adult personality and psychological types that it may not be a primary personality trait among many adult inmates.

Neurotic

With the exception of the I_5Na type, all of the neurotic types were validated by at least one other neurotic type in either the penitentiary or the prison camp (see table 6-7). Because three of the systems contain at least two neurotic types, we did not expect to see correlates across more than one type on each system; instead, we anticipated correlations with at least one type in each system, as was the case with the Quay Na type in the penitentiary sample.

Both the interview and the Jesness Inventory I-level systems distinguish between an acting-out/defended neurotic dimension and a

Table 6-6: Significant Divergent Relationships, Immature Dependent Measures

Classification Type		Divergent Correlates
Quay: Id	pen	Megargee Able = .15*
	camp	I_4Se = .13*
Megargee: Baker[a]	pen	none
	camp	none
Jesness: Aa[a]	pen	none
	camp	none
Jesness: Ap[a]	pen	none
	camp	none
Jesness: Cfm	pen	Able = .14**
		Foxtrot = .11*
		I_4Ci = .12*
	camp	Able = .19***

[a] Cell frequencies on this variable were limited to 5 or fewer cases.

  * $p \leq .10$

 ** $p \leq .05$

*** $p \leq .01$

Table 6-7: Correlation Matrix for Construct Validity Tests, Neurotic Measures

Classification Type		Quay	Megargee			Jesness		I-level				Anomalies[b]
		Na	Baker	George	Jupiter[c]	Nx	Na	I_4Nx	I_4Na	I_5Nx	I_5Na	
Quay: Neurotic[d]	pen	1.00	.14**	.05	.07	.01	.15**	.11*	.09	.15**	.08	Able .14**, I_4Ci .13*
	camp	1.00	.03	.05	.02	.05	.05	.15**	.03	.06	.03	How .15**, Jesness Cfm .33***
Megargee: Baker[c]	pen		1.00			.04	.04	.10	.02	.02	.05	I_4Ci .16**
	camp		1.00			.06	.06	.06	.04	.02	.05	Jesness Cfm .13**, I_4Se .16**
Megargee: George	pen			1.00		.16**	-.12*	.02	.01	.01	.03	Quay Id .23***
	camp			1.00		-.11*	.24***	.20***	.15**	.08	.09	none
Megargee: Jupiter[c]	pen				1.00	.19***	.05	.08	.08	.17**	.05	Quay Id .12*
	camp				1.00	.11*	.11*	.10*	.08	.08	.04	Quay Aa .32***
Jesness: Nx	pen					1.00		.03	-.10*	.08	.03	I_5Se .19***
	camp					1.00		.08	.01	.16**	.01	How .38***
Jesness: Na	pen						1.00	.07	.07	.02	.01	Able .15**, Foxtrot .12*
	camp						1.00	.07	.13**	.04	.01	Quay Aa .14*, Charlie .15**, Delta .13**
I-level: I_4Nx	pen							1.00				Quay Id .13**, Delta .16**, Jesness Aa .19**
	camp							1.00				How .16**, Jesness Aa .13**, Jesness Cfc .15**
I-level: I_4Na	pen								1.00			Quay Aa .16**, Able .21***, Jesness Cfc .15**
	camp								1.00			Quay Aa .12*, Charlie .15**

I-level: I_5Nx	pen	1.00	Foxtrot .11*
	camp	1.00	Quay Id .15*, Delta .24***
I-level: I_5Na	pen	1.00	Able .25***
	camp	1.00	Quay Id .14*, Able .21***

[a] Significant relationships (agreement) predicted.
[b] Convergent items predicted to be divergent.
[c] Cell frequencies on this variable were limited to 5 or fewer cases in both samples.
[d] Cell frequencies on this variable were limited to 5 of fewer cases in prison camp sample.

* $p \leq .10$
** $p \leq .05$
*** $p \leq .01$

more overtly anxious neurotic dimension. In the Megargee system, the distinction between Baker and George is less clear, but George, on the basis of type description, would appear to be the more overtly anxious of the two. Neither type evidences a defended style. We include Jupiter among the neurotic types because this type of inmate usually evidences a history of childhood deprivation. Inclusion of type Jupiter is more exploratory than definitive, however. One would think that these distinctions might produce a pattern of correlations in which perhaps the overt and the anxious neurotic types converge and the defended types converge. Such a pattern occurs between the Jesness Inventory and the interview I-level types for the prison camp sample, and type Jupiter correlates only with the anxious types in the penitentiary. In addition, a divergent or significant disagreement is observed in a relationship between Jesness Nx and I_4Na at the penitentiary. The remaining two measures, Quay Na and George, correlate with both the acting-out and the anxious types in other systems. This finding is not entirely surprising, because neither measure purports to make the distinction.

With the exception of the MMPI types George and (to a lesser extent) Jupiter, these correlations are not strong. Measurement considerations may offer some explanation for the Quay and the I-level interview findings. The Quay measures are obtained through observation in a setting that makes overt presentation of anxiety dangerous and less likely to be noticed. As a result, the proportion of neurotic inmates may be somewhat underestimated by the Quay system. The I-level interview, on the other hand, may place individuals in a neurotic category on the basis of childhood adversity, low self-esteem, or long-term anxiety, all of which may have been more observable in an interview than through other assessment methods. This possibility may explain why the I-level interview obtained the highest proportion of inmates diagnosed neurotic. Thus, definitional distinctions and measurement effects may have attenuated convergent relationships between various measures.

The anomalies shown on the right-hand side of the table produce important patterns, particularly in validating the anxious versus the acting-out traits discussed above. Interestingly, all of the I-level Na types correlate with Able in the penitentiary sample. These findings may be viewed as validating the acting-out, character-disorder qualities of Nas. Ables are described as "charming, impulsive, and manipulative." Their MMPI profile is a classic "4, 9" profile, tapping both the psychopathic deviate scales and the hypomania (emotional agitation) scales of the MMPI. For some, this characterization may also appear reminiscent of the "secondary psychopath," who demonstrates many of the impulsive behavioral traits of the psychopath as well as some neurotic traits (Karpman 1947). In fact, correlations with the I-level interview Na types and Able are stronger than correlations between Nas and other neurotic types. Further, the Na (acting-out) types often correlate weakly with other committed-criminal types such as Quay Aa, Charlie, and Jesness Cfc. Such findings suggest that the behavior pattern of neurotic acting-out offenders, while showing neurotic qualities is also one which can reflect committed criminal characteristics. The findings suggest a revision of the matches shown in table 6-2, perhaps to reflect a clearer link between Able and Nas, than between either of them and the other committed-criminal types or neurotic types, respectively.

Megargee How types were found to correlate with the overtly anxious types (e.g., Quay Na, Jesness Nx, and I_4Nx). Although these matches were not predicted, they confirm the more agitated aspects of the lives of some neurotic anxious individuals. Further, many individuals classified as neurotic anxious may indeed be more troubled than the type specifies, but the Quay and I-level systems do not purport to classify for more serious forms of psychological disturbance.

In a similar manner, anomalies occasionally occur with immature types such as Jesness Cfm and Quay Id, showing as we did in the section on immature measures that it is somewhat difficult to differentiate between the two, and the likely explanation is that the immature measures are tapping anxiety, low self-esteem and other traits that describe the neurotic, particularly the neurotic anxious individuals.

Observed correlations between the neurotic types and Megargee's Delta are difficult to explain. Delta evidences a "spike 4" (psychopathic deviate) MMPI profile, and the type description does not identify defended or anxious patterns. In addition, we observed a moderate correlation between I_5Se and Jesness Nx types in the penitentiary which also was anomalous. The remaining anomalous relationships occur among types for which too few inmates were available to test the hypotheses, as with Baker and Quay Na (at the prison camp).

The divergent relationships shown in table 6-8 appear to form a clear pattern. As frequently as type Able converges with the neurotic acting-out measure, it diverges from the neurotic anxious measures. Committed criminal types also diverge from neurotic anxious measures. With similar consistency, the neurotic acting-out types and situational types are often divergent.

Table 6-8: Significant Divergent Relationships, Neurotic Measures

Classification Type		Divergent Correlates
Quay: Neurotic[a]	pen	Jesness Cfc = .25***, I_4Se = .13**
	camp	none
Megargee: Baker[b]	pen	none
	camp	none
Megargee: George	pen	none
	camp	I_4Se = .11*
Megargee: Jupiter[b]	pen	none
	camp	Quay Si = .13*
Jesness: Nx	pen	Able = .11*
	camp	Able = .15**, How = .38***
Jesness: Na	pen	I_4Se = .12*
	camp	Easy = .11*, How = .11*
I_4Nx	pen	Quay Aa = .16**, Able = .12*
	camp	Easy = .11*, Jesness Mp = .14**
I_4Na	pen	Delta = .12*, Jesness Si = .14**
	camp	Quay Si = .15**, Jesness Si = .11* Item = .18**
I_5Nx	pen	Able = .10*, Jesness Cfc = .10*
	camp	Easy = .13**
I_5Na	pen	none
	camp	Foxtrot = .12*

[a] Cell frequencies on this variable were limited to 5 or fewer.

[b] Cell frequencies on this variable were limited to 5 or fewer at the prison camp.

* $p \le .10$

** $p \le .05$

*** $p \le .01$

In sum, the neurotic types appear to have converged, although not strongly. Anomalies are numerous, but with few exceptions they appear to display a pattern, which supports either the acting-out, defended qualities of the neurotic acting-out individuals or the overt and anxious qualities of the neurotic anxious types. Even so, this construct appears to be sensitive to the assessment process and is likely to overlap with immature, disturbed, and character-disorder types. On these measures as well, results for the penitentiary differ from those for the prison camp.

Manipulative

Convergent and divergent test results for the manipulative types are shown in tables 6-9 and 6-10, respectively. These systems identify only four manipulative types.[5] As shown in table 6-9, the Jesness Mp type and the Megargee Able type converge significantly in both samples. Delta and Quay Mp converge weakly and only in the prison camp sample.

Several anomalies were observed. Generally, the manipulative types are observed to correlate with both neurotic and committed-criminal types, and in one case with a disturbed type, Megargee's How. With respect to type Able, anomalies form a clear pattern of correlates with neurotic acting-out and committed-criminal types. This occurs in both samples, and they appear to portray Ables according to the secondary psychopathic characteristics presented in the discussion of the neurotic acting-out construct.

Type Delta is less clear. Tables 6-9 and 6-10 show contradictory correlates. Delta, for example, correlates with both the acting-out and anxious neurotic types. Weaker correlates with the committed-criminal types are also observed.

A much different description would be given for penitentiary Quay Mp inmates where the anomalies are primarily to committed-criminal types. Results show no neurotic correlates for the Quay Mp groups or for the Jesness Mp groups. Thus, if any of the four types appears to fit a manipulative construct, it would be these two.

Alternatively, we might speculate that manipulative types, like the immature/dependent types, are secondary characteristics to the neurotic acting-out and committed-criminal types. Perhaps the utility of a distinct manipulative type among adult male inmates should be questioned.

Table 6-9: Correlation Matrix for Construct Validity Tests, Manipulative Measures

		Hypothesized Convergent[a]				Anomalies[b]
		Quay Mp	Megargee Able	Megargee Delta	Jesness Mp	
Classification Type						
Quay: Mp	pen	1.00	.02	.10	.04	Megargee How .15*, Jesness Ci .21**, I_5Ci .13*
	camp	1.00	.02	.15**	.05	I_5Se .12*
Megargee: Able	pen		1.00		.31***	Quay Na .14**, Jesness Na .15**, I_5Na .21** I_5Ci .14**, I_5Na .25***
	camp		1.00		.14*	I_5Na .21***, Jesness Cfc .28***, I_5Ci .15**, I_5Ci .10*
Megargee: Delta	pen			1.00	.13*	Jesness Se .11*, I_4Nx .16*
	camp			1.00	.04	Jesness Na .13*, I_5Na .21***, I_5Nx .24**, Jesness Ci .12*
Jesness: Mp	pen				1.00	none
	camp				1.00	none

a Significant relationships (agreement) predicted.
b Convergent items predicted to be divergent.

* $p \leq .10$
** $p \leq .05$
*** $p \leq .01$

Table 6-10: Significant Divergent Relationships, Manipulative Measures

Classification Type		Divergent Correlates
Quay: Manipulator	pen	Megargee Easy = .17**
	camp	none
Megargee: Able	pen	Quay Id = .15**
		Jesness Cfm = .14**
		Jesness Nx = .11*
		I_4Nx = .12*
		I_4Se = .16**
		I_4Ci = .16**
		I_5Nx = .10*
		I_5Se = .13**
	camp	Jesness Cfm = .19***
		Jesness Nx = .15**
		I_4Se = .12*
Megargee: Delta	pen	Quay Id = .12*
		Jesness Cfc = .12*
		I_4Na = .12*
	camp	Quay Si = .17**
		I_4Se = .10*
Jesness: Mp	pen	Quay Si = .15**
		Charlie = .16**
		Easy = .14**
		How = .15**
	camp	Charlie = .10*
		How = .17**
		I_4Nx = .14**

* p ≤ .10
** p ≤ .05
*** p ≤ .01

Committed Criminal

Throughout this chapter we use the term "committed criminal type" to refer to types that are described as having an internalized deviant value system favoring criminal behavior. As with the pilot study, several of these types converge convincingly with at least one other similarly defined type (see table 6-11). Among the penitentiary inmates, the Quay Aa, Megargee Charlie, Jesness Cfc, and I_4Ci types correlate moderately to strongly with each other. In the prison camp, similar findings were observed for types Charlie, Jesness Cfc, and I_4Ci.

Results for criminal types Foxtrot, Asocial Aggressive, and I_5Ci are less consistent, possibly because they comprise smaller groups. The I_5Ci type, in particular, fails to correlate with any of the hypothesized matches. In fact, the only correlate for the penitentiary inmates is one with Megargee's Able. With the exception of this one, rather weak correlate, the qualities of the I_5Ci are unclear.

More of the convergent correlations appear in the penitentiary sample. This is likely to be due to the fact that the penitentiary is more likely to house the street-wise, antisocial offender with a lengthy criminal career.

An examination of the anomalies shows correlates with neurotic acting-out, immature, character-disordered, and situational types. Interrelationships between Able, the Neurotic Acting-out types, and the committed criminal types were discussed above and appear to tap a valid offender-personality construct. Anomalous correlates with types such as Jesness Ap, the situational types, How, and Quay Id, however, are less clear, except that we are more likely to observe such correlates for criminal types which were not strongly convergent and for those types that characterized few inmates and may have produced unstable results.

In support, table 6-12 shows situational correlates to be the most common divergent finding. Moreover, the situational divergent correlates are most likely to be observed for the convergent criminal types Quay Aa, Charlie, Jesness Cfc, and I_4Ci. The other common divergent correlate with neurotic anxious types was expected. We would anticipate that the committed criminal types would not show overt forms of anxiety.

In sum, we observe committed criminal types that converge strongly, but this occurs for only four of the seven types tested.

Table 6-11: Correlation Matrix for Construct Validity Tests, Committed Criminal Measures

Classification Type		Quay Aa	Megargee Charlie	Megargee Foxtrot	Jesness Aa	Jesness Cfc	I-level I_4Ci	I-level I_5Ci	Anomalies[b]
Quay: Aa	pen	1.00	.25***	.25***	.08	.16**	.15**	.05	I_4Na .16**
	camp	1.00	.10	.06	NC	.21**	.29**	.04	Delta .12*, Jesness Ap .12*, Jesness Na .14*, Able .15* I_4Na .12*
Megargee: Charlie	pen		1.00		.07	.28***	.14**	.04	Jesness Ap .13*
	camp		1.00		.02	.02	.02	.02	Jesness Ap .35***, I_4Na .15**, Jesness Na .15**
Megargee: Foxtrot	pen			1.00	.09	.11*	.00	-.10*	I_5Se .12*, Jesness Na .12*, I_5Na .11* Quay Id .19**, I_4Se .13**, I_5Na .12*
	camp			1.00	.02	.02	.06	.02	
Jesness Aa[c]	pen				1.00		NC	NC	How .15**, Quay Id .26**, I_4Nx .19**
	camp				1.00		NC	NC	none
Jesness: Cfc	pen					1.00	.23***	.00	Delta .12*, I_4Na .15*
	camp					1.00	.03	.05	Able .28***, I_4Na .15**
I-level: I_4Ci	pen						1.00	1.00	Quay Id .11*, Quay Na .13*, Quay Si .18** Baker .16**
	camp							1.00	Able .15**

[a] Hypothesized Convergent

Table 6-11: *(continued)*

Classification Type	Quay	Megargee		Jesness		I-level		Anomalies[b]
	Aa	Charlie	Foxtrot	Aa	Cfc	I_4Ci	I_5Ci	
I-level: I_5Ci^d pen							1.00	Able .14**
camp							1.00	Able .10*, Quay Mp .13*, Jesness Se .10*

[a] Significant relationships (agreement) predicted.
[b] Convergent items predicted to be divergent.
[c] Cell frequencies on this variable were limited to 5 or fewer cases in both samples.
[d] Cell frequencies on this variable were limited to 5 of fewer cases in prison camp sample.
NC: Not computed.

   * $p \leq .10$
  ** $p \leq .05$
 *** $p \leq .01$

Table 6-12: Significant Divergent Relationships, Committed Criminal Measures

Classification Type		Divergent Correlates
Quay: Aa	pen	Item = .17** Jesness Se = .16** I_4Se = .13* I_4Nx = .16**
	camp	Jesness Cfm = .14* Jesness Se = .13* I_4Se = .16** I_5Se = .12*
Megargee: Charlie	pen	Jesness Mp = .16** Jesness Se = .12*
	camp	Quay Si = .12* Jesness Mp = .10*
Megargee: Foxtrot	pen	Quay Na = .11* Jesness Cfm = .11* Jesness Se = .11*
	camp	none
Jesness Aa[a]	pen	none
	camp	none
Jesness: Cfc	pen	Quay Na = .25*** Easy = .11* I_5Nx = .10* I_5Se = .17**
	camp	none
I_4Ci	pen	Jesness Cfm = .12*
	camp	Jesness Nx = .11* Easy = .11* Able = .16**
I_5Ci[b]	pen	none
	camp	none

[a] Cell frequencies for this type were limited to fewer than 5 cases in both samples.
[b] Cell frequencies for this type were limited to fewer than 5 cases in prison camp sample.
* $p \leq .10$
** $p \leq .05$
*** $p \leq .01$

Cognitive Developmental Measures

As shown in table 6-13, all of the cognitive developmental measures converged in both the penitentiary and the prison camp. This finding supports earlier research among probationers diagnosed according to I-level and Moral Judgment (Van Voorhis 1984), and substantiates the findings from the pilot study for this research (Van Voorhis 1988). Earlier research, however, did not examine the construct validity of the Jesness Inventory measure of I-level among adults. This point is especially important, because this measure of I-level is actuarial rather than the product of a more open-ended and clinical assessment process. Some observers have questioned the possibility of obtaining valid measures of cognitive development through a closed-ended test format such as the Jesness Inventory or the Rest Defining Issues Test (for moral development). They maintain that because these developmental measures depict thinking processes, it may be necessary to observe those processes at work in order to measure them (Kohlberg 1958). In this study, however, we can support the construct validity of the developmental constructs of the Jesness Inventory measures.[6]

RESULTS OF THE FACTOR ANALYSES

Two analyses were conducted, one to test the construct validity of the personality measures and another to test the validity of the developmental measures. The tests of the personality constructs were limited by measurement and sample sizes, and thus were difficult to conduct. Because only the Jesness Inventory and the Quay methods offer interval scores for each type, this test was constrained to the analysis of dummy variables. The result was an ill-conditioned matrix and findings that are presented with caution. Moreover, the factor analysis of the personality variables was possible only with the penitentiary data; the more limited variability of the camp measures precluded this portion of the analysis altogether.

Factor analysis of the penitentiary personality variables produced three weak factors: (1) a situational factor with loadings of Quay Si, Megargee Easy, Jesness Cfm, Jesness Se, I_4Se, and I_5Se; (2) a committed criminal factor with loadings of Quay Aa, Quay Id, Megargee Charlie, Megargee Foxtrot, Jesness Aa, Jesness Cfc, and I_4Ci; and (3) a neurotic factor with loadings of Quay Id, Quay Na, Megargee Delta, and I_4Nx. These three factors, the most interpretable, explained only 21% of the variance and were the results of the initial principal-component analysis.

Table 6-13: Correlation Matrix for Construct Validity Tests, Cognitive Developmental Measures

Classification Type		Hypothesized Convergent[a]			
		CL3	CL5	I-level (Jesness)	I-level (Interview)
CL3	pen	1.00	.81***	.23***	.23***
	camp	1.00	.60***	.19***	.14*
CL5	pen		1.00	.20**	.17**
	camp		1.00	.29***	.22***
I-level: Jesness	pen			1.00	.29***
	camp			1.00	.17**
I-level: Interview	pen				1.00
	camp				1.00

[a] Significant relationships (agreement) predicted.

* $p \leq .10$
** $p \leq .05$
*** $p \leq .01$

Subsequent use of the principal-axis method with a varimax rotation compressed this picture considerably, but the three factors remained in the final statistics. In this second analysis, however, fewer variables loaded on the factors: (1) the situational factor included Quay Si and I_4Se; (2) the committed criminal factor included only Jesness Cfc, Megargee Charlie, and I_4 Ci; and (3) the neurotic factor contained only Quay Na and I_4Nx. These three factors accounted for only 14% of the variance, and communality figures were quite limited. We present these findings as suggestive at best.

Analysis of the developmental measures produced clearer results, as shown in table 6-14. As expected, one factor was produced for each data set (penitentiary and prison camp) and each measure loaded onto each factor. Communalities and proportion of explained variation were low, although not surprisingly so, in light of theoretical differences pertinent to the type of cognitive complexity being measured.

SUMMARY AND DISCUSSION

At the outset, the goals of these analyses were to learn more about each system and to discover more about the classification needs of this population. One question concerned the number of types needed to classify this population. From the preceding analyses and discussions, our cross-classification of types appears to have produced a convergence of four important personality types: (1) situational, (2) neurotic anxious, (3) committed criminal, and (4) a neurotic acting-out/character disorder type, as typified by Megargee's Able and Delta and by the I_4 and I_5 Na. Beyond this distinction, it would appear sensible to accommodate types that are not encompassed by the personality domains, such as cognitive-developmental types and Megargee's How. Although How did not have a theoretical match, it correlated with some measures that make theoretical sense.

We were able to isolate convergent constructs, but our exploration is constrained by the measures entered into these analyses. Obviously, we tap only the specific psychological domains addressed by previous classification research with these populations. Thus, our suggestion of four personality types is limited by the available measures as well as by the number of converging constructs. Nevertheless, we can argue convincingly that the manipulative and immature traits are less clear constructs among adults than they may be among juveniles; they may be secondary to the types enumerated above rather than types in themselves.

Table 6-14: Factor Analysis of Cognitive Development Measures

| | Penitentiary | | Prison Camp | |
	Factor	h^2	Factor	h^2
Jesness I-level	.53	.28	.45	.20
I-level (interview)	.52	.27	.37	.14
CL3	.19	.19	.42	.18
% of Total Variance Explained	25%		17%	
Jesness I-level	.56	.31	.47	.23
I-level (interview)	.50	.25	.35	.13
CL5	.35	.12	.61	.37
% of Total Variance Explained	23%		24%	

This analysis, of course, does not address completely the issue of how many types are needed to classify these populations. Indeed, the need for even a type with strong construct validity is questionable if that type fails to correlate with behavioral measures that convey important treatment and management implications. These questions are addressed in the following chapters.

The notable differences between the penitentiary and the prison camp results also have general implications for the classification of these populations. Only the cognitive-developmental measures and the neurotic anxious measures produced similarly convergent findings for both populations. Situational measures also converged in both populations, but the findings for the camp revealed more anomalous correlates than those for the penitentiary. Committed-criminal measures converged in the penitentiary but not in the prison camp.

Generally, the penitentiary findings support the research hypotheses more strongly. One could offer two possible explanations: (1) that measurement error and data-collection problems marred the prison camp data,or (2) that the prison camp sample is such an atypical prison sample that it is too far removed from the original norms for these classification systems.

Our results support the latter conclusion for several reasons. First, the data collection in the prison camp was much easier than in the penitentiary as far as inmates' cooperation and access to research were concerned. Second, the reliability measures and the response rates for the prison camp data were slightly better than those for the penitentiary. Third, distributions of inmates across the classification types differed in expected ways between the two samples. Finally, the developmental measures converged more strongly than the personality measures in both samples; this is an important distinction.

Theoretically, the developmental measures are presumed to be "universal" rather than specific to offender populations. The personality measures emerged empirically from offender populations, and thus are more likely to be sample-specific. Our findings may suggest that the personality-based classification systems are more sensitive to setting than their originators envisioned. At a minimum, these findings also support a need to develop norms for different types of prison populations: a description of a type in a maximum-security setting may not be applicable to the same type in a minimum-security setting. Alternatively, the findings may suggest a need for entirely different domains of classification across correctional settings.[7]

Another goal for this chapter was to validate each type and to perhaps describe it further. This process involved numerous bivariate correlations, the discussion of which could quickly become overwhelming. For the sake of organization, the research findings as they pertain to each classification type are summarized in table 6-15. The "Comments" column in the table offers additional type descriptors as they emerged from this research. This section may prove particularly valuable in light of the empirical, inductive nature of this technology and the limited validation research conducted to date.

One might argue that the results of this chapter are limited; correlations seldom surpassed .25, for example, and some anomalous correlations were detected. These arguments, however, may be countered with reminders of the constraints on these tests in light of the successful number and patterns of convergent findings. In view of the high potential for measurement error, as well as the observed measurement error, it is likely that the resultant error occurs in the direction of underestimating the magnitude of significant findings. Indeed, the challenges to these tests are more numerous than if we had correlated one measure (e.g., one obtained through a psychological inventory) with a similarly acquired measure (e.g., one obtained through another psychological inventory). Instead, a measure of neurosis/anxiety, for example, is compared across observation processes: One measure was obtained through staff observation, another similarly defined measure was obtained through a clinical interview, and yet two others through an inventory completed by the inmate. Some of these methods require the inmate to demonstrate spontaneously the trait being measured, whereas others probe for it; but the important point is that the differences may introduce a degree of measurement error (Rest 1976). Moreover, as presented in chapter 4, each assessment process incurred additional error because the reliability figures for the classification systems are not optimal. Finally, correlation figures can be sensitive to the metric of the measures correlated. A measure of association (phi) involving a dichotomous variable is likely to understate the magnitude of a relationship with respect to what it might have been if these results had been offered as interval/ratio levels of measurement.

The strength and the consistency of these findings, in light of the high level of actual and potential measurement error, suggest that these systems might be much more predictive and more powerful if greater attention were given to the development of training and retraining procedures and to scoring and rating structure. The reduction of error ultimately should improve the utility of these systems.

Table 6-15: Summary of Construct Validity Tests

Classification Type	Convergent[a]		Divergent[b]		Comments
	Pen	Camp	Pen	Camp	
Quay AIMS					
* Asocial Aggressive	Yes	Yes	Yes	Yes	Converges strongly with all other committed criminal measures. Diverges from situational measures
Immature Dependent	Weak[c]	No	Weak[c]	Weak[c]	May not be a useful classification in either setting. Difficult to distinguish from neurotic, disturbed (How), and criminal types.
Neurotic Anxious	Yes	Once[d]	Yes	Yes	Anomalous correlations with Able, How, Jesness Cfm, and I_4Ci.
Manipulative	No	Once[d]	Weak[c]	Weak[c]	Manipulative types were difficult to distinguish from others. In the penitentiary, they may be secondary characteristics to disturbed and committed criminal types.
* Situational	Yes	Yes	Yes	Yes	Converges strongly with other situational measures. May describe a naive type of situational offender.
Megargee MMPI-Based Typology					
* Able	Once[d]	Once[d]	Yes	Yes	Correlates highly with neurotic acting-out and weakly with some committed criminal measures. Though not supportive of research hypotheses as a manipulative type, is nevertheless an important classification type. Diverges from situational, neurotic anxious, and immature measures.
Baker	No	Once[d]	Yes	Yes	Correlates formed no meaningful patterns. Few Bakers identified in this population. As a result, these were not adequate validity tests for this type.

					Description
* Charlie	Yes	No	Yes	Yes	Converges strongly with other committed criminal types in the penitentiary. Not a meaningful type in minimum security setting. Some correlates with neurotic types in the prison camp.
Delta	Once[d]	Once[d]	Yes	Weak[c]	Correlates stronger with neurotic measures than with other manipulative measures. Diverges from situational types in the prison camp.
* Easy	Yes	Yes	Yes	Yes	Converges strongly with other situational measures. Anomalous correlations with Jesness Cfm in both samples suggests a more naive situational type. Diverges from criminal and neurotic anxious measures in the prison sample.
* Foxtrot	Yes	No	Weak[c]	Weak[c]	Converges strongly with other committed criminal types in the penitentiary. Anomalous correlations with situational and neurotic types. Not a meaningful type in minimum security.
George	Weak[c]	Yes	Yes	Yes	Converges most strongly with Quay Id in the penitentiary. Converges with neurotic measures in the prison camp.
How	NA[e]	NA[e]	NA[e]	NA[e]	Describes psychological disturbance rather than personality per se. Converges with neurotic, manipulative, and dependent types.
Item	Yes	Yes	Yes	Weak[c]	May be identifying a bright, more sophisticated, situational offender. Anomalies with criminal and neurotic acting-out measures in the camp.
Jupiter	Yes	Weak[c]	Yes	Yes	Correlates with neurotic types in the penitentiary, but few cases were identified and tests are limited.
Jesness Inventory I-level					
Asocial Aggressive (Aa)	NA[f]	NA[f]	NA[f]	NA[f]	Few cases were identified. Tests are limited. Correlates with How, neurotic anxious, and Quay Id in the penitentiary.

Table 6-15: *(continued)*

Classification Type	Convergent[a]		Divergent[b]		Comments
	Pen	Camp	Pen	Camp	
Ascial Passive (Ap)	NA[f]	NA[f]	NA[f]	NA[f]	Few cases were identified. Tests are limited. Correlates with How in the prison camp.
Immature Conformist (Cfm)	No	No	Weak[c]	Weak[c]	Correlates with neurotic and situational types and with How. Immature types do not converge in these samples and may not be useful in classifying adult offenders. Diverges from Able in both samples.
* Cultural Conformist (Cfc)	Yes	Yes	Yes	Yes	Converges strongly with other committed criminal types in the penitentiary sample. Anomalous correlations with Able (camp) and neurotic acting-out in both samples. Diverges from situational and neurotic anxious in the penitentiary.
Manipulator (Mp)	Yes	Once[d]	Yes	Yes	Converges better than other manipulative types in the penitentiary. Diverges from situational, committed criminal, How and neurotic types.
Neurotic Acting-out (Na)	Weak[c]	Yes	Yes	Yes	Converges better in the prison camp than in the penitentiary. Weak anomalous correlations with Able and committed-criminal types in both settings.
Neurotic Anxious (Nx)	Weak[c]	Weak[c]	Yes	Yes	Strong anomalous correlation with How (psychological disturbance) in the prison camp and with I_5Se in the penitentiary.
* Situational (Se)	Yes	Yes	Yes	Yes	Converges strongly in the penitentiary. May be tapping a less sophisticated type of situational offender. Diverges clearly from committed criminal, neurotic acting-out and disturbed measures.

Cultural Identifier (Ci)	Yes	Once[d]	Yes	Yes	Few cases. Tests are limited. Diverges from committed criminal and neurotic acting-out measures in both settings.
I-level (interview method)					
I_4 Neurotic Anxious (Nx)	Once[d]	Yes	Weak[c]	Weak[c]	Did not converge well in the penitentiary. Some divergent correlations with Delta, How, Jesness Aa, and Quay Id. Interviews are classifying more inmates as neurotic than are tests and observational measures.
I_4 Neurotic Acting-out (Na)	No	Weak[c]	No	No	Stronger correlations with divergent types (e.g., Able, Quay Aa, Charlie, and Cfc) than with neurotic types.
* I_4 Cultural Identifier (Ci)	Yes	Once[d]	Weak[c]	Weak[c]	Converges strongly with other committed criminal types in the penitentiary. Anomalous correlations with Able in the prison camp and with neurotic and situational measures in the penitentiary.
I_4 Situational (Se)	Once[d]	Yes	Yes	Yes	Converges with only Quay Si in the penitentiary. Anomalous correlation with Jesness Cfm in both samples suggests naive type of situational offender. Diverges from committed criminal and neurotic types in both samples.
I_5 Neurotic Anxious (Nx)	Yes	Once[d]	Yes	Yes	No convergent correlations are strong. Anomalous correlation with Delta in the camp sample.
I_5 Neurotic Acting-out (Na)	No	No	Yes	Yes	Only correlations are strong correlations with Able in both samples.
I_5 Cultural Identifier (Ci)	No	No	Yes	Yes	Anomalous correlation with Able in both samples and with Quay Mp and Jesness Se in the prison camp. Appears not to be a committed-criminal measure.

Table 6-15: *(continued)*

Classification Type	Convergent[a]		Divergent[b]		Comments
	Pen	Camp	Pen	Camp	
* I₅ Situational (Se)	Yes	Yes	Yes	Yes	Converges with measures of more highly functioning situational offenders. Anomalous relationship with Jesness Nx. Diverges from Able, Jesness Cfc, and Jesness Cfm.

[a] Significant relationships (agreement) predicted.
[b] Significant relationships (disagreement) or no relationship perdicted.
[c] Type correlated with only one other similarly defined type.
[d] Several (3 or more) anomalous correlations (or convergent items predicted to be divergent) and no pattern to the divergent correlations.
[e] Not applicable, because there were no matches to this type hypothesized.
[f] Not applicable, because cell sizes were limited.
* Type converged strongly with similarly defined types.

CHAPTER 7

PREDICTION OF
DISCIPLINARY-RELATED
PRISON OUTCOMES

This chapter examines the relationship between the classification types and measures of adjustment to prison. The focus here is on the criterion variables that measure those behaviors most relevant to managing an orderly and secure facility, such as disciplinary infractions, victimization experiences, drug and alcohol use, aggressive behavior, need for supervision, and quality of interactions with staff and fellow inmates.

The data analysis addresses two questions: (1) How well did the classification variables predict whether the inmates became involved in problem behaviors? and 2) How well did the classification types predict the extent or the frequency of these behaviors? The first question is assessed through cross-tabular analysis and probit analysis.[1] Multiple regression (OLS) is applied to the second question. Multiple regression analysis required transformation of the classification types into dummy variables; each type represents one variable and each regression equation contains only the types belonging to a single system. Thus, we generated one regression model for each classification system on each dependent variable. Each model contained all of the types (dummy variables) included in a given system; one type, of course, was omitted and was shown in the reference category (or constant). Results are identical to those that would have been obtained through analysis of variance, but they allowed us to examine multiple Rs for each model.[2] Further, the b-coefficients provided a way to compute the means for each type.

Given this plan, it is clear that the analyses became quite involved. Because their presentation is equally detailed, we reverse the traditional order of discussion and begin with a summary of the results. Readers who find the presentation of each test to be overly tedious may wish to read only this section and the discussion section at the end of the chapter. For others, the analyses follow this summary section.

SUMMARY OF THE FINDINGS

This research was designed not to select an optimum system from the five studied here, but to learn more about the technology of psychological classification. In retrospect, this intention makes good sense. As Wright (1988) observed for his New York State sample, each system has its own advantages and disadvantages. Moreover, as we argued earlier in this report, these psychological systems were designed primarily for treatment and case management. Accordingly, the results presented in the next chapter, which pertain to treatment implications, may be viewed by some as more relevant to the original intention of the systems than those presented in this chapter, which relate to security and custody concerns. Even so, much of the existing research has held these systems to the standard of predicting disciplinary problems.

This discussion is facilitated throughout by table 7-1, a summary of the most problematic types identified through these analyses.

Chapter 4 of this report detailed a number of problems with obtaining data on the **Quay AIMS** system. In addition, we expressed some concern for the interrater reliability of the measures. Despite these difficulties, we observe numerous significant relationships between this typology and important institutional behaviors. Moreover, the findings (with one exception) are consistent with the type descriptions. In both samples, the data show that Asocial Aggressive inmates and Manipulative inmates incur problems with aggressive behaviors, insubordination, and relations with other men. In both settings, staff members perceived these inmates as needing more supervision than others.

We observed a number of correlates for the Neurotic Anxious and the Quay Immature Dependent inmates, but their patterns are less clear. In the penitentiary, the Neurotic Anxious inmates showed a tendency to self-report aggressive behaviors, but that was the only indication of difficulty for these inmates on either the official or the self-reported penitentiary data. Penitentiary staff members, however, tended to rate these two groups at least as unfavorably as the Asocial Aggressives and the Manipulators, if not

Table 7-1: Most Problematic Types

Classification System/Type	Penitentiary	Prison Camp
	Official Data—All Disciplinaries	
Quay AIMS	none significant	none significant
Megargee MMPI	Able Charlie Delta How Item	none significant
Conceptual Level	none significant	CL3: Cl-2 & Cl-3 CL5: Cl-2 & Cl-3 (weak relationships)
Jesness Inventory	none significant	Level: I_2 & I_3 Personality: Cfc/Mp Na Ap/Cfm
I-level (interview)	none significant	none significant
	Official Data—Drug/Alcohol[a]	
Quay AIMS	Immature Dependent	not tested
Megargee MMPI	none significant	not tested
Conceptual Level	none significant	not tested
Jesness Inventory	none significant	not tested
I-level (interview)	none significant	not tested
	Official Data—Insubordination	
Quay AIMS	none significant	Asocial Aggressive Immature Dependent Manipulator
Megargee MMPI	Able Charlie	none significant
Conceptual Level	none significant	CL3: Cl-2 & Cl-3 CL5: Cl-2 & Cl-3 (weak relationships)
Jesness Inventory	none significant	Personality: Mp, Na
I-level (interview)	Personality: Ci, I_5Na, I_4Se	none significant

Table 7-1: *(continued)*

Classification System/Type	Penitentiary	Prison Camp
	Self-report—Non-Aggressive Reports	
Quay AIMS	none significant	not tested
Megargee MMPI	Able	not tested
	Charlie	
	Delta	
	Foxtrot	
	How	
Conceptual Level	none significant	not tested
Jesness Inventory	Level: I_2 & I_4	not tested
	Personality: Aa, Mp, Cfc, Na, Nx, Si	
I-level (interview)	Level: I_5	not tested
	Personality: I_5Ci	
	Self-Report—Aggressive Reports	
Quay AIMS	Asocial Aggressive Neurotic Anxious	none significant
Megargee MMPI	none significant	Able
		Charlie
		Delta
		Foxtrot
		How
Conceptual Level	CL3: Cl-2 & Cl-3	none significant
	CL5: Cl-2 & Cl-3	
Jesness Inventory	none significant	Personality: Mp, Cfc, Na, Nx
I-level (interview)	Level: I_4	Personality: Na, I_5Nx
	Personality: Na (n.s.)	
	Self-Report—Victimization Reports	
Quay AIMS	Situational	none significant
Megargee MMPI	none significant	Able
		Charlie
		Delta
		Easy
		Foxtrot
		How
		Item

Table 7-1: *(continued)*

Classification System/Type	Penitentiary	Prison Camp
	Self-Report—Vicltimization Reports *(continued)*	
Conceptual Level	CL3: Cl-2 & Cl-3 CL5: Cl-2 & Cl-3	CL3: Cl-2 & Cl-3 (n.s.) CL5: Cl-2 & Cl-3 (n.s.)
Jesness Inventory	none significant	none significant
I-level (interview)	none significant	Level: I_5
	Staff Ratings—Relations with Other Men	
Quay AIMS	Asocial Aggressive Immature Dependent Manipulator	Asocial Aggressive Manipulator
Megargee MMPI	none significant	Foxtrot (weak relationship)
Conceptual Level	CL3: Cl-1 & Cl-2 CL5: Cl-1 & Cl-2	Conflicting results
Jesness Inventory	Level I_3 Personality: Aa, Mp, Cfc, Cfm, Ap	none significant
I-level (interview)	Level: I_4	none significant
	Staff Ratings—Relations with Authority	
Quay AIMS	none significant	Manipulator
Megargee MMPI	none significant	none significant
Conceptual Level	CL5: Cl-1 CL5: Cl-1	CL5: Cl-1
Jesness Inventory	Personality: Aa, Mp, Nx	none significant
I-level (interview)	Personality: Na	none significant
	Staff Ratings—Aggressiveness	
Quay AIMS	Asocial Aggressive	none signifcant
Megargee MMPI	none significant	none significant
Conceptual Level	none significant	none significant
Jesness Inventory	Level: I_3 Personality: Aa, Mp, Cfc, Na	none significant
I-level (interview)	Personality: Na Level: I_4	Personality: Nx, Na

Table 7-1: *(continued)*

Classification System/Type	Penitentiary	Prison Camp
	Staff Ratings—Cooperativeness	
Quay AIMS	none significant	Asocial Aggressive Manipulator
Megargee MMPI	none significant	none significant
Conceptual Level	CL3: Cl-1 CL5: Cl-1	Conflicting results
Jesness Inventory	Level: I_2 & I_3 Personality: Aa, Mp, Cfc	none significant
I-level (interview)	Level: I_4	none significant
	Staff Ratings—Needs Supervision	
Quay AIMS	Asocial Aggressive Manipulator Neurotic Anxious	Asocial Aggressive Manipulator
Megargee MMPI	none significant	Foxtrot (weak relationship)
Conceptual Level	CL3: Cl-1 & Cl-2 CL5: Cl-1 & Cl-2	conflicting results
Jesness Inventory	Level: I_2 & I_3 Personality: Aa, Mp, Cfc	none significant
I-level (interview)	Personality: Na, I_4Nx, Ci	Level: I_4 (weak relationship)
	Staff Ratings—Responds to Supervision	
Quay AIMS	none significant	Immature Dependent Manipulator
Megargee MMPI	none significant	Foxtrot (weak relationship)
Conceptual Level	CL3: Cl-1 CL5: Cl-1	Conflicting results
Jesness Inventory	Level: I_3 Personality: Aa, Mp, Cfc	none significant
I-level (interview)	none significant	Conflicting results (level)

[a] Limited variation on this measure.
N.S. Relationship was high but not significant.

more so. Generalizations about the performance of the Immature Dependent and the Neurotic Anxious inmates at the prison camp are marred by low cell frequencies (N = 8). Nevertheless, they were rated favorably by the staff, except on their response to supervision.

The exception to the general trend of these findings pertains to the performance of the inmates classified as Situational in the penitentiary sample who were observed to have higher-than-expected rates of official infractions (not significantly higher ones, however). It is noteworthy that this finding parallels those for situationals and for most benign types on the other systems.

The fact that analyses of the Quay AIMS data produce results in expected directions, in spite of some concern for reliability problems, suggests that these results may underestimate the differences between the types. This suggestion is supported by the results of the construct validity tests reported in chapter 6. Thus the true findings are likely to be attenuated by the reliability problems. If this were not the case, our analysis probably would have resulted in a more persistent lack of correlates or in the observation of correlates that made no theoretical sense.

Findings for the **Megargee MMPI-based system** were somewhat disappointing. The lack of correlates, however, is confined largely to this chapter; we observed more positive results on tests of the system's construct validity as well as with the treatment-outcome variables reported in the next chapter. In this chapter, we noted many expected differences between types, but most of these distinctions did not reach significance. We might speculate on several reasons for this outcome. First and probably most important, this study was not an optimal test of the Megargee system. Most of the research conducted to date has involved large samples. In this study, tests were conducted on approximately 150 inmates but sometimes on as few as 107 inmates. This situation placed limitations on some cell frequencies and degrees of freedom. Quite possibly, our results would have been significant if our sample had been larger. The results were not improved, however, by analyses that involved collapsing the types and running tests only for those types with adequate Ns.

We also might speculate that our testing procedures were somehow flawed and thus rendered the results unreliable. Yet we observed no substantial differences between our test validity scores and those reported for other studies. In addition, a second analysis, which excluded tests with problematic scores on the validity scales of the MMPI, changed the results in only minimal ways.

Finally, predicting to disciplinary-related rather than treatment-related variables simply may not be one of the strengths of this system, particularly in this setting. In support of this point, comparable tests in the pilot study were positive but weak (tau_b = .20, p =. 07). Furthermore, most of the differences detected in the pilot study were attributable to the fact that the least disturbed types (Easy and Item) were much less likely than the other types to be cited for disciplinary infractions. Results for the remaining types were undifferentiated (Van Voorhis 1988). In the present study, however, Items incurred atypically high scores for disciplinary problems on the self-report, official, and staff measures. We observed earlier that this was part of a pattern among the situational and the least disturbed inmates on other classification systems as well.

As revealed in Tables 7-2 through 7-7, we found several positive findings in tests of the two measures of **Conceptual Level.** Regrettably, however, it is difficult to discern patterns. In the penitentiary, staff members typically rated the CL-1 inmates lower than the inmates classified at the higher developmental levels. Similar findings are not observed for the prison camp inmates. Penitentiary self-report data reveal a trend whereby inmates classified in the two higher levels, CL-2 and CL-3, report *more* aggressive behaviors and victimizations, but this trend is not supported by the prison camp data. CL-2 and CL-3 inmates were significantly more likely than CL-1 inmates to be cited for disciplinary infractions, but only at the prison camp. Finally, we find none of the CL-1 correlates with victimization experiences that the pilot study led us to expect (Van Voorhis 1988).

Results of the tests of the **Jesness Inventory** were quite promising. Although this system has not been used previously with adult inmates, tests generally revealed that the various types are relevant to the behaviors of adult male inmates. Most important, the results generate clear interpretations that often are supported across settings and outcome measures. Inmates diagnosed as aggressive on the I-level typology (Aa, Mp, Cfc) were found to be statistically more likely: to (1) be cited for disciplinary infractions and insubordination in the prison camp; (2) report aggressive behaviors in the prison camp and the penitentiary, and non-aggressive, problematic behaviors in the penitentiary; and (3) be evaluated unfavorably by staff in the penitentiary. In addition, Neurotic Acting-out inmates in both samples scored much higher than the other inmates on the self-report aggression scale, whereas both types of neurotic penitentiary inmates scored high on the self-report nonaggressive behavior scale. Penitentiary Nas also received relatively high ratings on the staff aggression scale.

Findings for the Situationals were mixed: favorable on staff ratings in the penitentiary and on self-report and official data in the prison camp and somewhat unfavorable on self-report and official penitentiary data. Yet these results form a pattern that is consistent with those observed for situational types identified by the other systems.

Tests of the effects of the Jesness developmental levels often were not significant; when they were significant, they typically found I_2 and I_3 inmates receiving the more unfavorable results. The only exceptions to the generally sensitive findings of the Jesness Inventory occur in the prison camp staff ratings, where none of the results were positive. As explained below, however, the prison camp staff data were not ideal.

Although tests of the **interview-based I-level** method did not often produce enlightening results, the results for the Nas and Cis should be noted. As in the Jesness Inventory, Neurotic Acting-out inmates scored higher than others on the self-report aggression index. This finding is noted in both samples, but the penitentiary test was not significant. In addition, penitentiary staff members tended to rate Nas as more aggressive than the other inmates. To a lesser extent, findings for Cis (Cultural Identifiers) in the penitentiary suggest a tendency to receive citations and to self-report more dysfunctional behaviors. Findings for level suggest that I_4 penitentiary inmates are more aggressive than I_5 inmates and that staff members rate them as more likely to have difficulty in relating to others and in cooperating. These results are somewhat more interpretable than the developmental levels identified by Conceptual Level and the Jesness Inventory. Specifically, I_4 appears to be an important construct.

Findings for the I-level interview method must be viewed in the context of administrative costs. This system required more complex training than the others, and incurred reliability problems in spite of time-consuming attempts to check reliability. As in the Quay AIMS data, these problems probably attenuated the findings. In the case of the I-level system, however, correction of the reliability problems is a more difficult task (see Harris 1988).[3] Prospective users should note that the Jesness Inventory taps many, but not all, of the same psychological domains as the I-level interview method and can be administered much more efficiently.

The discussion section of this chapter offers a more integrated discussion of these findings, particularly as they pertain to the psychological constructs common to the five systems. For ease of presentation and for greater clarity, the following analysis sections are presented separately for each sample.

PENITENTIARY

The Effects of the Classification Types on Officially Recorded Disciplinary Infractions

Moving to the results for the penitentiary sample, we examine the effects of the classification variables on officially recorded disciplinary infractions. Results of both the cross-tabular and the multiple regression analysis are shown in table 7-2. For each dependent variable and for each classification type, the percentage of inmates with at least one recorded disciplinary infraction is noted in the first column; the mean rate of infractions per month (multiplied by 100) is noted in the second column. The N for each type is noted in the third column.

For all but the tests of Conceptual Level, the classification types were collapsed for additional tests. We did this for three reasons: (1) to improve the degrees of freedom and the cell sizes; (2) in the cases of the two I-level systems, to test both the developmental and the personality constructs of the system; and (3) to correct for the fact that cell frequencies were limited in tests of the Megargee MMPI-based types and the Jesness Inventory and required us to collapse similar types. Thus, the tests of the uncollapsed types on the Jesness and the MMPI systems must be viewed with some caution, but are presented nevertheless for illustration.[4]

Table 7-2 reveals numerous instances in which the classification systems failed to correlate with any of the outcome measures: officially recorded disciplinary infractions, drug and alcohol infractions, and officially recorded incidents involving insubordination. The relationship between the psychological predictors and the disciplinary infractions was significant in only two instances: the relationship between the Quay AIMS types and drug and alcohol infractions and the relationship between the I-level (interview) subtypes and insubordination. In the former case, inmates diagnosed as Immature Dependent on the Quay AIMS systems were found through multiple regression analysis to have incurred significantly more drug infractions than other inmates, whereas the Quay Neurotic Anxious inmates incurred none, or significantly fewer than the other inmates. Cross-tabular analysis found that the

Table 7-2: Regression of Classification Variables on Official Disciplinary Variables, Penitentiary Sample

Classification System	All Disciplinaries[a]			Drug/Alcohol[a]			Insubordination[a]		
	%[b]	$\bar{X}$	N	%[b]	$\bar{X}$	N	%[b]	$\bar{X}$	N
Quay AIMS									
Asocial Agg.	27	5.7	21	5	.8	21	10	1.6	21
Immature Dep.	20	5.0	10	20	5.0	10	0	0.0	10
Neurotic Anx.	22	5.8	23	0	0.0	23	17	3.6	23
Manipulator	26	5.9	42	10	1.6	42	17	3.1	42
Situational	26	6.8	53	6	.9	53	13	2.5	53
				$F = 2.15*$					
				Mult. $R = .24$					
Quay AIMS (Collapsed Categories)									
Aa/Mp	27	5.8	63	8	1.3	63	14	2.6	63
Id/Na	21	5.6	33	6	1.5	33	12	2.5	33
Situational	26	6.8	53	6	.9	53	13	2.5	53
Megargee MMPI-Based Taxonomy									
Able	28	7.9	32	6	1.0	32	25	4.7	32
Baker	33	8.3	6	17	5.6	6	17	2.7	6
Charlie	46	9.0	13	8	1.3	13	23	5.1	13
Delta	39	8.0	23	13	2.2	23	17	2.9	23
Easy	18	3.0	11	0	0.0	11	9	1.5	11
Foxtrot	9	3.0	11	9	1.5	11	0	0.0	11
George	0	0.0	14	0	0.0	14	0	0.0	14
How	22	4.3	23	4	.7	23	13	2.8	23
Item	27	6.1	26	8	.8	26	15	3.2	26
Jupiter	25	8.3	4	25	8.3	4	0	0.0	4
Megargee (Collapsed Categories)									
Charlie/Foxtrot (Committed Criminal)	29	6.3	24	8	1.4	24	13	2.8	24
Able/Delta (Character Disorder)	33	8.0	55	9	1.5	55	22	4.0	55
How (Most Disturbed)	22	4.2	23	4	.7	23	13	2.8	23
Baker/George (Neurotic)	13	3.4	24	8	2.8	24	4	.7	24
Item/Easy (Least Disturbed)	24	5.2	37	5	.9	37	14	2.7	37
	($Tau_c = -.13*$)[c]						($Tau_c = -.12**$)[c]		
Conceptual Level—CL3									
CL-1	27	6.0	42	7	1.6	42	14	2.8	42
CL-2	26	6.2	82	10	1.6	82	13	2.6	82
CL-3	28	6.7	25	4	1.3	25	20	4.0	25

Table 7-2: *(continued)*

Classification	All Disciplinaries[a]			Drug/Alcohol[a]			Insubordination[a]		
	%[b]	$\overline{X}$	N	%[b]	$\overline{X}$	N	%[b]	$\overline{X}$	N
Conceptual Level—CL5									
CL-1	33	6.8	27	11	2.5	27	11	2.5	27
CL-2	24	5.7	102	8	1.3	102	14	2.6	102
CL-3	35	8.3	20	5	1.7	20	25	5.0	20
Jesness Inventory I-level									
I-2 Aa	40	6.9	5	20	3.3	5	20	2.9	5
I-2 Ap	33	5.6	3	0	0.0	3	33	5.6	3
I-3 Cfm	15	2.5	20	0	0.0	20	10	1.7	20
I-3 Mp	34	9.7	32	13	2.1	32	22	4.2	32
I-3 Cfc	28	6.1	43	12	1.2	43	9	2.3	43
I-4 Nx	14	2.4	7	14	2.4	7	0	0.0	7
I-4 Na	21	7.0	19	5	1.8	19	11	2.6	19
I-4 Si	35	5.8	20	0	0.0	20	30	5.0	20
I-4 Ci	33	5.6	3	0	0.0	3	33	5.6	3
Jesness Inventory (Collapsed Levels)									
I-2	38	6.0	8	13	2.2	8	25	3.9	8
I-3	27	6.7	95	10	1.9	95	14	2.9	95
I-4	27	7.0	49	4	1.8	49	18	3.8	49
Jesness Inventory (Collapsed Personality Subtypes)									
Aggressives (Aa, Cfc, Mp)	31	7.8	80	13	2.4	80	15	3.2	80
Neurotics (Na, Nx)	19	5.9	26	8	2.0	26	8	2.0	26
Dependents (Ap, Cfm)	17	3.0	23	0	0.0	23	13	2.3	23
Situational (Se, Ci)	35	5.9	23	0	0.0	23	30	5.2	23
I-level (Interview Method)									
I-4 Na	24	5.5	38	5	.9	38	13	2.2	38
I-4 Nx	25	5.2	32	9	1.6	32	6	1.0	32
I-4 Se	25	7.9	16	6	1.0	16	19	5.1	16
I-4 Ci	35	9.8	17	12	3.9	17	18	4.9	17
I-5 Na	24	8.0	17	6	1.0	17	18	4.0	17
I-5 Nx	29	6.3	24	8	1.3	24	17	2.8	24
I-5 Se	9	1.5	11	0	0.0	11	0	0.0	11
I-5 Ci	33	5.6	21	5	1.0	21	29	4.8	21
I-level (Collapsed Levels)									
I-4	26	6.5	103	8	1.6	103	13	2.5	103
I-5	26	5.6	73	6	1.0	73	18	3.2	73

Table 7-2: *(continued)*

Classification	All Disciplinaries[a]			Drug/Alcohol[a]			Insubordination[a]		
	%[b]	X̄	N	%[b]	X̄	N	%[b]	X̄	N
I-level (Collapsed Personality Subtypes)									
Ci (I-4 & I-5)	34	6.5	38	8	2.2	38	24	4.8	38
Na (I-4 & I-5)	24	6.2	55	6	1.0	55	15	2.7	55
Nx (I-4 & I-5)	27	5.7	56	9	1.5	56	11	1.8	56
Se (I-4 & I-5)	19	5.5	27	4	.6	27	11	3.0	27
							$Tau_c = .10$**		

[a] Rate per month × 100.
[b] Percent with at least one disciplinary report.
[c] Most valid cases, only.
* $p \leq .10$
** $p \leq .05$

I-level Cultural Identifiers and the Neurotic Acting-out inmates were significantly more likely to be cited for insubordination than were the inmates classified into other subtypes (tau$_c$ = .10, p ≤ .05). Both of these findings are consistent with type descriptions for Quay Immature Dependents and I-level Cultural Identifiers and Neurotic Acting-out types.

In several additional cases, findings were in the predicted direction. Inmates diagnosed as Able, Charlie, and Delta on the Megargee system, for example, were cited more often for disciplinary infractions than were most of the other types. Types Able and Charlie on the Megargee system were involved in a higher mean number of incidents of insubordination than the other inmates. Although initial tests proved insignificant, cross-tabular analysis of the collapsed MMPI types and the overall disciplinary and insubordination variables *were* significant when 40 cases flagged as potentially invalid were excluded from the analysis (tau$_c$ = −.13, p ≤ .10 and tau$_c$ = −.12, p ≤ .05 respectively).[5]

The aggressive subtypes on the Jesness system also incurred more overall disciplinary infractions and drug and alcohol infractions than the inmates diagnosed into the other categories. I$_4$Ci inmates (interview method) were more likely to be cited for disciplinary infractions and were cited more frequently than the other inmates. All of these findings make sense from the standpoint of the type descriptions, but they are not significant.

This is not to suggest that no anomalies existed. Most notably, inmates diagnosed as situational, or as least likely to be involved in difficulties, were cited far more frequently than one would predict. In fact, Quay AIMS Situationals have a substantially higher mean number of overall infractions than inmates classified into the other types. The Jesness I-level Situational and the Megargee Item groups are also atypically high on these measures. At the other extreme, inmates diagnosed as Foxtrot and How on the Megargee system were involved in far *less* difficulty than one would expect on the basis of prior research and their respective type descriptions.

As noted earlier, the official data forming the basis of the multiple regression analysis shown in table 7-2 were skewed. Sixty-five percent of the inmates with recorded disciplinary infractions were involved in only one incident. In response, we analyzed these data a second time, using log transformations of each of the dependent variables. The results, however, did not differ in any important way from those tests of the data which had not been transformed. In addition, we analyzed the data a third time by dichotomizing the dependent variables and executing a probit analysis, but results were similar. None of the chi-square goodness-of-fit values were significant.

The Effects of the Classification Types on
Self-Reported Disciplinary Problems

As shown in table 7-3 (and later in table 7-4), the picture changes substantially when other criterion measures are used. A cursory overview of table 7-3 reveals that when one tests the effects of the classification variables on self-report indices of nonaggressive infractions, aggressive behaviors, and self-reported victimization experiences, a number of significant findings emerge. These are discussed as they pertain to each system.

Cross-tabular analysis of the effects of the **Quay AIMS** types on aggressive behaviors revealed, as expected, that the Asocial Aggressive inmates were significantly more likely to report engaging in aggressive behaviors than were the inmates classified as other types (χ^2 = 8.8, p ≤ .05). A relatively high proportion of the Quay Neurotic Anxious inmates also evidenced high scores on this scale. At the same time, none of the Immature Dependent inmates reported engaging in aggressive behaviors.

Although one might have identified the Quay Neurotic and the Immature Dependent types to be at greater risk of victimizations, significantly more Situational inmates reported having been threatened and/or victimized during the initial months of incarceration (χ^2 = 9.9, p ≤ . 05). Yet this finding is not altogether surprising, because these inmates are also more likely to have less experience with the prison culture and with more strongly committed criminal lifestyles.

An inspection of the effects of the **Megargee MMPI-based** types on self-reported nonaggressive behaviors shows responses that occur in expected directions; yet only one of the six tests was significant. The committed criminal (Charlie and Foxtrot), character disorder (Able and Delta), and disturbed (How) inmates were far more likely to report nonaggressive problem behaviors than the more benign inmates (Easy and Item) and the neurotic inmates (Baker, George, and Jupiter). When the typology was collapsed, these results were significant (tau$_c$ = -.11, p ≤ .05). These five types were also more likely to report aggressive behaviors, but the means between the groups are not significantly different. One of

Table 7-3: Regression of Classification Variables on Self-Report Infraction and Victimization Measures, Penitentiary Sample

Classification	Nonaggressive[a]			Aggressive[b]			Victimized[c]		
	%[d]	$\bar{X}$	N	%[e]	$\bar{X}$	N	%[d]	$\bar{X}$	N
Quay AIMS									
Asocial Agg.	7	1.3	15	33	1.4	15	7	1.3	15
Immature Dep.	17	1.5	6	0	1.1	6	0	1.1	6
Neurotic Anx.	19	1.4	16	19	1.3	16	13	1.4	16
Manipulator	8	1.4	26	8	1.2	27	7	1.3	27
Situational	10	1.3	31	7	1.1	31	32	1.5	31
				$\chi^2 = 8.8^{**}$			$\chi^2 = 9.9^{**}$		
Quay AIMS (Collapsed Categories)									
Aa/Mp	7	1.3	41	17	1.3	41	7	1.3	41
Id/Na	18	1.4	22	14	1.2	22	9	1.3	22
Situational	10	1.3	31	6	1.2	31	32	1.5	31
				$Tau_c = -.10^*$			$\chi^2 = 9.4^{**}$		
							$Tau_c = .22^{***}$		
Megargee MMPI-Based Taxonomy									
Able	13	1.4	23	17	1.2	23	13	1.4	24
Baker	0	1.3	2	0	1.0	2	0	1.3	2
Charlie	13	1.5	8	25	1.4	8	38	1.8	8
Delta	20	1.5	15	27	1.3	14	13	1.2	15
Easy	0	1.2	5	0	1.1	5	0	1.1	5
Foxtrot	17	1.2	6	17	1.3	6	0	1.1	6
George	0	1.2	9	11	1.2	9	11	1.3	9
How	21	1.3	14	21	1.2	14	14	1.4	14
Item	5	1.3	22	23	1.3	22	14	1.3	22
Jupiter	0	1.2	3	0	1.1	3	33	1.6	3
Megargee (Collapsed Categories)									
Charlie/Foxtrot (Committed Criminal)	14	1.3	14	21	1.4	14	21	1.5	14
Able/Delta (Character Disorder)	16	1.4	38	21	1.2	38	13	1.3	39
How (Most Disturbed)	21	1.3	14	21	1.2	14	14	1.4	14
Baker/George (Neurotic)	0	1.2	14	7	1.1	14	14	1.4	14
Item/Easy (Least Disturbed)	4	1.3	27	18	1.2	27	11	1.3	27
	$Tau_c = -.11^{**}$								
Conceptual Level—CL3									
CL-1	10	1.3	30	7	1.1	30	7	1.3	30
CL-2	12	1.3	52	23	1.3	52	13	1.4	53
CL-3	14	1.4	22	32	1.3	22	23	1.4	22
				$\chi^2 = 5.5^*$			$Tau_c = .12^{**}$		
				$Tau_c = .19^{**}$					

Table 7-3: *(continued)*

Classification	Nonaggressive[a]			Aggressive[b]			Vicltimized[c]		
	%[b]	$\overline{X}$	N	%[b]	$\overline{X}$	N	%[b]	$\overline{X}$	N
Conceptual Level—CL5									
CL-1	15	1.4	20	10	1.1	20	15	1.3	20
CL-2	9	1.3	68	21	1.3	68	10	1.3	69
CL-3	19	1.4	16	31	1.3	16	25	1.4	16
				$Tau_c = .12*$					
Jesness Inventory I-level									
I-2 Aa	100	1.8	2	50	1.5	2	50	1.1	2
I-2 Ap	33	1.1	3	0	1.0	3	67	1.4	3
I-3 Cfm	8	1.1	12	33	1.2	12	50	1.3	12
I-3 Mp	41	1.3	22	23	1.2	22	40	1.2	23
I-3 Cfc	47	1.4	32	38	1.3	32	56	1.4	32
I-4 Nx	60	1.7	5	20	1.1	50	40	1.4	5
I-4 Na	85	1.6	13	62	1.5	13	46	1.4	13
I-4 Si	47	1.3	17	18	1.1	17	47	1.3	17
I-4 Ci	0	1.0	2	0	1.0	2	50	1.3	2
	$(\chi^2 = 8.5)*$	$F = 2.07**$							
		Mult. R = .38							
Jesness Inventory (Collapsed Personality Subtypes)									
Aggressives (Aa, Cfc, Mp)	46	1.3	56	32	1.3	56	49	1.3	57
Neurotics (Na, Nx)	78	1.6	18	50	1.4	18	44	1.4	18
Dependents (Ap, Cfm)	13	1.0	15	27	1.1	15	53	1.4	15
Situational (Se, Ci)	42	1.4	19	16	1.1	19	47	1.3	19
	$\chi^2 = 13.9***$								
		$F = 4.5***$							
		Mult. R = .34							
Jesness Inventory (Collapsed Levels)									
I-2	60	1.4	5	20	1.2	5	60	1.3	5
I-3	38	1.3	66	32	1.3	66	49	1.3	67
I-4	60	1.4	37	37	1.2	27	46	1.4	37
	$\chi^2 = 4.8*$								
	$Tau_c = .16**$								
I-level (Interview Method)									
I-4 Na	0	1.2	22	18	1.3	22	14	1.4	22
I-4 Nx	9	1.3	22	14	1.3	22	9	1.3	22
I-4 Se	0	1.2	0	22	1.3	9	33	1.6	9
I-4 Ci	30	1.6	10	20	1.3	10	10	1.3	10
I-5 Na	10	1.4	10	10	1.2	10	9	1.4	11
I-5 Nx	19	1.4	16	6	1.2	16	25	1.4	16
I-5 Se	11	1.3	9	0	1.0	9	11	1.3	9
I-5 Ci	18	1.4	11	0	1.2	11	9	1.1	11

Table 7-3: *(continued)*

Classification	Nonaggressive[a]			Aggressive[b]			Victimized[c]		
	%[b]	$\overline{X}$	N	%[b]	$\overline{X}$	N	%[b]	$\overline{X}$	N
I-level (Collapsed Levels)									
I-4	8	1.3	73	23	1.3	73	14	1.3	74
I-5	17	1.3	36	11	1.2	36	17	1.3	36
	Tau$_b$ = .13*			Tau$_b$ = –.15*					
I-level (Collapsed Personality Subtypes)									
Ci (I-4 & I-5)	24	1.5	21	19	1.2	21	10	1.2	21
Na (I-4 & I-5)	3	1.3	32	25	1.3	32	12	1.3	33
Nx (I-4 & I-5)	13	1.4	38	18	1.2	38	16	1.4	38
Se (I-4 & I-5)	6	1.2	18	11	1.2	18	22	1.4	18
	χ^2 = 6.3*								

[a] Scale includes gambling, illegal substances, and citation for missing work. Alpha = .58.
[b] Scale includes use of verbal threats, insults, and attacks on others. Alpha = .71.
[c] Scale includes inmates receiving physical and sexual threats, as well as a few inmates who reported being attacked by other inmates. Alpha = .75.
[d] Percentage scoring 2.0 and above on this scale, indicating infractions.
[e] Percentage scoring 1.7 and above on this scale, indicating infractions.
 * $p \leq .10$
 ** $p \leq .05$
 *** $p \leq .01$

the least disturbed groups (Item) actually account for a substantial proportion of inmates who responded affirmatively to the items tapping aggressive behaviors.[6]

Cross-tabular analysis of the relationship between **Conceptual Level** and self-report measures revealed that the inmates classified as CL-2 and CL-3 on the Conceptual Level system were most likely to report aggressive infractions (tau_c = .19, p ≤ .05) *and* victimization experiences (tau_c = .12, p ≤ .05). Previous research suggests that the highest and the lowest CL classifications are often associated with problem behaviors.[7] Our pilot study, however, which used official measures of victimization, noted no such relationship between CL and victimizations. In fact, the few victimized inmates were classified at CL-1 (Van Voorhis 1988).

A similar finding occurs with the I-level developmental system. Jesness I_2 and I_4 inmates were significantly more likely than others to report disciplinary infractions (tau_c = .16, p ≤ .05). I_5 inmates on the interview I-level system were also significantly more likely to report disciplinary infractions (tau_b = .13, p ≤ .10), but they were significantly *less* likely than the I_4 inmates to report the use of aggression (tau_b = –.15, p ≤ .10). Except for aggressive behavior, inmates classified into the higher developmental types on all of the developmental measures were more likely to report problems than their type descriptions might suggest.

For the most part, personality subtypes on the **Jesness I-level** classification system were related to the outcome measures in the expected manner. Neurotic Acting-out inmates, for example, reported the highest incidence of both non-aggressive and aggressive disciplinary behaviors. Inmates classified into Asocial Aggressive, Neurotic Anxious, Manipulative, and Cultural Conformist subtypes also were more likely than others to report nonaggressive infractions. When the subtypes were collapsed, both cross-tabular and multiple regression analysis detected significant relationships between the personality types and the nonaggressive index (χ^2= 13.9, p ≤ .01; multiple r = .34, p ≤ .01).[8]

The Situational inmates' rather high involvement in nonaggressive behaviors was not predicted. In response, Jesness suggested that this type may identify some inmates who produced invalid test results in addition to the valid Situational inmates. A second analysis to correct for this, however, failed to produce substantially different results.[9] Interestingly, neither the Jesness nor the AIMS situational inmates scored high on the aggression scale, but both are high on the victimization and the nonaggressive disciplinary scales. Again, these findings may relate to the lack of prison experience evidenced by these inmates.

Inmates' reports of nonaggressive disciplinary infractions were differentiated on the basis of **I-level (interview) personality** subtypes. Inmates in the Cultural Conformist (committed criminal) group were significantly more likely to report infractions than were members of the other groups (χ^2 = 6.3, p ≤ .10). Neurotic Acting-Out inmates and I_4 inmates were significantly more likely to engage in aggression, but results were not significant.

The Effects of the Classification Types
on Staff Ratings of Disciplinary Problems

Classification types often differentiated prison inmates on staff members' assessments of their behavior, and did so in predicted directions. As expected with the **AIMS** typology, for example, Asocial Aggressive, Neurotic Anxious, and Manipulative inmates scored significantly lower than other types in staff assessments of their relationships with other men (multiple r = .25, p ≤ .10). Immature Dependent and Situational inmates received significantly more favorable ratings on the aggression item, indicating nonaggressive tendencies (multiple r = .23, p ≤ .10). On the staff ratings, the aggressive, manipulative, and neurotic types were more likely to need supervision (multiple r = .24, p ≤ .10). Results are shown on Table 7-4.

None of the tests using the **Megargee MMPI** typology were significant. Controlling for validity problems or conducting the analysis without the least frequently observed types did not change the overall pattern of the MMPI findings.

In contrast to the tests using the self-report measures (table 7-3), inmates classified at the lowest **CL** category were consistently more likely to incur unfavorable staff ratings. By the same token, the CL-3 inmates were more likely to receive the most favorable ratings. These were noted on the measures pertaining to relations with other men, relations with authority, cooperation, need for supervision, and response to supervision.

The **Jesness Inventory** aggressive and dependent types incurred proportionately and significantly the lowest staff ratings of their ability to get along with other men. Aggressives also received unfavorable assessments of their ability to deal with authority, aggressiveness, cooperation, need for supervision, and response to supervision. In contrast, few of the inmates classified as situational received unsatisfactory ratings on any of the staff

Table 7-4: Effects of Classification Types on Staff Ratings, Penitentiary Sample

	Staff Ratings																	
	Relations/Other Men			Relations/Authority			Aggressiveness			Cooperation			Needs Supervision			Responds/Supervision		
Classification System	%[a]	$\bar{X}$	N	%[a]	$\bar{X}$	N	%[a]	$\bar{X}$	N	%[a]	$\bar{X}$	N	%[a]	$\bar{X}$	N	%[a]	$\bar{X}$	N
Quay AIMS																		
Asocial Aggressive	19	3.05	21	24	3.22	21	19	3.11	21	19	3.17	21	33	2.94	21	19	3.21	21
Immature Dependent	20	3.26	10	10	3.36	10	0	3.70	10	10	3.23	10	20	3.24	10	10	3.37	10
Neurotic Anxious	17	3.06	23	13	3.18	23	22	3.22	23	30	3.00	23	44	2.86	23	22	3.14	23
Manipulator	24	2.94	41	17	3.17	41	12	3.25	41	12	3.10	41	22	3.02	41	7	3.17	41
Situational	11	3.22	53	9	3.38	53	7	3.28	53	13	3.22	53	15	3.20	53	9	3.33	53
	Mult. R = .24*						Mult. R = .23*						χ^2 = 8.2* Mult. R = .24*					
Quay AIMS (Collapsed Categories)																		
Aa/Mp	23	2.98	62	19	3.19	62	15	3.20	62	15	3.13	62	26	2.99	62	11	3.18	62
Id/Na	18	3.12	33	12	3.24	33	15	3.37	33	24	3.07	33	36	2.97	33	18	3.20	33
Situational	11	3.22	53	9	3.38	53	8	3.27	53	13	3.23	53	15	3.19	53	9	3.32	53
	Tau_c = .11* Mult. R = .21**			Tau_c = .10*									χ^2 = 5.12* Mult. R = .19*					
Megargee MMPI-Based Taxonomy																		
Able	19	3.02	32	22	3.14	32	16	3.12	32	25	3.03	32	38	2.94	32	19	3.12	32
Baker	0	3.00	6	17	3.22	6	33	2.94	6	33	2.83	6	33	2.78	6	17	3.00	6
Charlie	8	3.05	13	8	3.20	13	8	3.05	13	8	3.18	13	8	3.13	13	8	3.07	13
Delta	26	3.07	23	13	3.30	23	17	3.28	23	13	3.25	23	26	3.13	23	13	3.29	23
Easy	0	3.23	11	0	3.23	11	0	3.23	11	0	3.20	11	0	3.06	11	0	3.16	11
Foxtrot	18	3.12	11	18	3.18	11	0	3.42	11	18	2.94	11	18	2.88	11	9	3.12	11
George	7	3.36	14	14	3.40	14	0	3.45	14	7	3.24	14	7	3.31	14	0	3.38	14

Table 7-4: (continued)

	Staff Ratings																	
	Relations/Other Men			Relations/Authority			Aggressiveness			Cooperation			Needs Supervision			Responds/Supervision		
Classification System	%[a]	$\bar{X}$	N	%[a]	$\bar{X}$	N	%[a]	$\bar{X}$	N	%[a]	$\bar{X}$	N	%[a]	$\bar{X}$	N	%[a]	$\bar{X}$	N
How	14	3.05	22	9	3.26	22	9	3.38	22	18	3.27	22	23	3.06	22	14	3.26	22
Item	22	3.04	27	15	3.22	27	19	3.14	27	22	3.04	27	33	3.05	27	18	3.27	27
Jupiter	0	3.21	4	25	3.21	4	0	3.56	4	0	3.21	4	0	3.08	4	0	3.16	4
Megargee MMPI-Based Taxonomy (Collapsed Categories)																		
Charlie/Foxtrot (Committed Criminal)	12	3.08	24	13	3.20	24	4	3.22	24	13	3.17	24	13	3.00	24	8	3.10	24
Able/Delta (Character Disorder)	22	3.04	55	18	3.21	55	16	3.18	55	20	3.12	55	32	3.01	55	16	3.19	55
How (Most Disturbed)	14	3.05	22	9	3.27	22	9	3.39	22	18	3.10	22	23	3.05	22	14	3.26	22
Baker/George/Jupiter (Neurotic)	4	3.24	24	15	3.33	24	8	3.34	24	12	3.13	24	13	3.13	24	4	3.25	24
Item/Easy (Least Disturbed)	16	3.09	38	11	3.23	38	13	3.17	38	16	3.08	38	24	3.05	38	13	3.25	38
Conceptual Level—CL3																		
CL-1	22	2.98	41	24	3.12	41	12	3.25	41	22	2.99	41	27	2.96	41	20	3.13	41
CL-2	17	3.06	82	11	3.20	82	12	3.17	82	17	3.05	82	26	3.01	82	11	3.13	82
CL-3	4	3.28	26	19	3.34	26	8	3.39	26	19	3.34	26	19	3.29	26	15	3.43	26
	$Tau_c = .12^{**}$ Mult. $R = .22^{**}$									Mult. $R = .21^{**}$			Mult. $R = .21^{**}$			Mult. $R = .21^{**}$		
Conceptual Level—CL5																		
CL-1	22	2.95	27	30	3.06	27	15	3.24	27	30	2.87	27	37	2.80	27	26	3.07	27
CL-2	17	3.09	102	12	3.24	102	11	3.21	102	16	3.11	102	23	3.06	102	11	3.19	102

CL-3	5 / 3.17 / 20	20 / 3.91 / 20	10 / 3.32 / 20	20 / 3.19 / 20	20 / 3.15 / 20	15 / 3.30 / 20	Total
	$Tau_c = .09^*$	$\chi^2 = 5.3^*$	$Tau_c = .07^*$	Mult. R = .18*	$Tau_c = .10^*$; Mult. R = .21**	$Tau_c = .07^*$	
Jesness Inventory I-level							
I-2 Aa	20 2.94	20 3.00	20 3.13	40 2.93	40 2.80	0 3.00	5
I-2 Ap	0 3.00	0 3.55	0 3.89	33 3.11	0 3.22	0 3.45	3
I-3 Cfm	21 3.07	16 3.12	5 3.35	5 3.22	16 3.23	16 3.15	19
I-3 Mp	31 3.04	28 3.19	19 3.08	31 2.96	41 2.94	22 3.18	32
I-3 Cfc	21 3.00	14 3.15	16 3.13	21 3.02	28 2.93	19 3.08	43
I-4 Nx	14 3.17	29 3.02	0 3.36	14 3.21	0 3.19	14 3.10	7
I-4 Na	5 3.11	16 3.30	16 3.20	16 3.10	16 3.03	16 3.18	19
I-4 Se	0 3.18	5 3.27	0 3.26	5 3.18	32 3.19	0 3.38	21
I-4 Ci	0 3.34	0 3.44	0 3.56	0 3.61	0 3.56	0 3.67	3
Jesness Inventory (Collapsed Levels)							
I-2	13 2.96	13 3.21	13 3.41	38 3.00	25 2.96	0 3.17	8
I-3	25 3.03	19 3.16	15 3.17	21 3.05	30 3.00	19 3.13	94
I-4	4 3.16	12 3.26	6 3.29	10 3.19	14 3.15	8 3.28	50
	$\chi^2 = 9.77^{**}$; $Tau_c = .16^{***}$		$Tau_c = .07^*$	$\chi^2 = 4.80^*$; $Tau_c = .13^{**}$	$Tau_c = .13^{**}$	$\chi^2 = 4.71^*$	
Jesness Inventory (Collapsed Personality Subtypes)							
Aggressives (Aa, Cfc, Mp)	25 3.06	20 3.17	18 3.11	26 2.99	34 2.93	19 3.11	80
Neurotics (Na, Nx)	8 3.12	19 3.23	12 3.24	15 3.13	27 3.07	15 3.15	26
Dependents (Ap, Cfm)	18 3.01	14 3.18	5 3.42	9 3.21	14 3.23	14 3.17	22

Table 7-4: *(continued)*

	Staff Ratings																	
	Relations/Other Men			Relations/Authority			Aggressiveness			Cooperation			Needs Supervision			Responds/Supervision		
Classification System	%[a]	$\bar{X}$	N	%[a]	$\bar{X}$	N	%[a]	$\bar{X}$	N	%[a]	$\bar{X}$	N	%[a]	$\bar{X}$	N	%[a]	$\bar{X}$	N
Jesness Inventory (Collapsed Personality Subtypes) (continued)																		
Situationals (Se, Ci)	0	3.20	24	4	3.30	24	0	3.34	24	4	3.24	24	0	3.24	24	0	3.41	24
	$\chi^2 = 10.11^{**}$ $Tau_c = .18^{***}$			$Tau_c = .11^{**}$			$\chi^2 = 6.08^{*}$ $Tau_c = .14^{**}$ Mult. R = .22**			$\chi^2 = 7.94^{**}$ $Tau_c = .19^{***}$			$\chi^2 = 13.03^{***}$ $Tau_c = .25^{***}$ Mult. R = .25**			$Tau_c = .12^{**}$		
I-level (Interview Method)																		
I-4 Na	24	3.09	37	22	3.24	37	19	3.10	37	19	3.09	37	30	3.09	37	16	3.25	37
I-4 Nx	28	3.03	32	16	3.28	32	19	3.21	32	25	3.15	32	28	3.04	32	16	3.26	32
I-4 Se	6	3.09	16	0	3.32	16	0	3.27	16	13	3.15	16	6	3.08	16	7	3.15	16
I-4 Ci	6	3.14	17	12	3.30	17	18	3.24	17	29	3.12	17	35	2.86	17	18	3.20	17
I-5 Na	11	2.99	18	22	2.99	18	17	3.05	18	17	2.99	18	28	2.91	18	17	2.99	18
I-5 Nx	13	3.23	24	17	3.33	24	0	3.42	24	8	3.23	24	13	3.15	24	13	3.21	24
I-5 Se	0	3.20	11	0	3.32	11	0	3.47	11	0	3.29	11	18	3.02	11	0	3.47	11
I-5 Ci	14	3.08	21	14	3.22	21	10	3.31	21	14	3.03	21	24	3.12	21	14	3.18	21
I-level (Collapsed Levels)																		
I-4	20	3.07	102	15	3.16	102	16	3.19	102	22	3.12	102	27	3.03	102	15	3.22	102
I-5	11	3.12	74	15	3.21	74	7	3.31	74	11	3.12	74	20	3.05	74	12	3.18	74
	$Tau_b = .12^{**}$						$Tau_b = .14^{**}$			$\chi^2 = 2.79^{*}$ $Tau_b = .14^{**}$								

I-level (Collapsed Personality Subtypes)

	%	Mean	N	%	Mean	N	%	Mean	N	%	Mean	N	%	Mean	N	%	Mean	N
Situational	4	3.12	27	0	3.29	27	0	3.35	27	7	3.20	27	11	3.10	27	4	3.27	27
Neurotic Anxious	21	3.11	56	16	3.30	56	11	3.30	56	18	3.18	56	21	3.09	56	14	3.23	56
Neurotic Acting-out	20	3.05	55	22	3.16	55	18	3.08	55	18	3.06	55	29	3.04	55	16	3.16	55
Cultural Identifier	11	3.10	38	13	3.25	38	13	3.27	38	21	3.07	38	29	2.96	38	16	3.18	38

$\chi^2 = 7.00$* $Tau_c = .10$** $Tau_c = .13$**

$Tau_c = .08$*   Mult. R = .20*

[a] Percentage rated below average (3.00) on this scale, indicating unsatisfactory performance.
[b] Scales range from negative behavior (1 and 2) to average (3) to positive behavior (4 and 5).

* $p \leq .10$
** $p \leq .05$
*** $p \leq .01$

assessments. When the personality subtypes are collapsed, relationships between the Jesness Inventory and all of the staff rating measures are significant. Although similar findings are not shown for the uncollapsed personality subtypes, a second analysis, which removed the least frequent subtypes, produced significant results for three of the six tests. Chi-square values were 10.9 (p ≤ .05) for the relationship between the Jesness types and relations with other men, 8.7 (p ≤ .07) for the relationship with cooperation, and 12.5 (p ≤ .01) for the relationship with need for supervision. Other regression tests were not significant.

The Jesness Inventory measure of I-level also was related to several of the ratings in an expected manner. I_2 and I_3 inmates were significantly more likely than others to receive low staff ratings.

Results of the **I-level** analysis (interview system) showed that both the I_4 and the I_5 Neurotic Acting-out inmates were significantly more likely than others to receive unfavorable staff ratings on measures pertaining to relations with authority (tau_c = .08, p ≤ .05) and aggressiveness (tau_c = .10, p ≤ .05). In addition, Cultural Conformist, Neurotic Anxious, and Neurotic Acting-out inmates were significantly more likely to be rated as needing supervision (tau_c = .13, p ≤ .05).

Finally, I_4 inmates were more likely than I_5 inmates to receive poor ratings on relations with other men (tau_b = .12, p ≤ .05), aggressiveness (tau_b =.14, p ≤ .05), and cooperation (tau_b = .14, p ≤ .05).

Regardless of the classification model, these tests produced none of the anomalies reported in tables 7-2 and 7-3. In no instance, for example, were situational or least disturbed inmates observed to have the worst scores. In fact, they typically received the best ratings. Further, the developmental classifications—I-level, Conceptual Level, and the Jesness I-level—were related to staff assessments in the expected or predicted manner. Those classified into the higher developmental types were more likely to receive positive ratings. The opposite occurred when the self-report dependent variables were used.

PRISON CAMP

The Effects of the Classification Types on
Officially Recorded Disciplinary Infractions

Table 7-5 shows results of the analysis of the relationship between the classification types and officially recorded disciplinary infrac-

Table 7-5: Effects of Classification Variables on Official Disciplinary Variables, Prison Camp

Classification System	All Disciplinaries[a]			Insubordination[a]		
	%[b]	$\bar{X}$	N	%[b]	$\bar{X}$	N
Quay AIMS						
Asocial Aggressive	33	8.3	9	33	8.3	9
Immature Dependent	60	14.0	5	40	7.3	5
Neurotic Anxious	0	0.0	3	0	0.0	3
Manipulator	23	7.8	22	23	6.2	22
Situational	18	4.2	80	14	3.0	80
Quay AIMS (Collapsed Categories)						
Aa/Mp	26	7.9	31	26	6.8	31
Id/Na	37	8.8	8	25	4.6	8
Situational	17	4.2	80	14	3.0	80
				$Tau_c = -.11^*$		
Megargee MMPI-Based Taxonomy						
Able	24	6.0	25	24	4.3	25
Baker	50	10.0	6	50	10.0	6
Charlie	0	0.0	7	0	0.0	7
Delta	0	0.0	7	0	0.0	7
Easy	29	5.3	17	12	2.0	17
Foxgtrot	75	17.0	4	50	8.3	4
George	19	6.8	16	13	3.1	16
How	7	2.4	14	7	2.4	14
Item	17	4.7	64	16	4.1	64
Jupiter	0	0.0	3	0	0.0	3
Megargee (Collapsed Categories)						
Charlie/Foxtrot (Committed Criminal)	27	6.1	11	18	3.0	11
Able/Delta (Character Disorder)	19	4.7	32	19	3.4	32
How (Most Disturbed)	7	2.4	14	7	2.4	14
Baker/George (Neurotic)	24	6.8	25	20	4.5	25
Item/Easy (Least Disturbed)	20	4.5	81	15	3.7	81
Conceptual Level—CL3						
CL-1	4	1.2	23	4	1.2	23
CL-2	21	5.6	122	16	3.9	122
CL-3	20	1.3	25	20	3.5	25
	$Tau_c = .07^*$			$Tau_c = .07^{**}$		

Table 7-5: *(continued)*

Classification System	All Disciplinaries[a]			Insubordination[a]		
	%[b]	$\bar{X}$	N	%[b]	$\bar{X}$	N
Conceptual Level - CL5						
CL-1	0	0.0	14	0	0.0	14
CL-2	20	5.1	144	16	3.6	144
CL-3	18	5.2	11	18	3.3	11
	$Tau_c = .06^*$			$Tau_c = .05^*$		
Jesness Inventory I-level						
I-2 Aa	—	—	1	—	—	1
I-2 Ap	20	6.7	5	20	6.7	5
I-3 Cfm	19	3.2	27	11	1.9	27
I-3 Mp	28	7.3	36	25	6.2	36
I-3 Cfc	23	6.0	31	13	2.9	31
I-4 Nx	6	1.3	16	6	1.3	16
I-4 Na	24	7.9	17	24	5.9	17
I-4 Si	11	2.6	28	11	1.9	28
I-4 Ci	0	0.0	6	0	0.0	6
Jesness Inventory (Collapsed Levels)						
I-2	17	5.6	6	17	5.6	6
I-3	23	5.7	94	17	3.9	94
I-4	12	3.4	67	12	2.6	67
	$Tau_c = -.10^{**}$					
Jesness Inventory (Collapsed Personality Subtypes)						
Aggressives (Aa, Cfc, Mp)	25	6.6	68	19	4.6	68
Neurotics (Na, Nx)	15	4.7	33	15	3.6	33
Dependents (Ap, Cfm)	19	3.8	32	13	2.6	32
Situational (Se, Ci)	9	2.2	34	9	1.6	34
	$Tau_c = -.14^{**}$			$Tau_c = -.08^*$		
I-level (Interview Method)						
I-4 Na	20	4.7	46	17	4.0	46
I-4 Nx	12	5.9	17	12	3.9	17
I-4 Se	20	4.2	35	17	3.2	35
I-4 Ci	22	5.7	18	17	4.7	18
I-5 Na	20	5.0	10	10	1.7	10
I-5 Nx	21	5.0	24	21	5.3	24
I-5 Se	12	3.0	26	8	1.4	26
I-5 Ci	0	0.0	2	0	0.0	2

Table 7-5: *(continued)*

Classification System	All Disciplinaries[a]			Insubordination[a]		
	%[b]	$\overline{X}$	N	%[b]	$\overline{X}$	N
I-level (Collapsed Levels)						
I-4	19	4.9	116	16	3.9	116
I-5	16	4.5	62	13	2.9	62
I-level (Collapsed Personality Subtypes)						
Ci (I-4 & I-5)	20	6.1	20	15	4.3	20
Na (I-4 & I-5)	20	4.9	56	16	3.6	56
Nx (I-4 & I-5)	17	6.1	41	17	4.7	41
Se (I-4 & I-5)	17	3.6	61	13	2.4	61

[a] Rate per month $\times$ 100.
[b] Percent with at least one disciplinary report.
  * $p \le .10$
 ** $p \le .05$

tions for the prison camp sample. In contrast to the comparable analysis of the penitentiary data, only two criterion variables are used. The drug variable is not incorporated into this phase of the analysis because of insufficient variation. Most of the disciplinary citations at the prison camp (82%) were for insubordination. Table 7-5 presents results of cross-tabular and multiple regression analysis. Again, the dichotomous variables for overall disciplinaries and insubordination were tested through probit analysis.[10]

Table 7-5 reveals more significant relationships between the classification variables and the official data than were noted for the penitentiary inmates. In addition, we observed few of the anomalous findings, particularly with respect to situational inmates.

Beginning with the **Quay AIMS** system, inmates classified as Immature Dependent were involved in proportionately more disciplinary infractions than inmates classified into the other types. This finding, however, must be viewed with caution, because only five inmates were classified as Immature Dependent. Clearly the irregular (albeit expected) distribution of inmates across the typology complicates these analyses. When the types are collapsed to improve cell frequencies, we find one of the tests to be significant—namely the relationship between the Quay AIMS types and the proportion of inmates involved in acts of insubordination (tau_c = -.11, p ≤ .10). In this case, the Asocial Aggressive/Manipulative and the Immature Dependent/Neurotic Anxious types are significantly more likely to be cited for insubordination than are the Situational types. These results are as expected.

We found no significant relationships between the **Megargee MMPI-based** types and disciplinary infractions. Again, the analysis is adversely affected by distribution irregularities and limited cell frequencies for some of the types. Types Able, Baker, Easy, and Foxtrot appear most likely to incur disciplinary-related difficulties, but differences were not significant. Further, Hows were involved in fewer infractions than one would expect on the basis of their type description, and Items and Easys were involved in more. At the same time, however, the insubordination mean rates and proportions for inmates classified as Item and Easy were similar to those observed for the penitentiary cases.[11]

Relationships between **Conceptual Level** and official data were significant but weak. CL-2 and CL-3 inmates were significantly more likely to be cited for disciplinary infractions than were the CL-1 inmates. In fact, CL-1 inmates incurred no infractions when the Conceptual Level classifications were determined by the CL-5 measure.

Inmates with the highest proportion and number of infractions on the **Jesness Inventory** system were those classified as I_3 Manipulators, I_3 Cultural Conformists, and I_4 Neurotic Acting-out. These findings are consistent with the type descriptions. When the types were collapsed to improve cell frequencies, the results were significant ($tau_c = -.14$, $p \leq .05$). The proportion of inmates cited for infractions was greatest for the aggressive types (Cfc and Mp), somewhat less for the neurotics (Na and Nx) and the dependents (Ap and Cfm), and substantially less for the situationals (Se and Ci). The relationship between the levels and overall disciplinary infractions was also significant. Inmates classified as I_2 and I_3 were significantly more likely to be cited than inmates classified as I_4 ($tau_c = -.10$, $p \leq .05$).[12]

Table 7-5 shows that the **I-level (interview method)** types were not related to either of the criterion variables. In fact, proportions and rates appear to be quite similar across the types.

The Effects of the Classification Types on
Self-Reported Disciplinary Problems

Survey results for the prison camp inmates produced two self-report indexes that tapped aggressive behaviors and victimizing experiences. In contrast to the penitentiary analysis, we do not present an index of nonaggressive infractions for this sample, because items pertaining to such behaviors failed to form an index with a sufficient degree of internal consistency.

As shown on table 7-6, we observed no significant findings in the analysis of the **Quay AIMS** typology and the self-report measures. As expected, a higher proportion of Immature Dependent inmates and Neurotic Anxious inmates reported victimizations, but a high proportion of Manipulative inmates also reported victimizations. As noted in the penitentiary sample, an atypically high proportion of Situational inmates reported both aggressive behaviors and victimizations.

When the types were collapsed, the **Megargee MMPI-based** types were related to both the aggression and the victimization index. Significantly more committed criminal types (Charlie and Foxtrot), character disorder inmates (Able and Delta), and Hows evidenced aggressive actions than did inmates typed as neurotic (Baker, George, and Jupiter) or least disturbed (Item and Easy) ($tau_c = -.20$, $p \leq .05$). These three types were also high on the victimization index, but the strength of the relationship is less,

Table 7-6: Effects of Classification Variables on Self-Reported Infraction and Victimization Measures, Prison Camp

Classification System	Aggression[a] %[c]	X̄	N	Victimization[b] %[d]	X̄	N
Quay AIMS						
Asocial Aggressive	43	1.3	7	0	1.0	6
Immature Dependent	25	1.3	4	50	1.5	4
Neurotic Anxious	0	1.0	3	33	1.3	3
Manipulator	13	1.1	15	48	1.5	15
Situational	23	1.2	56	31	1.3	54
Quay AIMS (Collapsed Categories)						
Aa/Mp	23	1.9	22	33	1.3	21
Id/Na	14	1.1	7	43	1.2	7
Situational	23	1.2	56	32	1.3	54
Megargee MMPI-Based Taxonomy						
Able	33	1.2	15	39	1.4	13
Baker	0	1.0	5	20	1.2	5
Charlie	29	1.3	7	43	1.4	7
Delta	50	1.5	4	75	1.8	4
Easy	18	1.2	11	36	1.4	11
Foxgtrot	33	1.3	3	67	1.7	3
George	27	1.2	11	20	1.2	10
How	43	1.4	7	29	1.3	7
Item	12	1.1	42	29	1.3	42
Jupiter	—	—	1	—	—	1
Megargee (Collapsed Categories)						
Charlie/Foxtrot (Committed Criminal)	30	1.3	10	50	1.5	10
Able/Delta (Character Disorder)	37	1.3	19	47	1.5	17
How (Most Disturbed)	43	1.4	7	29	1.3	7
Baker/George (Neurotic)	18	1.1	17	19	1.1	16
Item/Easy (Least Disturbed)	13	1.1	53	30	1.3	53
	$Tau_c = -.20$** (Mult. R = .41***)[e]			$Tau_c = -.13$* (Mult. R = .31*)[e]		
Conceptual Level—CL3						
CL-1	20	1.2	15	14	1.2	14
CL-2	24	1.2	79	34	1.3	77
CL-3	11	1.1	19	32	1.3	19

Table 7-6: *(continued)*

Classification System	Aggression[a]			Victimization[b]		
	%[c]	$\bar{X}$	N	%[d]	$\bar{X}$	N
Conceptual Level - CL5						
CL-1	22	1.1	9	13	1.1	9
CL-2	21	1.2	94	32	1.3	92
CL-3	22	1.2	9	44	1.5	9
Jesness Inventory I-level						
I-2 Aa	—	—	0	—	—	0
I-2 Ap	33	1.3	3	33	1.3	3
I-3 Cfm	5	1.1	21	33	1.3	21
I-3 Mp	24	1.2	25	32	1.2	25
I-3 Cfc	19	1.1	16	20	1.2	15
I-4 Nx	27	1.3	11	46	1.5	11
I-4 Na	62	1.6	13	36	1.4	11
I-4 Si	11	1.1	19	32	1.3	19
I-4 Ci	0	1.0	3	0	1.0	3

$(\chi^2 = 17.32^{**})^e$

Mult. R = .37**

Jesness Inventory (Collapsed Levels)						
I-2	33	1.3	3	33	1.3	3
I-3	16	1.2	62	30	1.3	61
I-4	28	1.3	46	34	1.4	44
Jesness Inventory (Collapsed Personality Subtypes)						
Aggressives (Aa, Cfc, Mp)	22	1.2	41	28	1.3	40
Neurotics (Na, Nx)	46	1.4	24	41	1.4	22
Dependents (Ap, Cfm)	8	1.1	24	33	1.3	24
Situational (Se, Ci)	9	1.1	22	27	1.3	22

$\chi^2 = .13^{***}$

$Tau_c = -.14^*$ Mult. R = .30**

I-level (Interview Method)						
I-4 Na	33	1.3	27	32	1.3	25
I-4 Nx	9	1.1	11	9	1.1	11
I-4 Se	21	1.2	24	30	1.3	24
I-4 Ci	0	1.0	9	0	1.0	9
I-5 Na	50	1.3	4	33	1.3	3
I-5 Nx	32	1.3	19	42	1.4	19
I-5 Se	0	1.0	17	47	1.5	17
I-5 Ci	50	1.5	2	50	1.5	2

Mult. R = .33**

Table 7-6: *(continued)*

Classification System	Aggression[a] %[b]	Aggression[a] X̄	Aggression[a] N	Victimization[a] %[b]	Victimization[a] X̄	Victimization[a] N
I-level (Collapsed Levels)						
I-4	21	1.2	71	23	1.2	69
I-5	21	1.2	42	44	1.4	41
				$\chi^2 = 5.2^{**}$		
				$Tau_b = .22^{**}$	Mult. R = .22**	
I-level (Collapsed Personality Subtypes)						
Ci (I-4 & I-5)	9	1.1	11	9	1.1	11
Na (I-4 & I-5)	36	1.3	31	32	1.3	28
Nx (I-4 & I-5)	23	1.2	30	30	1.3	30
Se (I-4 & I-5)	12	1.1	41	37	1.4	41
	$\chi^2 = 6.8^*$					
	$Tau_c = .12^*$					

[a] Scale includes use of verbal threats, insults, and attacks on others. Alpha = .63.
[b] Scale includes inmates receiving physical and sexual threats as well as a few inmates who reported being attacked by other inmates. Alpha = .70.
[c] Percent scoring 1.33 and above on this scale, indicating infractions.
[d] Percent scoring 1.50 and above on this scale, indicating infractions.
[e] Among more frequently observed types and most valid cases.
 * $p \leq .10$
 ** $p \leq .05$
 *** $p \leq .01$

because a high proportion of the Item and Easy group also reported victimizations (tau$_c$ = -.13,p ≤ .05). Multiple regression results were not significant, but they became significant when the potentially invalid cases were removed. The multiple r coefficient for the collapsed types was .41 (p ≤ .01) for the relationship with the aggression scale and .31 (p ≤ .10) for the relationship with the victimization scale.

The relationships between **Conceptual Level** and the self-report measures are not significant, whereas a much clearer pattern emerged for both of the **I-level** systems. Multiple regression analysis found the personality types on the **Jesness Inventory** to be related significantly to the aggression index. When the types were collapsed, neurotic and aggressive inmates were significantly more likely to report aggressive behaviors than the dependent and situational types (tau$_c$ = -.14,p ≤ .10; multiple r = .30, p ≤ .01).[13] Most of the difference is attributable to the I_4 Neurotic Acting-out inmates, whose mean index score far surpasses the scores of the other inmates. In addition, 63% of the I_4Na inmates scored in the upper portion of the index; the next highest proportion was 27% for the I_4 Neurotic Anxious inmates. Notably, findings for the I_4Na inmates in the penitentiary are similar to these. In another finding similar to the penitentiary results, neither the Jesness Inventory personality types nor the levels related significantly to the victimization index. In contrast to the penitentiary analysis, however, Situational inmates do not tend to score atypically high on these measures.

As shown in table 7-6, several of the tests of the **I-level (interview)** and self-report data produced significant findings. I_5 inmates, for example, were significantly more likely to report victimizations than I_4 inmates (tau$_b$ = .22, p ≤ .01; multiple r = .22, p ≤ .05). In addition, Neurotic Acting-out and Neurotic Anxious inmates were significantly more likely to report aggressive actions (tau$_c$ = .12, p ≤ .10).

*The Effects of the Classification Types on
Staff Ratings of Disciplinary Problems*

Table 7-7 shows tests of the relationships between the classification types and follow-up staff ratings. Across the various criterion variables, Asocial Aggressive and Manipulative inmates on the **Quay AIMS** system were fairly consistent in receiving poor staff ratings. At the same time, Situational inmates consistently received favorable ratings. This pattern is present in the relationship between the Quay types and relationships with other men, cooperation, and need for supervision. Correlations between the Quay types and relations with authority differed slightly in that only the Manipulative inmates were more likely than the others to receive an unfavorable rating. Finally, Immature Dependent inmates score significantly lower than other inmates on the staff ratings of their response to supervision. Seven of the twelve tests produced significant findings.

On the **Megargee MMPI-based** system, mean staff ratings for the committed criminal type Foxtrot were always lower than they were for the other inmates. Because only four inmates were classified as Foxtrot, these results must be viewed cautiously. Tests of the relationship between the Megargee types and the needs supervision variable and the response to supervision variable were significant (multiple $r = .32$, $p \leq .10$ for both tests). When the types were collapsed, we observed a significant relationship between the Megargee types and relationships with other men ($tau_c = . 06$, $p \leq .10$). In this instance, however, both the least disturbed and the committed criminal types received a higher proportion of the unfavorable ratings than the other types. These results for the least disturbed group were contradicted by the multiple regression results, which showed that the least disturbed group also received relatively high mean scores on the staff ratings of relationships with other men. The contradiction indicates that findings for the least disturbed group are inconclusive.[14]

Findings for the relationships between the **Conceptual Level** measures and staff ratings, shown in table 7-7, are unclear, because cross-tabular analysis occasionally produced results that differed from the multiple regression analysis. For example, significantly more CL-3 inmates were rated unfavorably on the relations with other men measure. Yet the mean score for this group was higher (more favorable) than for the other inmates. The latter finding, however, is not significant. Similar findings emerge in tests of the relationship between CL_3 and cooperation and between CL_3 and response to supervision. Again, the contradiction between the two tests (cross-tabular and multiple regression) suggests that it may be difficult to characterize the groups on this measure. The relationship between CL_5 and relations with authority was clearer: Inmates classified at a lower conceptual level (CL-1) were more likely to be rated unsatisfactory and to receive lower mean scores.

Table 7-7: Effects of Classification Types on Staff Ratings, Prison Camp Sample

	Staff Ratings																	
	Relations/Other Men			Relations/Authority			Aggressiveness			Cooperation			Needs Supervision			Responds/Supervision		
Classification System	%a	X̄	N	%a	X̄	N	%a	X̄	N	%a	X̄	N	%a	X̄	N	%a	X̄	N
Quay AIMS																		
Asocial Aggressive	11	3.13	9	0	3.30	9	0	3.37	9	11	3.28	9	22	3.11	9	0	3.36	9
Immature Dependent	0	3.29	5	0	3.37	5	0	3.37	5	0	3.30	5	0	3.37	5	17	3.17	5
Neurotic Anxious	0	3.00	3	0	3.50	3	0	3.17	3	0	3.17	3	0	3.16	3	0	3.33	3
Manipulator	19	3.32	21	19	3.28	21	14	3.38	21	14	3.31	21	24	3.20	21	14	3.26	21
Situational	4	3.62	78	1	3.67	77	4	3.67	77	0	3.65	78	0	3.57	78	3	3.65	78
	Mult. R = .26*			χ^2 = 18.4***						χ^2 = 12.07**			χ^2 = 9.28**			Mult. R = .26*		
				Mult. R = .26**						Mult. R = .28*			Mult. R = .26*					
Quay AIMS (Collapsed Categories)																		
Aa/Mp	17	3.27	30	13	3.28	30	10	3.36	30	13	3.30	3	23	3.18	30	10	3.27	30
Id/Na	0	3.18	8	0	3.42	8	0	3.29	8	0	3.25	8	0	3.29	8	13	3.23	8
Situational	4	3.63	78	1	3.68	77	4	3.62	78	0	3.65	78	5	3.58	78	0	3.65	78
	χ^2 = 6.18**			χ^2 = 7.90**						χ^2 = 11.88***			χ^2 = 9.27***			Tau_C = .07**		
	Tau_C = .09**			Tau_C = .09***						Tau_C = .10***			Tau_C = .13***			Mult. R = .26**		
	Mult R = .24**			Mult. R = .26**						Mult. R = .28**			Mult. R = .26**					
Megargee MMPI-Based Taxonomy																		
Able	0	3.61	22	0	3.65	22	0	3.53	22	0	3.63	22	5	3.60	22	5	3.61	22
Baker	0	3.93	5	0	3.87	5	0	3.77	5	0	3.87	5	0	3.73	5	0	3.93	5
Charlie	0	3.61	6	17	3.55	6	0	3.36	6	0	2.39	6	17	3.17	6	0	3.41	6
Delta	0	3.28	7	14	3.05	7	14	3.05	7	0	3.33	7	14	3.10	7	14	3.09	7
Easy	0	3.39	12	0	3.44	12	17	3.31	12	0	3.63	12	17	3.30	12	8	3.41	12
Foxtrot	25	2.91	4	25	2.88	4	25	2.87	4	25	3.27	4	50	2.84	4	25	2.79	4

Table 7-7: (continued)

Classification System	Staff Ratings																	
	Relations/Other Men			Relations/Authority			Aggressiveness			Cooperation			Needs Supervision			Responds/Supervision		
	%[a]	X̄	N	%[a]	X̄	N	%[a]	X̄	N	%[a]	X̄	N	%[a]	X̄	N	%[a]	X̄	N
George	0	3.43	16	0	3.48	16	6	3.31	16	6	3.43	16	13	3.28	16	0	3.43	16
How	7	3.51	15	7	3.50	15	7	3.55	15	0	3.31	15	7	3.37	15	0	3.40	15
Item	11	3.62	62	5	3.70	61	3	3.64	62	3	3.66	62	7	3.63	62	5	3.66	62
Jupiter	0	3.83	3	0	3.67	3	0	3.50	3	0	3.50	3	0	3.83	3	0	3.83	3
													Mult. R = .32*			Mult. R = .32*		
Megargee MMPI-Based Taxonomy (Collapsed Categories)																		
Charlie/Foxtrot (Committed Criminal)	10	3.32	10	20	3.28	10	10	3.17	10	10	3.30	10	30	3.03	10	10	3.17	10
Able/Delta (Character Disorder)	0	3.53	29	3	3.50	29	3	3.41	29	0	3.56	29	7	3.47	29	7	3.49	29
How (Most Disturbed)	7	3.51	15	7	3.50	15	7	3.55	15	0	3.31	15	7	3.36	15	0	3.40	15
Baker/George/Jupiter (Neurotic)	0	3.59	24	0	3.58	24	4	3.43	24	4	3.53	24	8	3.44	24	0	3.59	24
Item/Easy (Least Disturbed)	10	3.58	74	4	3.66	73	5	3.59	74	3	3.66	74	8	3.58	74	5	3.62	74
	Tauc = .06*												Mult. R = .32*			Mult. R = .32*		
Conceptual Level—CL3																		
CL-1	0	3.42	24	8	3.49	24	8	3.35	24	0	3.47	24	8	3.19	24	0	3.40	24
CL-2	5	3.56	112	3	3.57	110	4	3.53	112	3	3.55	112	11	3.51	112	3	3.59	112
CL-3	18	3.62	22	9	3.71	22	9	3.55	22	9	3.72	22	5	3.65	22	18	3.61	22
	χ^2 = 8.15** Tauc = .09***									Tauc = .04**						χ^2 = 11.75*** Tauc = .09***		

Conceptual Level - CL5

	n	Mean	N	n	Mean	N	n	Mean	N	n	Mean	N	n	Mean	N	n	Mean	N
CL-1	0	3.41	15	13	3.46	15	7	3.29	15	0	3.45	15	7	3.31	15	0	3.37	15
CL-2	5	3.53	131	4	3.56	129	5	3.50	131	3	3.53	131	11	3.47	131	5	3.55	131
CL-3	18	3.86	11	0	4.03	11	9	3.80	11	0	3.86	11	0	3.88	11	9	3.93	11
	$Tau_c = .05^{**}$			$Tau_c = .04^{**}$ Mult. R = $.20^{**}$									Mult. R = $.17^{*}$					

Jesness Inventory I-level

	n	Mean	N	n	Mean	N	n	Mean	N	n	Mean	N	n	Mean	N	n	Mean	N
I-2 Aa	—	—	1	—	—	1	—	—	1	—	—	1	—	—	1	—	—	1
I-2 Ap	20	3.57	5	0	3.64	5	0	3.74	5	0	3.53	5	0	3.47	5	0	3.50	5
I-3 Cfm	0	3.73	25	4	3.80	23	4	3.71	25	0	3.77	25	8	3.65	25	4	3.80	25
I-3 Mp	9	3.62	33	6	3.64	33	6	3.59	33	6	3.65	33	9	3.54	33	6	3.60	33
I-3 Cfc	3	3.43	30	10	3.39	30	7	3.42	30	0	3.41	30	17	3.41	30	0	3.46	30
I-4 Nx	0	3.44	15	0	3.56	15	13	3.33	15	0	3.55	15	0	3.40	15	0	3.44	15
I-4 Na	6	3.42	16	0	3.35	16	7	3.40	16	13	3.22	16	19	3.45	16	6	3.37	16
I-4 Se	11	3.69	28	4	3.76	28	7	3.57	28	4	3.64	28	7	3.67	28	11	3.68	28
I-4 Ci	0	3.67	4	0	3.67	4	0	3.67	4	0	3.66	4	0	3.67	4	0	3.67	4

Jesness Inventory (Collapsed Levels)

	n	Mean	N	n	Mean	N	n	Mean	N	n	Mean	N	n	Mean	N	n	Mean	N
I-2	17	3.64	6	0	3.69	6	0	3.61	6	0	3.45	6	0	3.31	6	0	3.42	6
I-3	5	3.57	88	7	3.59	86	3	3.55	88	2	3.60	88	11	3.36	88	3	3.61	88
I-4	6	3.51	63	2	3.56	63	8	3.42	63	5	3.50	63	8	3.44	63	6	3.49	63

Jesness Inventory (Collapsed Personality Subtypes)

	n	Mean	N	n	Mean	N	n	Mean	N	n	Mean	N	n	Mean	N	n	Mean	N
Aggressives (Aa, Cfc, Mp)	6	3.54	64	8	3.52	64	3	3.50	64	3	3.53	64	12	3.47	64	3	3.54	64
Neurotics (Na, Nx)	3	3.55	31	0	3.54	31	10	3.48	31	6	3.43	31	10	3.45	31	3	3.52	31
Dependents (Ap, Cfm)	3	3.70	30	4	3.76	28	3	3.71	30	0	3.73	30	7	3.59	30	3	3.47	30

Table 7-7: (continued)

	Staff Ratings																
	Relations/Other Men			Relations/Authority			Aggressiveness			Cooperation			Needs Supervision			Responds/Supervision		
Classification System	%[a]	$\bar{X}$	N	%[a]	$\bar{X}$	N	%[a]	$\bar{X}$	N	%[a]	$\bar{X}$	N	%[a]	$\bar{X}$	N	%[a]	$\bar{X}$	N
Jesness Inventory (Collapsed Personality Subtypes) (continued)																		
Situationals (Se, Ci)	9	3.47	32	3	3.58	32	6	3.37	32	3	3.57	32	6	3.43	32	9	3.75	32
I-level (Interview Method)																		
I-4 Na	7	3.47	44	7	3.52	44	4	3.42	44	4	3.48	44	11	3.42	44	5	3.47	44
I-4 Nx	0	3.30	16	6	3.25	16	12	3.24	16	0	3.20	16	6	3.10	16	0	3.19	16
I-4 Se	3	3.67	32	3	3.64	31	0	3.61	32	0	3.66	32	13	3.51	32	0	3.73	32
I-4 Ci	6	3.58	16	0	3.68	16	0	3.67	16	0	3.55	16	0	3.67	16	0	3.60	16
I-5 Na	11	3.48	9	0	3.71	8	11	3.55	9	0	3.72	9	11	3.54	9	0	3.60	9
I-5 Nx	8	3.65	24	8	3.57	24	8	3.47	24	4	3.54	23	13	3.57	23	13	3.52	24
I-5 Se	9	3.77	22	0	3.81	22	4	3.77	22	9	3.75	23	5	3.73	22	9	3.77	22
I-5 Ci	0	3.50	2	0	3.50	2	0	3.50	2	1	3.83	2	0	3.67	2	0	3.83	2
I-level (Collapsed Levels)																		
I-4	5	3.52	108	5	3.54	107	4	3.48	108	2	3.51	108	9	3.43	108	2	3.52	108
I-5	9	3.66	57	4	3.68	56	7	3.59	57	5	3.66	57	9	3.63	57	9	3.63	57
												Mult. R = .14*			$\chi^2 = 2.86*$		
															$Tau_c = -.16**$		

I-level (Collapsed Personality Subtypes)

Situational	6	3.72	54	2	3.71	53	2	3.68	54	4	3.70	54	9	3.60	54	4	3.75	54
Neurotic Anxious	5	3.51	40	8	3.44	40	10	3.38	40	3	3.41	40	10	3.38	40	8	3.39	40
Neurotic Acting-out	8	3.47	53	6	3.55	52	6	3.44	53	4	3.52	53	11	3.44	53	4	3.49	53
Cultural Identifier	6	3.57	18	0	3.67	18	0	3.66	18	0	3.58	18	0	3.67	18	0	3.63	18
							Mult. R = .20*											

---

[a] Percentage rated below average (3.00) on this scale, indicating unsatisfactory performance.
[b] Scales range from negative behavior (1 and 2) to average (3) to positive behavior (4 and 5).

* $p \le .10$
** $p \le .05$
*** $p \le .01$

Results for tests of both the **Jesness Inventory** and the **interview measures of I-level** were generally insignificant. None of the tests for the Jesness Inventory were significant.[15] I_5 inmates (interview method) were found to have consistently higher mean scores on the staff ratings, but these results were significant only for the relationship between I-level and need for supervision (multiple r = .14, p ≤ .10). An additional test of the relationship between I-level (interview) and staff ratings produced results similar to those noted above for CL. I_5 inmates were significantly more likely to be rated unfavorably on the response to supervision variable (tau$_c$ = −.16, p ≤ .05), but as a group they received higher, or more favorable, mean scores. The latter test, a multiple regression test, was not significant. Finally, a multiple regression test of the relationship between the I-level (interview) personality types and aggressiveness found that both the Situational inmates and the Cultural Identifiers received significantly higher (more favorable) mean scores than either of the neurotic types (multiple r = .20, p ≤ .10).

DISCUSSION

Findings presented in this chapter suggest that the psychological systems differentiate adult male prison inmates on the basis of official disciplinary data, staff ratings of inmates' behavior, and self-report measures of prison infractions and victimization experiences. Our first endeavor to organize the results of this portion of the analysis appears in an earlier summary section. Two additional issues are important to consider at this concluding point: (1) the relevance of the criterion measures to the research outcomes and (2) the potential contributions of psychological constructs to a more thorough understanding of prison inmates.

The Importance of Criterion Measures

One of the first generalizations that one might offer from these findings concerns the fact that the results varied according to the criterion variables employed in the analysis. In some cases this occurred because the criterion construct changed, but similar constructs were measured differently in other cases (e.g., aggression, victimizations, insubordination).[16] In these instances, it appeared that findings depended as heavily on the measurement of the criterion variable as on the psychological classifications. This conclusion certainly supports those who assert the importance of multiple indicators of outcome (e.g., Farrington 1987; Gottfredson 1987a).

In the penitentiary data, the systems correlate in a manner consistent with type descriptions primarily upon analysis of the staff ratings and (to a lesser extent) of the self-report data.[17] We offer a number of explanations for this finding. It may be attributable to the fact that staff members were rating more precise behaviors than were tapped in the self-report or official data. In contrast, self-report and official measures often tapped a composite or a variety of behaviors, especially the official measure identifying all disciplinaries. Alternatively, staff variables may have been more sensitive from a measurement perspective, as two-dimensional indicators of performance ranging from poor to excellent, whereas the other measures were unidimensional, ranging from no problems to problem behaviors.

More likely, our findings may support those who warn us that official disciplinary records may not be the most accurate indicators of adjustment to prison (Light 1991; Schafer 1984). Indeed, official prison data, like other official forms of crime measurement, may be highly sensitive to reporting irregularities. Especially in maximum-security prisons, such data are particularly vulnerable to inmate codes that discourgage "snitching," or informing prison authorities of the infractions committed by fellow inmates. The fact that we observe correlates with official data in the prison camp does not contradict our concern for the validity of the penitentiary data, because the disciplinary data from the prison camp measured a much more unitary, more observable behavior. At the prison camp, the main disciplinary problem was insubordination. By definition, insubordination is observable; in this case, the victim or the observer was almost always a staff member. Finally, in using official data, we may be attempting to tap behaviors that are too infrequent to be analyzed statistically in any but the largest samples. In contrast, the self-report and staff ratings were more sensitive measures. Surveys tapped behaviors that staff did not observe, as well as those which staff may not have viewed as serious. Staff data may also have tapped tendencies as well as completed actions.[18]

Specific Constructs

In some instances, a comparison of findings across different follow-up measures and classification systems increases our understanding of the general psychological constructs. Most important, situational types in the penitentiary often were observed to perform poorly on official-record measures and self-report measures but quite well on staff ratings. Moreover, in a comparison of situational correlates across the systems, we note a pattern that suggests that the situationals in each system typically incurred difficulties with insubordination and victimizations rather than with perhaps more intentional aggressive behaviors or drug and alcohol infractions. Yet these inmates were more likely to be rated by the staff as (1) having good relationships with other inmates and with authority, (2) being more cooperative, (3) being less aggressive, (4) showing less need for supervision, and (5) being more responsive to supervision.

This pattern may suggest that the difficulties encountered by situationals stems in part from their lack of prison experience. Indeed, a number of sources inform us that staying out of trouble in prison is highly dependent upon one's knowledge of how to "do time" (Irwin 1980; Sykes 1958). In this environment, lack of skill and perhaps lack of familiarity with the more committed criminal personality types, may override the fact that situationals otherwise are described as least troublesome.

Findings for the prison camp may bolster this environmental interpretation. Situational and least disturbed (Megargee's Item and Easy) inmates in the prison camp evidenced the favorable results that typically are attributed to these groups. Yet the prison camp environment was much less aversive and more likely to house inmates with less prison experience. Here, familiarity with traditional inmate subculture and unfamiliar codes of conduct may have been less crucial to staying out of trouble. If this explanation is true, one might expect to see the situational penitentiary inmates improve over time as they become more familiar with their surroundings. The treatment implication is clear, however. Until these inmates gain prison experience, they risk incurring problems that may affect both their own personal safety and their ratings on those internal classification instruments that reclassify an inmate's risk of further incidents according to past disciplinary records. If situationals' adjustment problems are temporary, such security-based reclassifications would be misleading.

As we pointed out elsewhere in this chapter, it is not easy to infer any patterns from these data which help us to understand the relevance of *cognitive developmental levels* (CL and I-level) to these inmates. In a comparison of the developmental measures using the penitentiary data, however, inmates diagnosed at higher developmental levels appeared to do poorly on self-report measures and better (as predicted) on staff measures of prison adjustment. Similar findings occur for the prison camp self-report data, but inmates at higher levels did not receive higher staff ratings in the prison camp sample. As stated earlier, however, the camp staff data evidence somewhat limited variability. Nevertheless, one might ask at this point whether the self-report data taps something other than behavior. The most likely answer is that these measures may be highly sensitive to idiosyncratic perceptions of what constitutes behavior that crosses over the line to qualify as threatening, aggressive, or in violation of the institutional policies. Such perceptions in themselves may vary according to personality and emotional states, and by cognitive complexity, but this situation is more obvious in regard to the cognitive- developmental measures. If we examine only the official and the staff data, we observe that the inmates classified in the lower I-level categories tend to be difficult, especially in tests relevant to relationships with others. This is less true of the Conceptual Level classifications.

The preceding discussion of the developmental classification still leaves us with results that may not be perceived as meaningful to correctional practitioners. We do not mean to cast doubt on the existence of differences among inmates in terms of cognitive complexity. Indeed, the construct was validated strongly in chapter 6. In these settings, however, developmental differences do not appear to point to meaningful behavioral differences in and of themselves.

The most frequently observed correlates of behavioral problems occurred among committed criminal and character disorder types (e.g., Quay's Asocial Aggressive and Manipulator; Megargee's Able, Charlie, Delta, and Foxtrot; I-level Cultural Identifiers; Jesness's Mps and Cfcs). These correlates were expected, as were those for inmates diagnosed as neurotic. The findings for neurotic inmates, however, warrant further observation because the danger they pose to institutional settings is important. Indeed, Na and Nx (I-level) inmates consistently scored higher than other inmates on measures of aggression. The importance of these findings is underscored by the nature of the definition of neurotic personality: Their behavior has a private meaning (Warren et al. 1966) and is more likely to manifest itself in an idiosyncratic manner than to be predicted by life events, environmental conditions, or, for that matter, by risk-assessment instruments. In fact, these individuals may or may not have the long records that committed criminal types evidence, and therefore may not be identified as high-risk on security-based classification measures. Accordingly, they represent a classification and management option that is unique to the psychological systems.

CHAPTER 8

PSYCHOLOGICAL CORRELATES OF TREATMENT-RELATED OUTCOMES

This chapter examines the relationship between the classification types and the measures relevant to treatment issues. Three sources of criterion data are used: (1) ratings extracted from the intake interviews, (2) follow-up survey/self-report data, and (3) follow-up staff ratings obtained from the Megargee Adjustment Ratings and the Megargee Work Performance Ratings. This analysis makes no attempt to address all possible issues of treatment and case management; we have chosen measures that are likely to have greater implications for clinicians than for administrators. More specifically, most measures pertain to inmates' adjustment to prison life, such as their specific needs, stresses, fears, and interactions with others. In addition, we present some measures designed to identify inmates' amenability to treatment, such as desire to participate, initiative, and ability to learn.

As in chapter 7, we address two questions: (1) Did the classification systems differentiate inmates according to whether a factor pertains to them? and (2) Did the classification systems differentiate inmates according to the extent of these experiences? With the exception of the interview data, we assess the first question through cross-tabular analysis and the second through multiple regression (OLS). Thus, for the self-report and staff data, these analyses are identical to those used in chapter 7. The ordinal interview data are analyzed through cross-tabular analysis. Also similar to the format used in chapter 7, we begin with a summary of our findings. More detailed accounts of the analyses follow this overview.

SUMMARY OF THE FINDINGS

For review and organization, the findings observed in this chapter are summarized in table 8-1. We observed rather generous criteria in selecting the items to be included in the table as correlates of a specific classification type. Occasionally we included an outcome characteristic that was relatively high or low for a type even though the relationship was not significant. Such findings are not mentioned unless they support similar but significant findings for a similar type on another system or unless they support significant findings for the same type in the other sample. Moreover, we present them not as definitive but rather as suggestive and supportive of further inquiry in subsequent research. In this way, we overcompensated for some limited cell sizes which sometimes prevented substantial differences from reaching significance.

An overview of findings for **situational and least disturbed** inmates tends to support observations that we put forward in chapter 7. These inmates experience some degree of difficulty, particularly in the penitentiary. Although the pattern is not evident among the Megargee MMPI-based least disturbed types, the Quay AIMS and the I-level interview situational types at the penitentiary evidence high stress and fear, concern for their safety, and some tendency to isolate themselves and to limit their level of participation. The Jesness situational inmates (Se and Ci) showed the same tendency toward isolation but none of the stress symptoms. In some cases, situational inmates showed a need for programmatic support at the beginning of their stay, but gave evidence of very little actual participation upon follow-up four months later.[1] At the same time, these inmates looked quite good to the staff; as a group, situational inmates typically received the highest staff ratings on measures such as emotional control, maturity, initiative, and ability to learn. We continue to conclude that their problems are primarily the adjustment difficulties of a group of inmates who have not had much prison experience but who, nevertheless, are faced suddenly with the task of adjusting to an adverse environment. In support of this conclusion, we do not see similar adjustment difficulties among situational minimum-security inmates to their less severe environment; yet we found positive staff ratings in both settings.

Committed criminal types (e.g., Asocial Aggressive, Manipulative, MMPI Charlie, MMPI Foxtrot, Jesness Mp, Jesness Cfc, and I-level Ci) showed few adjustment difficulties in the form of

Table 8-1: Summary of Treatment-Related Correlates of Classification Types

Classification Type	Institutional Setting	
	Penitentiary	Prison Camp
	Quay AIMS	
Asocial Aggressive	institutionalized poor emotional control participates in programs	immature poor emotional control
Immature Dependent	low need for social stimulation institutionalized few friends participates in programs high stress follows crowd	low need for programmatic support limited participation in programs poor emotional control
Neurotic Anxious	need for programmatic support few friends participates in programs poor emotional control immature follows crowd	low need for programmatic support limited participation in programs
Manipulator	limited communication with staff limited participation in programs	poor emotional control
Situational	need for privacy need for safety need for programmatic support sees others as willing to help limited communication with staff limited participation in programs high stress	need for programmatic support sees others as willing to help
	Megargee MMPI-Based System	
Able		low stress
Baker	need for programmatic support	limited communication with staff
Charlie	institutionalized	sees others as willing to help immature oriented to rehabilitation goals
Delta		poor emotional control few friends (n.s.) immature
Easy		need for privacy

Table 8-1: *(continued)*

	Institutional Setting	
Classification Type	Penitentiary	Prison Camp

Megargee MMPI-Based System (continued)		
Foxtrot	few friends low initiative	sees others as willing to help immature poor emotional control
George	need for programmatic support (n.s.) has friends sees others as willing to help (n.s.) high initiative	limited communication with staff few friends (n.s.)
How	high fear (n.s.) high stress has friends limited communication with staff (n.s.)	need for privacy high stress others are *not* willing to help limited communication with staff
Item	has friends high initiative	
Jupiter	need for programmatic support (n.s.) sees others as willing to help	

Conceptual Level		
CL-1	need for safety need for programmatic support oriented to rehabilitation goals participates in programs high fear high stress low initiative	need for structure oriented to rehabilitation goals sees others as willing to help (n.s.) immature poor emotional control
CL-2	need for privacy need for safety oriented to rehabilitation goals limited participation in programs	need for structure oriented to rehabilitation goals sees others as willing to help (n.s.)
CL-3	need for privacy need for social stimulation need for programmatic support limited participation in programs good emotional control mature high initiative	not oriented to rehabilitation high fear does not seek help limited participation in programs mature

Table 8-1: *(continued)*

Classification Type	Institutional Setting	
	Penitentiary	Prison Camp
	Jesness Inventory I-level	
I-2	need for programmatic support (n.s.) sees others as willing to help institutionalized high stress (n.s.) few friends (n.s.) limited participation in programs	need for programmatic support sees others as willing to help needs emotional feedback (n.s.) need for structure high stress (n.s.) high fear (n.s.) oriented to rehabilitation goals
I-3	sees others as willing to help	
I-4	need for emotional feedback good emotional control high initiative high ability to learn mature (n.s.)	
	Jesness Inventory I-level: Personality Types[a]	
I-3 Cfm	need for safety need for programmatic support sees others as willing to help high stress (n.s.) few friends	need for programmatic support limited participation in programs sees others as willing to help (n.s.)
I-3 Mp	need for safety limited participation in programs has friends poor emotional control low initiative	
I-3 Cfc	not a loner need for safety limited participation in programs has friends	
I-4 Se	limited participation in programs low stress good emotional control mature (n.s.) high initiative loner high ability to learn	need for programmatic support limited praticipation in programs
I-4 Na	need for programmatic support few friends high ability to learn high stress	high stress

Table 8-1: *(continued)*

| Classification Type | Institutional Setting | |
	Penitentiary	Prison Camp
	Jesness Inventory I-level: Personality Types[a] (continued)	
I-4 Nx	need for safety need for programmatic support high stress high ability to learn high initiative	stress
	I-level (Interview Method)	
I-4 Ci	limited participation in programs good emotional control mature (n.s.) high initiative high ability to learn loner	need for programmatic support limited participation in programs
I-4 Na	poor emotional control some problems learning	
I-4 Nx	need for emotional feedback participates in programs high stress poor emotional control	need for programmatic support high initiative high stress few friends
I-4 Se	need for emotional feedback need for safety limited participation in programs high fear high stress mature sees others as willing to help (n.s.)	need for programmatic support will seek help from others has friends high stress high initiative communicates with staff high ability to learn
I-4 Ci	institutionalized (n.s.) high fear high stress communicates with staff	does not seek help from others few friends limited communication with staff low stress high initiative few friends
I-5 Na	need for privacy (n.s.) high fear some learning problems communicates with staff	

Table 8-1: *(continued)*

Classification Type	Institutional Setting	
	Penitentiary	Prison Camp
	I-level (Interview Method) (continued)	
I-5 Nx	need for emotional feedback (n.s.) need for programmatic support participates in programs high stress high fear	need for programmatic support high initiative high ability to learn high stress
I-5 Se	need for emotional feedback need for safety limited participation in programs high stress mature good emotional control high initiative high ability to learn	need for programmatic support will seek help from others has friends high initiative communicates with staff high ability to learn
I-5 Ci	good emotional control high ability to learn	does not seek help from others few friends limited communication with staff low stress high initiative
	I-level (Collapsed Levels)	
I-4	institutionalized high fear high stress poor emotional control	fewer friends poor emotional control
I-5	need for programmatic support oriented to rehabilitation goals high initiative high ability to learn	high fear will seek help from others communicates with staff mature high initiative high ability to learn

n.s.: The finding is reported even though results are not significant. This option is chosen in instances where the group differences were substantial and/or results support findings for a similarly defined type.

[a] Jesness I_2 subtypes are not summarized because of insufficient number of observations.

stress, fear, or isolation. Yet these inmates, in the assessment of the interview raters, were most likely to appear to be institutionalized. Sometimes the staff considered them to be immature and to evidence poor emotional control. Findings with respect to their participation and interaction with others were less consistent across systems. It was somewhat surprising to find these inmates, rather than the dependent or neurotic types, more likely candidates for becoming institutionalized. On the other hand, in accordance with their type descriptions, the committed criminal types in this study had more extensive prison experience than others.

The most common trait of the **neurotic** types (e.g., Quay Neurotic Anxious, MMPI George, MMPI Jupiter, MMPI Baker, I-level Neurotic Anxious, and I-level Neurotic Acting-out) was their need for programmatic support, but both I-level systems identify neurotic inmates who evidence difficulties with stress and fear. Moreover, the I-level interview system appears to differentiate the Neurotic Anxious from the Neurotic Acting-out inmates. In both settings, the Neurotic Anxious inmates showed a willingness to participate in programs and a desire for emotional feedback from others. Yet perhaps in keeping with a pattern of outrunning anxiety, Neurotic Acting-out inmates showed less stress but more problems with emotional control and learning. The Quay and MMPI neurotic types failed to show stress-related correlates, possibly because this dimension is tapped by another type. Indeed, Quay Immature Dependents and Megargee Hows also were described as likely candidates for stress and anxiety. Our study found stress correlates for both the Quay Immature Dependents and the Megargee Hows. In addition, Quay Immature Dependent penitentiary inmates showed dependent characteristics such as institutionalized traits, few friends, a tendency to follow a crowd, and a low need for social stimulation. Moreover, How inmates, noted as most disturbed on the Megargee MMPI system, showed both anxiety and tendencies toward isolation.

In chapter 7, we concluded that the **cognitive developmental** types offered little help in differentiating inmates on the basis of disciplinary characteristics. Exactly the opposite occurred with the treatment characteristics, and the patterns are clearer. Inmates classified into the lower developmental stages generally had a more difficult time adjusting to prison. They were more likely to display high stress and fear, and to show poor emotional control. At the same time, they appeared to need more from the prison experience than the inmates diagnosed at higher stages. For example, inmates at lower levels evidenced a higher need for safety, structure, help from others, and programmatic support. They were more likely to be institutionalized. In contrast, correlates for the more developed inmates emphasized their social and intellectual skills, such as high initiative, maturity, good emotional control, and ability to learn. Participation correlates were not consistent across the systems for the inmates diagnosed at higher stages, but it is not clear whether the participation measure tapped a reluctance to participate or limited opportunities to participate (see note 1, in this chapter). The sections that follow present a more detailed account of the analyses that produced these findings.

PENITENTIARY

The Effects of the Classification Types on
Interview-Based Measures of Inmates' Needs

As shown in table 8-2, we used six dependent variables in this analysis: (1) need for privacy, (2) need for structure (a clear system of rules and expectations), (3) need for emotional feedback, (4) need for social stimulation, (5) need for safety, and (6) need for support (in the form of programs and activities) (Toch, 1977). Our research design called for additional rating items, such as "need for a high level of activity," but these were not used in this analysis because of limited variability or poor interrater reliability.[2] In contrast to the measures obtained from the inmate survey or the staff ratings, interview items register an inmate's tendency to express a "need" spontaneously, either in response to the question "Do you expect any difficulties while you are in here?" or in other parts of the interview.

Cross-tabular analysis of the relationship between the **Quay AIMS** types and the inmates' needs items reveals a pattern for Situational inmates that is relevant to findings observed in chapter 7. That is, Situationals are significantly more likely than others to evidence needs for privacy ($tau_c = -.21$, $p \leq .001$), safety ($tau_c = -.14$, $p \leq .05$), and programmatic support ($tau_c = -.19$, $p \leq .05$). With few exceptions, differences across the other types are minimal; significant relationships are attributable largely to the results for the Situationals. One noteworthy exception is found in the test of the relationship between the Quay types and support, where a high proportion of Immature Dependent and Neurotic Anxious inmates (combined) also show a need for programmatic support. An addi-

Table 8-2: Cross-Tabular Analysis of the Relationship between Classification Types and Inmates' Needs, Penitentiary Sample

| | Prison-Based Needs | | | | | | | | | | | |
| | Privacy | | Structure | | Feedback | | Social Stimulation | | Safety | | Support | |
Classification System	$\%^a$	N^b	$\%^a$	N^b	$\%^c$	N^b	$\%^c$	N^b	$\%^a$	N^b	$\%^c$	N^b
Quay AIMS												
Asocial Aggressive	30	20	25	20	15	20	15	20	25	20	50	20
Immature Dependent	20	10	10	10	0	10	0	10	30	10	40	10
Neurotic Anxious	23	22	14	22	23	22	14	22	18	22	55	22
Manipulator	15	41	20	41	17	41	22	41	24	41	37	41
Situational	42	52	19	52	27	52	23	52	40	52	62	52
	$\chi^2 = 9.51^{**}$											
Quay AIMS (Collapsed Categories)												
Aa/Mp	20	61	21	61	16	61	20	61	25	61	41	61
Id/Na	22	32	13	32	16	32	9	32	22	32	50	32
Situational	42	52	19	52	27	52	23	52	40	52	62	52
	$\chi^2 = 7.92^{**}$								$\chi^2 = 4.55^{*}$		$\chi^2 = 4.75^{*}$	
	$\mathrm{Tau}_c = -.21^{***}$								$\mathrm{Tau}_c = -.14^{**}$		$\mathrm{Tau}_c = -.19^{**}$	
Megargee MMPI-Based Taxonomy												
Able	36	31	10	31	16	31	19	31	26	31	52	31
Baker	17	6	0	6	0	6	17	6	17	6	68	6
Charlie	33	12	25	12	42	12	8	12	42	12	50	12
Delta	17	23	17	23	17	23	17	23	17	23	48	23
Easy	46	11	27	11	27	11	0	11	36	11	46	11
Foxtrot	18	11	27	11	18	11	18	11	9	11	55	11
George	15	13	15	13	8	13	8	13	46	13	46	13

How	21	19	11	19	16	19	11	19	32	19	53	19
Item	21	24	25	24	21	24	25	24	29	24	29	24
Jupiter	25	4	0	4	0	4	25	4	25	4	100	4
Megargee MMPI-Based Taxonomy (Collapsed Categories)												
Charlie/Foxtrot (Committed Criminal)	26	23	26	23	30	23	13	23	26	23	52	23
Able/Delta (Character Disorder)	28	54	13	54	17	54	19	54	22	54	50	54
How (Most Disturbed)	21	19	11	19	16	19	11	19	32	19	52	19
Baker/George/Jupiter (Neurotic)	17	23	9	23	4	23	13	23	35	23	61	23
Item/Easy (Least Disturbed)	27	35	26	35	23	35	17	35	31	35	34	35
Conceptual Level—CL3												
CL-1	13	39	15	39	18	39	8	39	36	39	62	39
CL-2	33	77	22	77	18	77	18	77	31	77	49	77
CL-3	24	25	8	25	28	25	28	25	12	25	32	25
	$\chi^2 = 5.29^*$						$\chi^2 = 4.61^*$		$\chi^2 = 4.59^*$		$\chi^2 = 5.32^*$	
	$Tau_c = -.11^*$						$Tau_c = -.14^{**}$		$Tau_c = .15^{**}$		$Tau_c = .20^{**}$	
Conceptual Level—CL5												
CL-1	12	25	20	25	20	25	4	25	48	25	64	25
CL-2	30	97	20	97	18	97	18	97	28	97	50	97
CL-3	21	19	5	19	32	19	32	19	11	19	32	19
							$\chi^2 = 5.87^{**}$		$\chi^2 = 7.58^{**}$		$\chi^2 = 4.54^*$	
							$Tau_c = -.14^{**}$		$Tau_c = .20^{***}$		$Tau_c = .17^{**}$	

Table 8-2: (continued)

	Prison-Based Needs											
	Privacy		Structure		Feedback		Social Stimulation		Safety		Support	
Classification System	%ᵃ	Nᵇ	%ᵃ	Nᵇ	%ᶜ	Nᵇ	%ᶜ	Nᵇ	%ᵃ	Nᵇ	%ᶜ	Nᵇ
Jesness Inventory I-level												
I-2 Aa	25	4	25	4	25	4	0	4	25	4	75	4
I-2 Ap	33	3	0	3	0	3	0	3	33	3	67	3
I-3 Cfm	24	17	0	17	6	17	24	17	29	17	77	17
I-3 Mp	27	30	17	30	23	30	23	30	30	30	50	30
I-3 Cfc	28	43	23	43	16	43	14	43	35	43	40	43
I-4 Se	20	20	15	20	25	20	15	20	15	20	40	20
I-4 Na	24	17	24	17	18	17	18	17	18	17	65	17
I-4 Nx	29	7	27	7	43	7	14	7	57	7	57	7
I-4 Ci	33	3	33	3	33	3	0	3	0	3	0	3
Jesness Inventory (Collapsed Levels)												
I-2	27	7	14	7	14	7	0	7	29	7	71	7
I-3	27	90	17	90	17	90	19	90	32	90	50	90
I-4	23	47	21	47	26	47	15	47	21	47	49	47
					Tau$_c$ = −.08*							
Jesness Inventory (Collapsed Personality Subtypes)												
Aggressives (Aa, Cfc, Mp)	27	77	21	77	20	77	17	77	33	77	41	77
Neurotics (Na, Nx)	25	24	25	24	25	24	17	24	29	24	63	24
Dependents (Ap, Cfm)	25	20	0	20	5	20	20	20	30	20	75	20
Situationals (Se, Ci)	22	23	17	23	26	23	13	23	13	23	35	23
									Tau$_c$ = .12*		χ^2 = 9.24**	

I-level (Interview Method)

	(1)	(2)	(3)	(4)	(5)	(6)	N
I-4 Na	26	14	11	14	26	31	35
I-4 Nx	29	26	19	13	29	48	31
I-4 Se	33	7	27	27	47	47	15
I-4 Ci	6	13	25	13	31	50	16
I-5 Na	44	17	22	29	22	67	18
I-5 Nx	24	10	29	19	29	71	21
I-5 Se	18	27	18	9	27	36	11
I-5 Ci	24	24	5	14	19	48	21

I-level (Collapsed levels)

	(1)	(2)	(3)	(4)	(5)	(6)	N
I-4	25	17	19	16	31	42	97
I-5	28	18	18	18	24	58	71

$\chi^2 = 3.33^*$
$Tau_b = -.15^{**}$
$Tau_c = .09^*$ (col 3) $Tau_c = .09^*$ (col 5)

I-level (Collapsed Personality Subtypes)

	(1)	(2)	(3)	(4)	(5)	(6)	N
Situational	27	15	23	19	39	42	26
Neurotic Anxious	27	19	23	15	29	58	52
Neurotic Acting-out	32	15	15	19	25	43	53
Cultural Identifier	16	19	14	14	24	49	37

$Tau_c = .09^*$

a Percent yes (there is a need or some indication of a need).

b Number of inmates in the category.

c Percent yes (there is a need).

 * $p \leq .10$

 ** $p \leq .05$

 *** $p \leq .01$

tional finding concerns the low proportion of Immature Dependent and Neurotic Anxious types (combined) who expressed any need for social stimulation. This relationship, however, was not significant.

Table 8-2 shows that none of the twelve tests of the relationships between the **Megargee MMPI-based** types and inmates' needs were significant. Although a high proportion (61%) of the neurotic types (Baker, George, and Jupiter) expressed a need for support in the form of programs, the relationship was not significant.[3]

Seven of 12 tests of the relationship between **Conceptual Level** and inmates' needs produced significant results. Proportionately more inmates classified as CL-2 and CL-3 showed a need for privacy (tau$_c$ = -.11, p ≤ .10) and social stimulation (tau$_c$ = -.14, p ≤ .05), whereas inmates classified as CL-1 and CL-2 were significantly more likely to express concern for their safety (tau$_c$ =. 15, p ≤ .05) and a need for support (tau$_c$ = .20, p ≤ .05). The latter two findings were strongest for the CL-1 inmates.

Relationships between prison needs and both the **Jesness Inventory and the interview-based measures of I-level** were weak to nonexistent. In contrast to inmates classified as situational on other systems, proportionately fewer Jesness Inventory Situational inmates evidenced a need for safety than the other types (tau$_c$ = .12, p ≤ .10). The opposite was true for the Situational inmates classified according to the I-level interview measure, who showed a slightly greater need for safety (tau$_c$ = .09, p ≤ .10).

Jesness Situational inmates also were less likely than others, particularly the Jesness neurotic and dependent types, to express a need for programmatic support (χ^2 = 9.24, p ≤ .05). I$_4$ inmates were significantly more likely to be rated as having a need for emotional feedback (tau$_c$ = -.08, p ≤ .08), a finding that is partially supported by similar results for Conceptual Level tests. Finally, proportionately more inmates classified as I$_5$ by the interview method showed a need for programmatic support.

The Effects of the Classification Types on Interview-Based
Measures of Inmates' Attitudes toward
Treatment and Incarceration

This portion of the analysis examines relationships with inmates' adherence to the notion of rehabilitation, whether inmates perceive others (inmates and staff) as willing to help, and whether the raters viewed interview responses as indicative of an "institutionalized" person whose skills of decision making and independent living appeared to have been impaired by exposure to the intense structure and the deprivations of prison life.

Results of these cross-tabular analyses are shown in table 8-3. We begin with a discussion of the relationship between the **Quay AIMS** types and these measures. Two of six tests produced significant results. Situational inmates were significantly more likely than the other types to perceive others as willing to help ($tau_c = -.20$, $p \leq .05$); and Asocial Aggressive and Immature Dependent inmates were significantly more likely to be rated as institutionalized ($\chi^2 = 11.64$, $p \leq .05$).[4]

We observe few results for the **MMPI-based** measures. As in the findings for the Quay analysis above, the committed criminal types (Charlie and Foxtrot) were significantly more likely than others to be rated as institutionalized.[5] Conducting these analyses a second time, while controlling for possible validity problems, produced similar results except that proportions for the How inmates again were somewhat higher than those shown in table 8-3.

Analysis of the **Conceptual Level** data found lower levels (CL-1 and CL-2) to be significantly more likely than the CL-3 inmates to perceive rehabilitation or treatment as an important purpose of their sentence. Tau_c measures of association were .20 ($p \leq .01$) and .18 ($p \leq .01$), respectively, for the Cl_3 and the Cl_5 measures. CL-1 and Cl-2 inmates also were more likely than the CL-3 inmates to view others as willing to help; the results were not significant, however.

Inmates diagnosed at the lower two I-levels on the **Jesness I-level system** also were more likely to see others as willing to help. These results, however, *were* significant ($tau_c = .12$, $p \leq .10$). Not surprisingly, I_2 inmates were more likely to be rated as institutionalized. Again, the I_2 category was small (only six inmates); thus, the results may be unstable. The only personality distinction occurred on the test of the relationship between the collapsed personality types and perceptions of others' willingness to help: Dependent types were substantially more likely to perceive others as willing to help ($\chi^2 = 7.73$, $p \leq .05$). This latter finding may bring into question whether the criterion measure differentiates inmates who seek help from those who view it as available, regardless of whether they seek it.

When we used the **I-level interview method,** two tests of the relationship between level and interview measures were signifi-

Table 8-3: Cross-Tabular Analysis of the Relationship between Classification Variables and Additional Treatment-Related Measures, Penitentiary Sample

Classification System	Interview Measures					
	Sees Others as Willing to Help		Institutionalized		Oriented to Rehabilitation	
	%[a]	N	%[a]	N	%[b]	N
Quay AIMS						
Asocial Aggressive	39	18	21	19	30	20
Immature Dependent	38	8	20	10	20	10
Neurotic Anxious	30	20	10	20	14	22
Manipulator	33	36	2	41	30	40
Situational	56	48	2	50	27	49
			$\chi^2 = 11.64^{**}$			
Quay AIMS (Collapsed Categories)						
Aa/Mp	35	54	8	60	30	60
Id/Na	32	28	13	30	16	32
Situational	56	48	2	50	26	49
	$\chi^2 = 6.13^{**}$					
	$Tau_c = -.20^{**}$					
Megargee MMPI-Based Taxonomy						
Able	45	29	7	31	17	29
Baker	33	6	17	6	33	6
Charlie	46	11	25	12	18	11
Delta	46	22	14	22	17	23
Easy	33	9	0	11	27	11
Foxtrot	30	10	10	10	64	11
George	64	11	0	13	33	12
How	44	16	0	17	21	19
Item	23	23	0	23	25	24
Jupiter	67	3	0	4	50	4
Megargee MMPI-Based Taxonomy (Collapsed Categories)						
Charlie/Foxtrot (Committed Criminal)	38	21	18	22	41	22
Able/Delta (Character Disorder)	45	51	9	53	17	52
How (Most Disturbed)	44	16	0	17	21	19
Baker/George/Jupiter (Neurotic)	55	20	4	23	36	22
Item/Easy (Least Disturbed)	25	32	0	34	26	35
			$\chi^2 = 9.12^{**}$			
			$Tau_c = -.13^{***}$			

Table 8-3: *(continued)*

Classification System	Sees Others as Willing to Help %[a]	N	Institutionalized %[a]	N	Oriented to Rehabilitation %[b]	N
Conceptual Level—CL3						
CL-1	49	35	8	36	40	38
CL-2	46	70	4	76	31	75
CL-3	30	23	8	25	8	24
					$\chi^2 = 7.07^{**}$	
					$Tau_c = .20^{***}$	
Conceptual Level—CL5						
CL-1	41	22	5	22	42	22
CL-2	46	89	5	96	31	95
CL-3	35	17	11	19	6	18
					$\chi^2 = 6.75^{**}$	
					$Tau_c = .18^{***}$	
Jesness Inventory I-level						
I-2 Aa	25	4	50	4	0	4
I-2 Ap	100	3	50	2	0	3
I-3 Cfm	67	15	0	17	41	17
I-3 Mp	52	27	3	29	31	29
I-3 Cfc	40	38	2	43	31	42
I-4 Se	47	19	5	20	15	20
I-4 Na	24	17	20	15	25	16
I-4 Nx	50	4	0	7	50	6
I-4 Ci	33	3	0	3	33	3
Jesness Inventory (Collapsed Levels)						
I-2	57	7	50	6	0	7
I-3	49	80	2	89	33	88
I-4	37	43	9	45	24	45
	$Tau_c = .12^*$		$\chi^2 = 21.98^{***}$			
Jesness Inventory (Collapsed Personality Subtypes)						
Aggressives (Aa, Cfc, Mp)	44	69	5	76	29	75
Neurotics (Na, Nx)	29	21	14	22	32	22
Dependents (Ap, Cfm)	72	18	5	19	35	20
Situationals (Se, Ci)	46	22	4	23	17	23
	$\chi^2 = 7.73^{**}$					

Interview Measures

Table 8-3: *(continued)*

Classification System	Sees Others as Willing to Help		Institutionalized		Oriented to Rehabilitation	
	%[a]	N	%[a]	N	%[b]	N
I-level (Interview Method)						
I-4 Na	25	28	9	34	25	35
I-4 Nx	37	27	10	30	24	29
I-4 Se	67	15	0	15	13	15
I-4 Ci	33	15	25	16	13	16
I-5 Na	50	18	6	18	24	17
I-5 Nx	41	17	0	19	38	21
I-5 Se	27	11	10	10	27	11
I-5 Ci	53	19	0	21	40	20
I-level (Collapsed Levels)						
I-4	38	85	11	95	21	95
I-5	45	65	3	68	33	69
			$Tau_b = -.14^{**}$		$Tau_b = -.14^{**}$	
I-level (Collapsed Personality Subtypes)						
Situational	50	26	4	25	19	26
Neurotic Anxious	39	44	6	49	30	50
Neurotic Acting-out	35	46	8	52	25	52
Cultural Identifier	44	34	11	37	29	36

[a] Percent yes.
[b] Percent yes or somewhat.
* $p \le .10$
** $p \le .05$
*** $p \le .01$

cant. I_4 inmates were slightly more likely to be rated as institution-alized (tau_b = -.14, p ≤ .05) but less likely to be oriented to the notion of rehabilitation (tau_b = -.14, p ≤ .05). Unfortunately, none of the relationships between collapsed personality types and inter-view measures proved significant. Some differences, however, sup-port findings for similar types on the other systems. The finding that more Cultural Identifiers were rated as institutionalized, for example, also was noted for the Quay and the MMPI types. As on the Quay tests, Situational inmates were more likely to see others as willing to help.

*The Effects of the Classification Types on Self-Report
Indices of Stress and Interaction Patterns*

The self-report scales used as criterion measures in this portion can be subdivided into those that identify the level and nature of inmates' interactions within the institution and those that pertain to the fear and stress experienced by the inmates. Presumably, both experiences provide important information to prison practitioners. For both samples, the analyses incorporate three stress measures and four interaction measures. Results show the value of using related rather than single indicators of each concept. Even though some indices appear to measure similar constructs (e.g., "Sees Help" and "Has Friends"), findings differed across the related indicators and overall provided a richer, more meaningful picture of the prison experiences of the personality and developmentally defined classification types. Definitions of the survey indices were presented in chapter 4, but are reviewed here as follows:

A. Interaction Measures

1. Sees Help: Measures the extent to which inmates report having been helped by staff and other inmates.

2. Has Friends/Support: Measures whether or not the inmate has established close, supportive friendships in the institution.

3. Communicates: Measures whether the inmate commu-nicates with staff.

4. Participates: Measures whether the inmate participates in programs and activities that help one to cope with prison life.

B. Stress Measures

1. Fear: Measures extent to which the inmate is afraid of other inmates with regard to his physical safety.

2. CESD stress scale (Center for Epidemiologic Studies Depression Scale) (Radloff 1977): Measures general, not situational, life stress.

3. Stress: An ordinal measure in which the inmate indicates the level of stress experienced while incarcerated, on the following scale: (1) no stress; (2) sometimes worries, but can cope; (3) worries often but usually can cope; (4) worries a lot and has difficulty coping; (5) worries so much that he often gets sick.

Table 8-4 shows that in several instances, types identified by the **Quay AIMS** system differentiated inmates on these measures. We find, for example, that the Asocial Aggressive and the Manipulative inmates were least likely to report stress. Cross-tabular tests of the relationships between the collapsed AIMS types and both the CESD stress scale and the ordinal stress measure show that the Situational inmates and the combined Immature Dependent and Neurotic Anxious inmates were significantly more likely to report problems with stress than the inmates classified as Asocial Aggressive or Manipulative. Mean scores on the CESD scale also were lower for the Asocial Aggressive and Manipulative inmates, but not significantly so. The relationship between the Quay types and perceptions of fear was not significant.

Results differed across the interaction measures, but in meaningful ways. Most notably, combined Immature Dependent and Neurotic Anxious inmates were significantly less likely to form supportive friendships with other inmates ($\chi^2 = 5.14$, $p \leq = .10$) but significantly more likely to indicate that participation in prison programs helped them to cope with prison ($\chi^2 = 5.40$, $p \leq .10$). Thus, three tests for the Immature Dependent/Neurotic Anxious inmates tell us that these inmates (*a*) do not establish supportive

Table 8-4: Effects of Classification Types on Self-Report Prison Experience Measures, Penitentiary Sample

	Prison Experience Measures																				
	Fear			Sees Help			Has Friends			Communicates			Participates			Stress (CESD)			Stress	
Classification System	%[a]	$\bar{X}$	N[b]	%[b]	$\bar{X}$	N[b]	%[c]	$\bar{X}$	N[b]	%[d]	$\bar{X}$	N[b]	%[e]	$\bar{X}$	N[b]	%[f]	$\bar{X}$	N[b]	%,[g]	N[b]
Quay AIMS																				
Asocial Aggressive	40	1.42	15	53	2.10	15	43	2.78	14	20	2.86	15	53	2.57	15	33	32.42	15	13	15
Immature Dependent	50	1.61	6	50	1.88	6	83	2.25	6	50	2.33	6	50	2.29	6	67	41.66	6	50	6
Neurotic Anxious	38	1.45	16	56	1.95	16	63	2.64	16	47	2.54	15	40	2.36	15	38	35.35	16	38	16
Manipulator	26	1.51	27	65	1.82	26	42	2.81	26	77	2.09	26	82	1.72	27	37	33.33	27	19	27
Situational	39	1.49	31	66	1.91	29	39	2.90	31	70	2.33	30	69	2.07	29	61	42.03	31	36	31
										$\chi^2 = 15.49$***			$\chi^2 = 8.9$*							
										Mult. R = .35**			Mult. R = .35**							
Quay AIMS (Collapsed Categories)																				
Aa/Mp	31	1.48	40	61	1.92	41	43	2.80	40	56	2.38	41	71	2.03	42	36	33.68	42	17	42
Id/Na	41	1.50	22	55	1.93	22	68	2.52	22	48	2.48	22	43	2.34	21	46	37.24	22	41	22
Situational	39	1.49	31	66	1.91	29	39	2.91	31	70	2.34	30	69	2.06	29	61	42.03	31	36	31
							$\chi^2 = 5.14$*						$\chi^2 = 5.40$*			$\chi^2 = 4.70$*			$\chi^2 = 5.30$*	
																Tau$_c$ = .24*			Tau$_c$ = .19**	
Megargee MMPI-Based Taxonomy																				
Able	29	1.50	24	50	1.92	24	48	2.68	23	57	2.30	23	64	1.94	22	21	26.75	24	13	24
Baker	0	1.16	2	0	2.36	2	50	3.00	2	100	2.08	2	100	1.50	2	50	30.00	2	50	2
Charlie	75	1.90	8	75	1.82	8	57	2.72	7	38	2.64	8	63	2.72	8	63	53.57	8	38	8
Delta	33	1.36	15	53	1.98	15	53	2.77	15	64	2.35	14	78	1.94	14	47	42.31	15	33	15
Easy	40	1.46	5	20	1.95	5	100	2.10	5	60	2.43	5	40	2.25	5	40	31.00	5	40	5
Foxtrot	17	1.39	6	33	1.91	6	83	2.25	6	67	2.53	6	67	2.38	6	33	30.00	6	17	6

Table 8-4: *(continued)*

	Prison Experience Measures																			
	Fear			Sees Help			Has Friends			Communicates			Participates			Stress (CESD)			Stress	
Classification System	%[a]	X̄	N[b]	%[b]	X̄	N[b]	%[c]	X̄	N[b]	%[d]	X̄	N[b]	%[e]	X̄	N[b]	%[f]	X̄	N[b]	%[g]	N[b]
George	14	1.50	9	63	1.82	8	44	2.75	9	63	2.29	8	67	1.97	9	22	31.25	9	0	9
How	36	1.60	14	46	1.99	13	50	2.87	14	71	2.38	14	54	2.34	13	86	50.45	14	54	13
Item	32	1.29	22	55	1.91	20	27	3.13	22	68	2.25	22	73	1.99	22	46	33.75	22	23	22
Jupiter	33	1.89	3	67	1.67	3	33	2.67	3	67	2.33	3	33	2.34	3	100	50.00	3	67	3
																(Mult. R = .46***)				
Megargee MMPI-Based Taxonomy (Collapsed Categories)																				
Charlie/Foxtrot (Committed Criminal)	50	1.67	14	57	1.85	14	69	2.50	13	50	2.59	14	64	2.56	14	50	42.69	14	29	14
Able/Delta (Character Disorder)	31	1.44	39	51	1.94	39	50	2.71	38	60	2.31	37	69	1.98	36	31	32.88	39	21	39
How (Most Disturbed)	36	1.61	14	46	1.99	13	50	2.86	14	71	2.38	14	54	2.34	13	86	50.45	14	54	13
Baker/George/Jupiter (Neurotic)	36	1.54	14	54	1.86	13	43	2.77	14	69	2.27	13	64	1.98	14	43	35.38	14	21	14
Item/Easy (Least Disturbed)	33	1.32	27	48	1.91	25	41	2.92	27	68	2.29	27	67	2.04	27	44	33.20	27	26	27
							$Tau_c = .17*$									$\chi^2 = 12.71**$ Mult. R = .30*				
Conceptual Level—CL3																				
CL-1	43	1.55	30	54	1.90	26	48	2.74	29	66	2.35	29	59	2.33	29	53	42.39	30	38	29
CL-2	34	1.51	53	47	1.90	53	46	2.87	52	62	2.39	52	64	2.10	52	45	36.20	53	25	53
CL-3	23	1.26	22	50	2.08	22	41	2.92	22	57	2.27	21	70	1.89	20	36	30.53	22	14	22
	$Tau_c = -.15**$															$Tau_c = -.18**$				

Conceptual Level—CL5

CL-1	45 1.74 20	59 1.90 17	42 2.82 19	60 2.44 20	53 2.12 19	65 49.64 20	42	19
CL-2	33 1.45 69	47 1.97 68	42 2.85 68	64 2.37 67	64 2.38 67	44 35.16 69	23	69
CL-3	25 1.29 16	56 2.07 16	44 2.86 16	53 2.23 15	73 1.84 15	31 30.00 16	19	16

$Tau_c = -.12^*$; $Tau_c = -.12^*$; $Tau_c = -.20^{**}$; $Tau_c = -.14^{**}$; Mult. $R = .29^{**}$

Jesness Inventory I-level

I-2 Aa	0 1.00 2	100 1.71 2	50 2.75 2	100 2.00 2	50 2.75 2	50 54.99 2	50	2
I-2 Ap	33 1.17 3	67 1.64 3	67 2.75 3	33 2.42 3	50 2.50 2	67 30.00 3	67	3
I-3 Cfm	42 1.58 12	11 2.03 9	58 2.62 12	58 2.73 12	33 2.50 12	58 35.00 12	46	11
I-3 Mp	17 1.29 23	52 1.90 23	32 3.12 22	57 2.43 23	73 1.86 22	30 31.19 23	9	23
I-3 Cfc	47 1.57 32	59 1.82 32	48 2.73 31	69 2.25 32	74 2.22 31	50 37.61 32	28	32
I-4 Se	29 1.31 17	44 2.14 16	53 2.71 17	50 2.48 14	71 2.10 17	24 30.36 17	18	17
I-4 Na	31 1.50 13	46 2.04 13	62 2.54 13	69 2.31 13	50 2.33 12	62 43.75 13	31	13
I-4 Nx	60 2.13 5	60 1.63 5	20 3.30 5	80 2.17 5	80 1.75 5	100 57.99 5	40	5
I-4 Ci	0 1.00 2	50 2.00 2	100 2.00 2	50 2.25 2	100 1.00 2	0 17.50 2	0	2

$Tau_c = -.16^*$

Jesness Inventory (Collapsed Levels)

I-2	20 1.08 5	80 1.68 5	60 2.75 5	60 2.21 5	50 2.63 4	60 45.00 5	60	5
I-3	36 1.47 67	50 1.88 64	45 2.86 65	63 2.38 67	66 2.09 65	45 35.00 67	24	66
I-4	32 1.48 37	42 2.03 36	54 2.70 37	62 2.36 34	67 2.03 36	46 38.64 37	24	37

Jesness Inventory (Collapsed Personality Subtypes)

Aggressives (Aa, Cfc, Mp)	33 1.44 57	46 1.85 57	42 2.88 55	65 2.31 57	73 2.07 55	42 35.76 57	21	57
Neurotics (Na, Nx)	39 1.69 18	44 1.92 18	50 2.76 18	72 2.26 18	59 2.16 17	72 47.94 18	33	18
Dependents (Ap, Cfm)	40 1.50 15	33 1.95 15	60 2.65 15	53 2.66 15	36 2.37 14	60 35.00 15	50	14
Situationals (Se, Ci)	26 1.26 19	63 2.12 19	58 2.62 19	50 2.45 16	74 1.89 19	21 28.75 19	16	19

$\chi^2 = 7.69^{**}$; $\chi^2 = 11.28^{**}$; $\chi^2 = 6.46^*$

Table 8-4: *(continued)*

	Fear			Sees Help			Has Friends			Communicates			Participates			Stress (CESD)			Stress	
Classification System	%[a]	$\bar{X}$	N[b]	%[b]	$\bar{X}$	N[b]	%[c]	$\bar{X}$	N[b]	%[d]	$\bar{X}$	N[b]	%[e]	$\bar{X}$	N[b]	%[f]	$\bar{X}$	N[b]	%[g]	N[b]
I-level (Interview Method)																				
I-4 Na	32	1.35	22	55	1.90	20	55	2.77	20	64	2.21	22	77	1.82	21	46	31.50	22	14	22
I-4 Nx	36	1.38	22	50	1.95	20	46	2.63	22	70	2.27	20	48	2.47	21	55	46.66	22	41	22
I-4 Se	56	1.84	9	56	1.66	9	44	3.35	9	89	2.29	9	89	1.53	9	56	37.50	9	38	8
I-4 Ci	60	1.67	10	60	1.78	10	33	3.22	9	30	2.85	10	60	2.38	10	60	43.89	10	40	10
I-5 Na	27	1.71	11	36	2.08	11	60	2.33	10	40	2.70	10	64	2.05	11	36	32.23	11	18	11
I-5 Nx	44	1.69	16	44	1.95	16	38	2.93	16	56	2.45	16	53	2.18	15	56	41.00	16	31	16
I-5 Se	22	1.19	9	33	2.19	9	44	2.94	9	56	2.61	9	67	2.11	9	44	35.00	11	33	9
I-5 Ci	9	1.12	11	82	1.67	11	64	2.38	11	82	1.83	11	79	2.05	9	9	20.00	11	0	11
	Mult. R = .36*									χ^2 = 11.90*						Mult. R = .39**				
										Mult. R = .38**										
I-level (Collapsed levels)																				
I-4	41	1.46	63	54	1.93	59	47	2.73	62	64	2.41	62	66	2.16	62	52	38.48	63	31	62
I-5	28	1.48	47	49	1.88	47	50	2.88	46	59	2.32	46	64	2.01	44	38	34.39	47	21	47
	Tau$_b$ = -.14*															Tau$_b$ = -.14*				
I-level (Collapsed Personality Subtypes)																				
Situtional	39	1.49	18	50	1.94	18	44	3.09	18	72	2.46	18	78	1.84	18	50	36.18	18	35	17
Neurotic Anxious	40	1.51	38	40	1.95	38	42	2.77	38	64	2.36	36	50	2.34	36	55	44.08	38	37	38
Neurotic Acting-out	30	1.46	33	49	1.96	33	56	2.64	32	56	2.35	32	73	1.90	33	42	31.78	33	15	33
Cultural Identifier	33	1.39	21	48	1.72	21	50	2.80	20	57	2.34	21	68	2.22	19	33	31.94	21	19	21
													Mult. R = .25*			Tau$_c$ = -.16**	Tau$_c$ = -.18**			
																Mult. R = .28**				

[a] Percent scoring above 1.40, indicating relatively high fear.

[b] Percent scoring below 1.85, indicating inability or reluctance to seek help from others.

[c] Percent scoring below 2.67, indicating limited tendencies to form supportive friendships with other inmates.

[d] Percent scoring below 2.67, indicating limited communication with staff.

[e] Percent scoring below 2.50, indicating limited participation in prison activities as a coping strategy.

[f] Percent scoring above 38.00 on the CESD Stress Scale, indicating relatively high stress.

[g] Percent reporting stress ranging from excessive worrying to stress that interferes with living.

* $p \leq .10$

** $p \leq .05$

*** $p \leq .01$

ties with other inmates, (*b*) are more likely to find that program participation helps them to cope with imprisonment, and (*c*) still experience significant problems with stress. Together, the findings suggest that these inmates may be an important group to target for supportive programming.

As discussed earlier, limited cell sizes for the **Megargee MMPI-based system** complicated the task of interpreting results for the uncollapsed types. When we collapsed similar types, however, one of the most obvious findings concerned the high stress scores and stress levels reported by inmates classified as How. Average CESD scores were significantly higher (multiple r = .30, p ≤ .10; χ^2 = 12.71, p ≤ .05) than for the other inmates. In addition, 54% of the How types reported difficulty in coping with stress, whereas proportions for the other types did not exceed 30%. This finding strongly supports Megargee's description of type How and confirms previous research.

A test of the relationship between the collapsed MMPI types and "Has Friends" reveals that the least disturbed inmates (Easy and Item) and those classified into the neurotic types (Baker, George, and Jupiter) were significantly more likely than others to form friendships with other inmates (tau$_c$ = .17, p ≤ .10). The inmates least likely to report support or help from others were types Charlie and Foxtrot, the committed criminal types. This finding is interesting in light of the observation that the committed criminal types are also higher than expected on reports of fear and stress. One would expect them to be somewhat more experienced with prison life.[6]

Across tests of **Conceptual Level** and stress, more low-CL inmates (CL-1) than others appear to indicate difficulties. CL-1 inmates were significantly more likely than others to report high levels of fear (tau$_c$ = -.15, p ≤ .05) and stress (on the CL$_5$ measure) (tau$_c$ = -.20, p ≤ .05, multiple r = .29, p ≤ .05). In addition, the relationship between Conceptual Level and the ordinal measure of level of stress experienced in the prison setting was significant for both the CL$_3$ measure (tau$_c$ = -.18, p ≤ .05) and the CL$_5$ measure (tau$_c$ = -.14, p ≤ .05). Although most tests of the relationship between Conceptual Level and participation in programs and activities were insignificant, we found that CL-1 inmates were significantly more likely than others to report that participation helped them (tau$_c$ = -.12, p ≤ .10).

Analyses of the **Jesness Interview I-level** types were plagued by some of the same distribution difficulties that were evident for the Megargee MMPI-based data. Cell frequencies for six of the nine types were less than 15. This situation is particularly frustrating because a cursory overview of findings for the uncollapsed types revealed that I_4 Neurotic Anxious (Nx) inmates, in particular, experienced comparatively high levels of fear and stress, but it is not possible to make inferences for as few as five cases. A similar result occurs for the measures of level. With only five I_2 inmates, none of the tests were significant; yet these five inmates appeared to have high stress scores and limited abilities to interact and participate in ways that would help them cope with prison life. Combining them with the next highest level would serve only to obscure their distinctiveness. Despite their small numbers, I_2s may be evidencing some important patterns. Results for both the Nx and the I_2 inmates are consistent with their type descriptions.

When personality types are collapsed, results are significant for four tests. As with the similar types on other systems, neurotics (Nx and Na) and dependents (Ap and Cfm) were significantly more likely than others to report problems with stress ($\chi^2 = 6.46$, p ≤ .10) and to receive comparatively high scores on the CESD stress scale ($\chi^2 = 11.28$, p ≤ .05). They also were higher on the measure of fear than inmates classified into either the situational or the aggressive types, but the differences are not significant. In addition, however, the neurotic and the dependent groups were more likely to participate in prison programs and activities that they found to be helpful ($\chi^2 = 7.69$, p ≤ .05).

Finally, we observed a weak relationship ($tau_c = -.16$, p ≤ .10) between the collapsed personality types and the measure of friendships with other inmates, finding that the aggressive inmates (Aa, Cfc, and Mp) were slightly more likely to form friendships than inmates in the other groups, especially the dependent and the situational groups.

As shown in table 8-4, several significant relationships are observed between the **interview-based I-level** types and these dependent variables. Moreover, cell frequencies are slightly higher, though not ideal; thus, statistical tests and interpretations for uncollapsed types are less precarious.

Again, inmates experiencing high levels of fear and stress are those whom we would expect to have such difficulties. For example, I_4Se, I_4Ci, I_5Na, and I_5Nx inmates had significantly higher scores on the fear scale than other inmates (multiple r = .36, p ≤ .10). A significant relationship was also observed between the uncollapsed types and the CESD stress measure (multiple r = .39,

$p \leq .05$). Here I_4Nx, I_4Se, I_4Ci, I_5Nx, and I_5Se inmates scored higher than others on the CESD scale. The tests of collapsed types show, as expected, that Situational and Neurotic Anxious inmates had significantly higher CESD scores (Multiple $r = .28$, $p \leq .05$) and also evidenced significantly greater difficulties with stress as they coped with prison life ($tau_c = -.18$, $p \leq .05$). Inmates also were differentiated on the fear and stress measure according to their level classifications. Significantly more I_4 inmates had high fear scores ($tau_b = -.14$, $p \leq .10$) and high CESD stress scores ($tau_b = -.14$, $p \leq .10$) than the inmates diagnosed as I_5.

We also observed significant relationships in tests of the effects of I-level on interactions. Inmates most likely to state that they communicated with staff were those classified as I_4Ci and I_5Na (multiple $r = .38$, $p \leq .10$). Those most likely to report that they participated in prison programs to help themselves cope were the Neurotic Anxious inmates (multiple $r = .25$, $p \leq .10$).

The Effects of the Classification Types on Staff Ratings

Criterion variables for this portion of the analysis were extracted from the Megargee Adjustment Ratings and the Megargee Work Performance Ratings. For the penitentiary sample, we used four 5-point scales and two nominal measures. As noted earlier, the scale scores represent sums of evaluations given at 4-, 5-, and 6-month intervals. The scales tap such qualities as emotional control, maturity, initiative, and ability to learn. In addition, staff members also were asked to indicate (yes or no) whether they had observed the inmate to be a loner or one who followed a crowd. The resulting measures show whether any of the evaluation forms furnished an affirmative answer to these two questions.

Table 8-5 shows classification correlates of the staff assessment for the penitentiary inmates. Beginning with the results for the **Quay AIMS** categories, we find significant relationships between the types and emotional control, maturity, and inmates' tendencies to follow a crowd. In all instances, Situational inmates are observed as less likely to be rated negatively than other types. A view of the uncollapsed types shows that Quay Asocial Aggressive, Neurotic Anxious, and Manipulative inmates obtained lower mean ratings on scales measuring emotional control than inmates diagnosed as Immature Dependent and Situational (multiple $r = .26$, $p \leq .05$). In keeping with the category descriptions for both types, the Immature Dependent and the Neurotic Anxious inmates were more

Table 8-5: Effects of Classification Types on Staff Ratings, Penitentiary Sample

	Staff Ratings																	
	Emotional Control			Maturity			Initiative			Learning Ability			Loner		Follows Crowd	
Classification System	%[a]	$\bar{X}$	N[c]	%[a]	$\bar{X}$	N[c]	%[a]	$\bar{X}$	N[c]	%[a]	$\bar{X}$	N[c]	%[d]	N[c]	%[d]	N[c]
Quay AIMS																
Asocial Aggressive	29	2.94	21	19	3.06	21	14	3.41	21	14	3.51	21	14	21	19	21
Immature Dependent	10	3.20	10	20	3.10	10	10	3.48	10	10	3.31	10	10	10	40	10
Neurotic Anxious	30	2.92	23	39	2.95	23	9	3.64	23	0	3.68	23	22	23	22	23
Manipulator	20	3.02	41	15	3.09	41	15	3.50	41	10	3.51	41	7	41	12	41
Situational	9	3.19	53	13	3.21	53	9	3.46	53	6	3.60	53	11	53	6	53
	Mult. R = .26**			$\chi^2 = 7.75*$											$\chi^2 = 10.26**$	
Quay AIMS (Collapsed Categories)																
Aa/Mp	23	2.99	62	16	3.07	62	15	3.47	62	11	3.51	62	10	62	15	62
Id/Na	24	3.00	33	33	3.00	33	9	3.59	33	3	3.57	33	18	33	27	33
Situational	9	3.19	53	13	3.21	53	9	3.46	53	6	3.60	53	11	53	6	53
	$Tau_c = .12**$ Mult. R = .21**			$\chi^2 = 5.91**$											$\chi^2 = 7.81**$	
Megargee MMPI-Based Taxonomy																
Able	19	3.02	32	28	3.07	32	16	2.34	32	9	3.51	32	15	32	6	32
Baker	17	2.94	6	33	2.78	6	17	3.33	6	17	3.33	6	0	6	33	6
Charlie	15	3.00	13	8	3.03	13	15	3.30	13	23	3.33	13	0	13	15	13
Delta	13	3.17	23	17	3.23	23	13	3.42	23	4	3.56	23	13	23	9	23
Easy	0	3.11	11	0	3.20	11	0	3.33	11	9	3.43	11	9	11	18	11
Foxtrot	18	3.00	11	18	2.94	11	27	3.48	11	9	3.64	11	0	11	36	11

Table 8-5: *(continued)*

	Staff Ratings															
	Emotional Control			Maturity			Initiative			Learning Ability			Loner		Follows Crowd	
Classification System	%^{a}	X̄	N^c	%^{a}	X̄	N^c	%^{a}	X̄	N^c	%^{a}	X̄	N^c	%^{d}	N^c	%^{d}	N^c
George	7	3.14	14	14	3.21	14	0	3.71	14	7	3.66	14	21	14	0	14
How	14	3.05	22	23	3.05	22	13	3.63	23	9	3.66	23	14	22	4	23
Iem	22	3.07	27	19	3.16	27	4	3.74	26	4	3.77	26	15	27	15	26
Jupiter	0	3.08	4	25	2.96	4	25	3.64	4	0	3.58	4	0	4	25	4
Megargee MMPI-Based Taxonomy (Collapsed Categories)																
Charlie/Foxtrot (Committed Criminal)	17	3.00	24	13	2.99	24	21	3.39	24	17	3.47	24	0	24	25	24
Able/Delta (Character Disorder)	16	3.08	55	24	3.14	55	15	3.38	55	7	3.53	55	15	55	7	55
How (Most Disturbed)	14	3.05	22	23	3.04	22	13	3.64	23	9	3.65	23	14	22	4	23
Baker/George/Jupiter (Neurotic)	8	3.08	24	21	3.06	24	8	3.61	24	8	3.56	24	13	24	13	24
Item/Easy (Least Disturbed)	16	3.08	38	13	3.17	38	3	3.62	37	5	3.67	37	13	38	16	37
							Tau$_c$ = .13***									
Conceptual Level—CL3																
CL-1	17	3.05	41	20	3.02	41	17	3.38	41	12	3.49	41	12	41	12	41
CL-2	15	3.01	82	20	3.03	82	11	3.51	82	6	3.59	82	9	82	12	82
CL-3	12	3.23	26	19	3.36	26	4	3.72	26	12	3.71	26	23	26	15	26
	Mult. R = .20**			Mult. R = .23**			Tau$_c$ = .09**									

Conceptual Level—CL5

CL-1	22	2.97	27	26	2.92	27	15	3.41	26	12	3.60	26	7	27	15	26
CL-2	13	3.06	102	19	3.10	102	12	3.50	103	8	3.42	103	13	102	12	103
CL-3	15	3.18	20	15	3.25	20	5	3.67	20	10	3.63	20	15	20	15	20

Jesness Inventory I-level

I-2 Aa	0	3.13	5	40	2.93	5	0	3.40	5	20	3.00	5	6	5	20	5
I-2 Ap	33	3.00	3	0	3.00	3	0	3.67	3	33	3.22	3	33	3	0	3
I-3 Cfm	11	3.09	19	21	3.03	19	10	3.58	20	15	2.46	20	11	19	15	20
I-3 Mp	34	2.98	32	31	3.02	32	23	3.45	31	13	3.56	31	16	32	3	31
I-3 Cfc	16	3.00	43	12	3.06	43	14	3.31	43	9	3.44	43	2	43	19	43
I-4 Se	0	3.20	21	10	3.23	21	0	3.73	21	5	3.73	21	19	21	14	21
I-4 Na	16	3.08	19	26	3.09	19	11	3.47	19	5	3.70	19	5	19	16	19
I-4 Nx	14	2.95	7	29	3.02	7	0	3.87	7	0	3.86	7	27	7	0	7
I-4 Ci	0	3.44	3	0	3.67	3	0	4.11	3	0	4.22	3	33	3	0	3

$Tau_c = .10**$

Jesness Inventory (Collapsed Levels)

I-2	13	3.08	8	25	2.96	8	0	3.50	8	13	3.08	8	25	8	13	8
I-3	21	3.01	94	20	3.04	94	16	3.41	94	21	3.48	94	9	94	13	94
I-4	8	3.13	50	18	3.28	50	4	3.67	50	8	3.76	50	16	50	12	50

$Tau_c = .10**$ $\chi^2 = 5.76*$ $Tau_c = .07*$ $Tau_c = .10**$
$Mult. R = .18*$ $Mult. R = .26***$

Jesness Inventory (Collapsed Personality Subtypes)

Aggressives (Aa, Cfc, Mp)	23	3.00	80	21	3.04	80	17	3.37	79	11	3.46	79	9	80	13	79
Neurotics (Na, Nx)	15	3.04	26	27	3.07	26	8	3.58	26	4	3.74	26	12	26	12	26
Dependents (Ap, Cfm)	14	3.08	22	18	3.03	22	9	3.59	23	17	3.42	23	14	22	13	23
Situationals (Se, Ci)	0	3.23	24	8	3.28	24	0	3.78	24	4	3.79	24	21	24	13	24

$\chi^2 = 7.00$ $Tau_c = .13**$ $Tau_c = -.08*$
$Tau_c = .16***$ $Mult. R = .22**$
$Mult. R = .20*$ $Mult. R = .22***$

Table 8-5: (continued)

	Staff Ratings																	
	Emotional Control			Maturity			Initiative			Learning Ability			Loner		Follows Crowd			
Classification System	%[a]	X̄	N[c]	%[a]	X̄	N[c]	%[a]	X̄	N[c]	%[a]	X̄	N[c]	%[d]	N[c]	%[d]	N[c]		
I-level (Interview Method)																		
I-4 Na	30	2.96	37	19	3.12	37	13	3.48	38	16	3.54	38	16	37	5	38		
I-4 Nx	22	3.09	32	28	3.05	32	10	3.44	31	7	3.53	31	9	32	19	31		
I-4 Se	13	2.98	16	0	3.15	16	13	3.44	16	6	3.47	16	6	16	6	16		
I-4 Ci	18	2.98	17	24	3.12	17	12	3.33	17	6	3.31	17	6	17	24	17		
I-5 Na	17	3.08	18	33	2.95	18	17	3.39	18	17	3.42	18	17	18	22	18		
I-5 Nx	13	3.18	24	17	3.09	24	13	3.47	24	4	3.57	24	4	24	4	24		
I-5 Se	0	3.11	11	0	3.35	11	0	4.15	11	0	4.27	11	27	11	27	11		
I-5 Ci	0	3.16	21	19	3.05	21	14	3.70	21	5	3.78	21	10	21	5	21		
	($\chi^2 = 12.19^*$)						Mult. R = .27*			Mult. R = .32**					($\chi^2 = 12.04^*$)			
I-level (Collapsed Levels)																		
I-4	23	3.02	102	20	3.07	102	12	3.42	102	23	3.49	102	11	102	13	102		
I-5	8	3.12	74	19	3.13	74	12	3.63	74	8	3.72	74	12	74	12	74		
	$\chi^2 = 5.49^{**}$						Mult. R = .14*			$\chi^2 = 5.49^{**}$								
	$Tau_b = .19^{***}$									$Tau_b = .19^{***}$								
										Mult. R = .17**								
I-level (Collapsed Personality Subtypes)																		
Situational	7	3.03	27	0	3.23	27	7	3.73	27	4	3.80	27	15	27	15	27		
Neurotic Anxious	18	3.13	56	23	3.07	56	11	3.46	55	6	3.55	55	7	56	13	55		
Neurotic Acting-out	26	2.99	55	24	3.06	55	14	3.45	56	16	3.50	56	16	55	11	56		
Cultural Identifier	8	3.08	38	21	3.08	38	13	3.54	38	5	3.57	38	8	38	13	38		
	$\chi^2 = 6.95^*$			$\chi^2 = 7.74^{**}$						$\chi^2 = 6.08^*$								
				$Tau_c = -.11^{**}$														

a Percent rated below average, 3.00, on this scale

b Scales range from negative behavior (1 and 2) to average (3) to positive behavior (4 and 5)

c N in the category.

d Percent identified by staff.

* $p \leq .10$

** $p \leq .05$

*** $p \leq .01$

likely to receive low scores on staffs' ratings of maturity, and the Situational group was more likely to receive high ratings (χ^2 = 7.75, p ≤ .10). Also as expected on the basis of category descriptions, Immature Dependent inmates were more likely to be viewed as following the crowd. When types were collapsed, differences between the combined Immature Dependent and Neurotic Anxious inmates and the other types were clearer (χ^2 = 7.81, p ≤ .05).[7]

The only relationship between the **Megargee MMPI-based** types and staff ratings occurred when we collapsed types and tested the relationship between the types and staff assessments of initiative (tau$_c$ = 13, p ≤ .01). The most favorable ratings were received by the combined neurotic types (Baker, George, and Jupiter) and by the combined least disturbed types (Easy and Item). Patterns and results from the other tests were less clear.[8]

Significant findings for tests of the relationships between **Conceptual Level** and staff ratings are attributable primarily to the fact that CL-3 inmates received higher ratings than CL-1 or CL-2 inmates on most measures. Results were significant for three of the tests, namely tests of the relationship between CL$_3$ and: (*a*) emotional control (multiple r = .20, ≤ .05), (*b*) maturity (multiple r = .23, p ≤ .05), and (*c*) initiative (tau$_c$ = .09, p ≤ .05). The last of these relationships was weak.

Similar findings were observed on another cognitive developmental construct, the **Jesness Inventory** measure of I-level. Again, inmates classified at I$_4$, the highest level on the system, were more likely than others to receive favorable staff ratings of emotional control (tau$_c$ = .10. p ≤ .05), initiative (multiple r = .18, p ≤ .10), and learning ability (multiple r = .26, p ≤ .01). Mean maturity scale scores for this group were also higher, but the results were not significant.

Tests of the collapsed Jesness personality types showed a pattern in which situational inmates again received substantially higher evaluations than other inmates, including significantly higher ratings of emotional control (multiple r = .20, p ≤ .10), initiative (multiple r = .22, p ≤ .05), and learning ability (multiple r = .22, p ≤ .05). Differences on the maturity scale were once again apparent but not significant. A test of the relationship between personality types and staff evaluations showed that situational inmates had a somewhat greater tendency to be viewed as loners and that aggressive inmates were least likely to be viewed as such (tau$_c$ = .08, p ≤ .10).

We observed several significant findings for tests of the relationship between the **I-level interview** system and staff ratings. Here, type frequencies and variabilities were adequate for multiple regression tests of the uncollapsed types. Two multiple regression tests were observed to be significant: the relationships between I-level and initiative (multiple r = .27,p ≤ .10) and between I-level and learning ability (multiple r = .32, p ≤ .05). Results showed that I_5 inmates generally received higher ratings than I_4 inmates, but I_5 Situational inmates in particular were rated substantially higher than others. Chi-square tests of the uncollapsed types are reported with caution because the expected cell frequencies were limited. Even so, we find proportionately more I_4Na and I_4Nx inmates having difficulty with emotional control and proportionately fewer I_5Se and I_5Ci inmates receiving low ratings (χ^2 =12.19, p ≤ .10). The relationship between I-level and the measure "Follows Crowd" was also significant, but in ways that are difficult to interpret.

Tests of collapsed personality types revealed significant and expected findings. Not surprisingly, Neurotic Acting-out inmates, followed by Neurotic Anxious inmates, had proportionately more unfavorable ratings on the emotional control scale than others (χ^2 = 6.95, p ≤ .10). None of the Situational inmates at either level received unfavorable ratings on the maturity scale (tau_c = -.11, p ≤ .05). Further, inmates diagnosed as Neurotic Acting-out were slightly more likely to be rated as having a limited ability to learn (χ^2 = 6.08, p ≤ .10).

Tests of the relationship between the developmental levels and staff measures showed a pattern whereby I_4 inmates were more likely to receive lower ratings of their emotional control, maturity, initiative, and learning ability. These findings are similar to those observed for inmates classified at lower stages on the other developmental measures, on Conceptual Level, and on the Jesness Inventory I-level measures.

PRISON CAMP

The Effects of the Classification Types on
Interview-Based Measures of Inmates' Needs

For the prison camp, this analysis involved only five dependent measures. Not surprisingly, the sixth measure, inmates' need for safety, characterized very few inmates in this minimum-security setting. Table 8-6 shows that few of the tests produced significant results.

Table 8-6: Cross-Tabular Analysis of the Relationship between Classification Types and Inmates' Needs, Prison Camp Sample

	Prison-Based Needs									
	Privacy		Structure		Feedback		Social Stimulation		Support	
Classification System	%[a]	N[b]	%[a]	N[b]	%[c]	N[b]	%[c]	N[b]	%[c]	N[b]
Quay AIMS										
Asocial Aggressive	56	9	44	9	11	9	22	9	22	9
Immature Dependent	50	6	0	6	0	6	17	6	0	6
Neurotic Anxious	33	3	0	3	67	3	0	3	0	3
Manipulator	36	22	18	22	32	22	23	22	9	22
Situational	35	82	20	82	20	82	21	82	29	82
Quay AIMS (Collapsed Categories)										
Aa/Mp	42	31	26	31	26	31	23	31	13	31
Id/Na	44	9	0	9	22	9	11	9	0	9
Situational	35	82	20	82	20	82	21	82	29	82
									$\chi^2 = 6.30$**	
									$Tau_c = -.16$**	
Megargee MMPI-Based Taxonomy										
Able	31	26	27	26	19	26	19	26	15	26
Baker	17	6	17	6	17	6	22	6	17	6
Charlie	14	7	29	7	43	7	43	7	27	7
Delta	25	8	38	8	25	8	0	8	50	8
Easy	63	16	6	16	19	16	6	16	38	16
Foxtrot	0	4	0	4	0	4	0	4	25	4
George	44	18	11	18	22	18	28	18	11	18

	C1	C2	C3	C4	C5	Total
How	50	19	19	13	31	16
Item	32	20	17	19	14	65
Jupiter	0	50	50	0	50	2
Megargee MMPI-Based Taxonomy (Collapsed Categories)						
Charlie/Foxtrot (Committed Criminal)	9	18	27	27	27	11
Able/Delta (Character Disorder)	29	29	21	15	24	34
How (Most Disturbed)	50	19	19	13	31	16
Baker/George/Jupiter (Neurotic)	35	15	23	27	15	26
Item/Easy (Least Disturbed)	38	17	17	16	19	81
$Tau_c = -.11*$						
Conceptual Level—CL3						
CL-1	31	19	8	12	19	26
CL-2	37	22	22	20	21	123
CL-3	29	4	21	17	21	24
$Tau_c = .07*$						
Conceptual Level—CL5						
CL-1	35	18	12	12	24	17
CL-2	35	21	21	21	21	145
CL-3	30	0	10	10	20	10

Table 8-6: (continued)

					Prison-Based Needs					
	Privacy		Structure		Feedback		Social Stimulation		Support	
Classification System	%a	Nb	%a	Nb	%c	Nb	%c	Nb	%c	Nb
Jesness Inventory I-level										
I-2 Aa	50	2	0	2	0	2	0	2	50	2
I-2 Ap	20	5	60	5	60	5	20	5	60	5
I-3 Cfm	46	28	14	28	11	28	11	28	29	28
I-3 Mp	32	37	14	37	27	37	27	37	11	37
I-3 Cfc	28	32	16	32	9	32	6	32	19	32
I-4 Se	35	29	21	29	14	29	14	29	31	29
I-4 Na	50	16	25	16	19	16	31	16	19	16
I-4 Nx	25	16	19	16	31	16	25	16	6	16
I-4 Ci	20	5	40	5	20	5	20	5	20	5
Jesness Inventory (Collapsed Levels)										
I-2	29	7	43	7	43	7	14	7	57	7
I-3	35	97	14	97	17	97	16	97	19	97
I-4	35	66	23	66	20	66	21	66	21	66
			$\chi^2 = 4.53^*$						$\chi^2 = 8.21^{**}$	
	$Tau_c = -.08^*$									
Jesness Inventory (Collapsed Personality Subtypes)										
Aggressives (Aa, Cfc, Mp)	31	71	14	71	18	71	17	71	16	71
Neurotics (Na, Nx)	37	32	22	32	25	32	28	32	13	32
Dependents (Ap, Cfm)	42	33	21	33	18	33	12	33	33	33
Situationals (Se, Ci)	32	34	24	34	15	34	15	34	29	34
									$\chi^2 = 7.12^*$	
									$Tau_c = -.14^{**}$	

I-level (Interview Method)

	%	%	%	%	%	n[b]
I-4 Na	40	17	23	15	13	48
I-4 Nx	32	11	32	16	21	19
I-4 Se	29	19	11	22	36	36
I-4 Ci	33	14	14	19	19	21
I-5 Na	30	40	10	20	10	10
I-5 Nx	50	33	21	21	25	24
I-5 Se	24	8	24	24	20	25
I-5 Ci	50	0	0	0	0	2

I-level (Collapsed Levels)

	%	%	%	%	%	n[b]
I-4	34	16	19	18	22	124
I-5	36	23	20	21	20	61

I-level (Collapsed Personality Subtypes)

	%	%	%	%	%	n[b]
Situational	26	15	16	23	30	61
Neurotic Anxious	42	23	26	19	23	43
Neurotic Acting-out	38	21	21	16	12	58
Cultural Identifier	35	13	13	17	17	23

$Tau_c = .14$***

[a] Percent yes (there is a need or some indication of a need).
[b] Number of inmates in the category.
[c] Percent yes (there is a need).
* $p \leq .10$
** $p \leq .05$
*** $p \leq .01$

As with previous tests of the **Quay AIMS** prison camp data, these tests were marred by limited variability; very few inmates were classified as Immature Dependent, Asocial Aggressive, or Neurotic Anxious. As in the findings for the penitentiary sample, however, Situational inmates were significantly more likely to express a need for programmatic support (tau_c = -.16, p ≤ .05).

With the exception of one test, the **Megargee MMPI-based** system did not differentiate inmates according to prison needs. Fifty percent of inmates classified as How were rated as having a need for privacy. This proportion was considerably higher than among the other types (tau_c = -.11, p ≤ .10).[9]

We find only one significant relationship between the **Conceptual Level** types and prison needs, namely the test of the relationship between CL_3 and need for structure. Inmates classified as CL-3 were significantly less likely to show a need for structured rules and expectations. Although this relationship was weak, it is consistent with the data for the penitentiary sample and pertinent to the principles of Conceptual Level theory (Hunt 1971).

Significant relationships between the **Jesness** measures of I-level and prison needs for structure and programmatic support must be viewed with caution, because most of the difference is attributable to seven inmates diagnosed as I_2. Nevertheless, the results support those observed for the Conceptual Level tests.

Two relationships between collapsed personality types and prison needs were significant. Aggressive inmates (Aa, Cfc, and Mp) were significantly less likely to show a need for structure than the other inmates (tau_c = -.08, p ≤ .10). Also situational (Ci and Se) and dependent (Ap and Cfm) inmates were more likely to evidence a need for programmatic support (tau_c = -.14, p ≤ .05).

Findings for the **I-level interview method** occasionally were observed to occur in the expected direction, but only one test was significant: the relationship between collapsed personality types and need for programmatic support. In this case, Situational and Neurotic Anxious inmates were significantly more likely than others to show a need for such support.[10]

The Effects of the Classification Types on Interview-Based
Measures of Inmates' Attitudes toward
Treatment and Incarceration

We include only two dependent variables for this analysis because, again, very few minimum-security inmates were considered by raters to be institutionalized. A cursory overview of table 8-7 shows few noteworthy findings based on tests of either the **Quay AIMS** or the **MMPI** data. Although both tests of the collapsed MMPI types produced significant results, the differences are attributable to the committed criminal types (Charlie and Foxtrot), a category that included only eleven inmates. In both cases, inmates in the Charlie/Foxtrot category were more likely to see others as willing to help and to be oriented to the notion of rehabilitation.[11]

On tests of the **Conceptual Level** types, we find results that mirror those for the penitentiary. That is, inmates classified as CL-1 and CL-2 were more likely to see others as willing to help (not significant) and significantly more likely to place a priority on the notion of rehabilitation ($tau_c = .18$, $p \le .01$).

Both of the **Jesness I-level** tests of the effects of level were significant. Once again, however, most of the difference is attributable to I_2, which contained only seven inmates and thus rendered the tests unstable. Tests of the collapsed personality types once again find dependent types more likely than the other types to view others as helpful. These results, however, are not significant.

Most tests of the **I-level interview** measures were found insignificant, except for a test of the relationship between the collapsed personality types and orientation to rehabilitation. Neurotic Acting-out inmates and Cultural Identifiers were slightly more likely than others to view rehabilitation as a priority for their sentences.

The Effects of the Classification Types on Self-Report Indices of Stress and Interaction Patterns

Table 8-8 shows relationships between the classification types and self-report indices measuring stress and interactions. Two tests of the **Quay AIMS** system produced significant results. Situational inmates were more likely than the other types of inmates to seek or obtain help from others ($tau_c = .15$, $p \le .10$). In contrast to the penitentiary sample, Immature Dependent and Neurotic Anxious inmates (combined) were less likely to report that program participation helped them do time. Only seven inmates, however, were classified as these types. None of the tests using stress measures as criterion variables produced significant results. Although Immature Dependent and Neurotic Anxious inmates reported difficulties with stress in this setting as well as in the penitentiary,

Table 8-7: Cross-Tabular Analysis of the Relationship between Classification Variables and Additional Treatment-Related Measures, Prison Camp Sample

Classification System	Interview Measures			
	Sees Others as Willing to Help		Oriented to Rehabilitation	
	%[a]	N	%[b]	N
Quay AIMS				
Asocial Aggressive	22	9	11	9
Immature Dependent	50	6	17	6
Neurotic Anxious	50	2	0	3
Manipulator	32	22	18	22
Situational	23	82	21	81
Quay AIMS (Collapsed Categories)				
Aa/Mp	29	31	16	31
Id/Na	50	8	11	9
Situational	23	82	21	81
Megargee MMPI-Based Taxonomy				
Able	31	26	27	26
Baker	50	6	33	6
Charlie	71	7	71	7
Delta	38	8	25	8
Easy	13	16	13	16
Foxtrot	50	4	0	4
George	11	18	28	18
How	13	15	13	16
Item	22	65	11	65
Jupiter	50	2	0	2
Megargee MMPI-Based Taxonomy (Collapsed Categories)				
Charlie/Foxtrot (Committed Criminal)	64	11	46	11
Able/Delta (Character Disorder)	32	34	27	34
How (Most Disturbed)	13	15	13	16
Baker/George/Jupiter (Neurotic)	23	26	27	26
Item/Easy (Least Disturbed)	20	81	11	81

$\chi^2 = 12.01**$ $\chi^2 = 10.99**$

$Tau_c = .17***$ $Tau_c = .18***$

Table 8-7: *(continued)*

Classification System	Sees Others as Willing to Help		Oriented to Rehabilitation	
	%[a]	N	%[b]	N
Conceptual Level—CL3				
CL-1	28	25	36	25
CL-2	30	122	18	123
CL-3	13	24	0	24
			$\chi^2 = 10.75^{***}$	
			$Tau_c = .18^{***}$	
Conceptual Level—CL5				
CL-1	25	16	47	17
CL-2	29	144	15	144
CL-3	10	10	0	10
			$\chi^2 = 12.88^{***}$	
			$Tau_c = .15^{***}$	
Jesness Inventory I-level				
I-2 Aa	0	2	50	2
I-2 Ap	60	5	60	5
I-3 Cfm	37	27	15	27
I-3 Mp	32	37	16	37
I-3 Cfc	22	32	22	32
I-4 Se	24	29	10	29
I-4 Na	13	15	25	16
I-4 Nx	31	16	6	16
I-4 Ci	0	5	20	5
Jesness Inventory (Collapsed Levels)				
I-2	43	7	57	7
I-3	30	96	18	96
I-4	22	65	14	66
	$Tau_c = .10^{*}$		$\chi_2 = 8.21^{**}$	
			$Tau_c = .10^{**}$	
Jesness Inventory (Collapsed Personality Subtypes)				
Aggressives (Aa, Cfc, Mp)	27	71	20	71
Neurotics (Na, Nx)	23	31	16	32
Dependents (Ap, Cfm)	41	32	22	32
Situationals (Se, Ci)	21	34	12	32

Table 8-7: *(continued)*

Classification System	Interview Measures			
	Sees Others as Willing to Help		Oriented to Rehabilitation	
	%[a]	N	%[b]	N
I-level (Interview Method)				
I-4 Na	17	47	21	48
I-4 Nx	16	19	5	19
I-4 Se	39	36	14	36
I-4 Ci	33	21	24	21
I-5 Na	40	10	30	10
I-5 Nx	33	24	25	24
I-5 Se	25	24	12	25
I-5 Ci	50	2	0	2
I-level (Collapsed Levels)				
I-4	26	123	17	124
I-5	32	60	20	61
I-level (Collapsed Personality Subtypes)				
Situational	33	60	13	61
Neurotic Anxious	26	43	16	43
Neurotic Acting-out	21	57	22	58
Cultural Identifier	35	23	22	23
			$Tau_c = -.09*$	

[a] Percent yes.

[b] Percent yes or somewhat.

* $p \le .10$

** $p \le .05$

*** $p \le .01$

Table 8-8: Effects of Classification Types on Self-Report Prison Experience Measures, Prison Camp Sample

	Prison Experience Measures																				
	Fear			Sees Help			Has Friends			Communicates			Participates			Stress (CESD)			Stress	
Classification System	%[a]	X̄	N[b]	%[b]	X̄	N[b]	%[c]	X̄	N[b]	%[d]	X̄	N[b]	%[e]	X̄	N[b]	%[f]	X̄	N[b]	%[g]	N[b]
Quay AIMS																				
Asocial Aggressive	29	1.16	7	71	1.93	7	50	3.42	6	57	2.30	7	29	2.21	7	29	35.00	7	14	7
Immature Dependent	50	1.25	4	75	2.03	4	75	2.50	4	50	2.85	4	100	1.69	4	75	27.86	4	50	4
Neurotic Anxious	33	1.25	3	33	2.28	3	0	4.00	3	33	2.70	3	100	1.00	3	0	30.00	2	50	2
Manipulator	47	1.26	15	53	2.08	15	67	2.82	15	53	2.41	15	47	2.54	15	43	36.43	14	53	15
Situational	29	1.15	56	43	2.18	54	48	3.28	56	49	2.62	55	45	2.31	53	27	32.75	56	30	56
				Tau$_c$ = .15*									(Mult. R = .33*)							
Quay AIMS (Collapsed Categories)																				
Aa/Mp	41	1.24	22	59	2.03	22	62	3.00	22	55	2.38	22	41	2.44	22	38	36.00	21	41	22
Id/Na	43	1.22	7	57	2.12	7	43	3.28	7	43	2.62	7	100	1.46	7	50	40.00	6	50	6
Situational	29	1.16	56	43	2.18	54	48	3.00	56	49	2.80	55	45	2.31	53	27	32.75	56	30	56
													χ^2 = 8.16** Mult. R = .30**							
Megargee MMPI-Based Taxonomy																				
Able	33	1.13	15	47	2.05	15	53	3.33	15	33	2.82	15	47	2.38	15	20	26.33	15	13	15
Baker	0	1.00	5	60	1.94	5	20	3.30	5	8	2.40	5	40	2.50	5	60	46.00	5	60	5
Charlie	29	1.24	7	43	2.12	7	43	3.28	7	57	2.32	7	43	2.68	7	29	35.00	7	14	7
Delta	67	1.55	3	50	2.19	4	100	2.33	4	50	2.20	4	50	2.84	4	50	41.66	4	25	4
Easy	46	1.18	11	9	2.57	11	46	3.50	11	36	2.65	11	11	2.53	9	9	31.11	11	36	11
Foxtrot	33	1.11	3	67	2.00	3	67	2.33	3	33	2.80	3	67	2.17	3	33	26.67	3	0	3
George	18	1.08	11	73	1.76	11	70	2.50	10	82	2.00	11	55	1.88	11	30	38.12	10	36	11

Table 8-8: (continued)

Classification System	Fear %ᵃ	Fear X̄	Fear Nᵇ	Sees Help %ᵇ	Sees Help X̄	Sees Help Nᵇ	Has Friends %ᶜ	Has Friends X̄	Has Friends Nᵇ	Communicates %ᵈ	Communicates X̄	Communicates Nᵇ	Participates %ᵉ	Participates X̄	Participates Nᵇ	Stress (CESD) %ᶠ	Stress (CESD) X̄	Stress (CESD) Nᵇ	Stress %ᵍ	Stress Nᵇ
Megargee MMPI-Based Taxonomy (continued)																				
How	27	1.13	7	29	2.08	7	57	2.70	7	67	2.12	6	71	2.15	7	67	45.00	6	67	6
Item	31	1.14	42	53	2.14	40	45	3.26	42	43	2.65	42	58	2.13	41	36	35.88	42	38	42
Jupiter	(100	1.33	1)	(100	2.43	1)	(100	3.00	1)	(0	3.00	1)	(0	2.50	1)	(0	35.00	1)	(0	1)
Megargee MMPI-Based Taxonomy (Collapsed Categories)																				
Charlie/Foxtrot (Committed Criminal)	30	1.20	10	50	2.08	10	50	3.00	10	50	2.46	10	50	2.52	10	30	32.50	10	10	10
Able/Delta (Character Disktorder)	39	1.20	18	47	2.07	19	63	3.17	19	37	2.71	19	47	2.46	19	26	28.89	19	16	19
How (Most Disturbed)	29	1.13	7	29	2.08	7	57	2.70	7	67	2.12	6	71	2.15	7	67	45.00	6	67	6
Baker/George/Jupiter (Neurotic)	18	1.07	17	65	1.88	17	56	2.83	16	77	2.21	17	47	2.14	17	38	40.71	16	41	17
Item/Easy (Least Disturbed)	34	1.15	53	43	2.22	51	45	3.31	53	42	2.64	53	50	2.20	50	30	35.00	53	38	53
										$\chi^2 = 8.20^*$						$\chi^2 = 9.01^*$ $Tau_c = -.17^{**}$				
Conceptual Level—CL3																				
CL-1	20	1.13	15	40	2.06	15	73	2.94	15	57	2.26	14	46	2.45	13	31	35.00	13	31	13
CL-2	32	1.15	78	46	2.16	77	50	3.16	78	47	2.59	79	49	2.27	78	35	36.02	78	34	79
CL-3	42	1.24	19	61	2.03	18	53	3.12	19	47	2.64	19	71	2.18	17	21	30.59	19	26	19
	$Tau_c = .11^*$			$Tau_c = -.11^*$									$Tau_c = -.13^*$							

Conceptual Level - CL5

	n	M	%	n	M	%	n	M	%	n	M	%	n	M	%	n	M	%		
CL-1	33	1.15	9	33	2.07	9	67	3.08	9	56	2.27	9	50	2.33	8	25	35.84	8	13	8
CL-2	31	1.22	93	50	2.12	91	52	3.14	93	48	2.55	93	51	2.29	91	34	35.12	92	34	93
CL-3	44	1.25	9	33	2.23	9	56	3.31	9	33	2.95	9	75	2.03	8	11	29.38	9	22	9

Jesness Inventory I-level

	n	M	%	n	M	%	n	M	%	n	M	%	n	M	%	n	M	%		
I-2 Aa	0	0	0	0	0	0	0	0	0	0	0	0	0	0	0	0	0	0	0	0
I-2 Ap	33	1.34	3	33	2.00	3	67	2.83	3	67	2.00	3	100	1.66	3	67	51.67	3	33	3
I-3 Cfm	28	1.23	21	37	2.21	19	43	3.40	21	43	2.71	21	56	2.10	18	20	29.37	20	40	20
I-3 Mp	38	1.14	25	63	1.97	24	60	2.85	25	40	2.66	25	48	2.45	25	44	35.83	25	28	25
I-3 Cfc	37	1.15	16	50	2.13	16	44	3.41	16	50	2.45	16	44	2.42	16	27	32.33	15	25	16
I-4 Se	8	1.14	19	47	2.19	19	58	3.29	19	47	2.66	19	59	2.07	17	17	32.65	18	33	18
I-4 Na	46	1.06	13	23	2.31	13	67	2.90	12	62	2.41	13	46	2.21	13	31	39.08	13	23	13
I-4 Nx	50	1.27	11	46	2.18	11	64	2.75	11	50	2.32	10	55	2.14	11	55	44.00	11	55	11
I-4 Ci	0	1.17	2	67	2.14	3	33	4.00	3	68	2.20	3	67	2.08	3	0	20.00	3	0	3

Jesness Inventory (Collapsed Levels)

	n	M	%	n	M	%	n	M	%	n	M	%	n	M	%	n	M	%		
I-2	67	1.33	3	33	2.00	3	67	3.09	3	67	2.00	3	100	1.67	3	67	51.66	3	33	3
I-3	32	1.17	62	51	2.09	59	50	3.16	62	44	2.62	62	49	2.39	59	32	33.00	60	31	61
I-4	31	1.15	45	41	2.22	46	60	2.83	45	53	2.51	45	55	2.13	44	29	36.62	45	33	45

Jesness Inventory (Collapsed Personality Subtypes)

	n	M	%	n	M	%	n	M	%	n	M	%	n	M	%	n	M	%		
Aggressives (Aa, Cfc, Mp)	32	1.15	41	58	2.03	40	54	3.06	42	44	2.58	41	46	2.47	41	38	34.49	40	27	41
Neurotics (Na, Nx)	25	1.16	24	33	2.25	24	65	2.83	23	57	2.42	23	50	2.13	24	42	41.43	24	38	24
Dependents (Ap, Cfm)	38	1.24	24	36	2.18	22	46	3.37	24	46	2.60	24	62	2.09	21	26	32.90	23	39	23
Situationals (Se, Ci)	38	1.14	21	50	2.19	22	55	3.37	22	50	2.61	22	60	2.13	20	14	31.32	21	29	21

$Tau_c = -.14**$ $Tau_c = -.19**$

Table 8-8 (continued)

Classification System	Prison Experience Measures																				
	Fear			Sees Help			Has Friends			Communicates			Participates			Stress (CESD)			Stress	
	%[a]	X̄	N[b]	%[b]	X̄	N[b]	%[c]	X̄	N[b]	%[d]	X̄	N[b]	%[e]	X̄	N[b]	%[f]	X̄	N[b]	%[g]	N[b]
I-level (Interview Method)																				
I-4 Na	26	1.10	27	52	2.04	27	46	3.07	26	56	2.56	27	44	2.34	25	40	36.59	25	35	26
I-4 Nx	36	1.24	11	70	1.78	10	82	2.79	11	70	1.97	10	80	1.75	10	40	36.43	10	30	10
I-4 Se	21	1.14	24	30	2.29	23	38	3.50	24	42	2.66	24	48	2.35	23	17	29.77	24	46	24
I-4 Ci	33	1.15	9	89	1.73	9	67	2.72	9	68	2.04	9	33	2.22	9	33	32.78	9	11	9
I-5 Na	50	1.17	4	50	1.96	4	75	2.12	4	50	2.29	4	75	2.00	4	25	35.00	4	0	4
I-5 Nx	47	1.25	19	42	2.16	19	58	3.00	19	42	2.70	19	58	2.21	19	42	38.16	19	42	19
I-5 Se	31	1.16	16	31	2.41	16	42	3.60	17	29	2.83	17	63	2.18	16	24	30.00	17	29	17
I-5 Ci	50	1.16	2	50	2.00	2	100	3.00	2	50	2.90	2	0	3.24	2	50	42.50	2	0	2
	Tau$_b$ = .15**			(Mult. R = .44***)			(Mult. R = .36*)			(Mult. R = .36*)										
I-level (Collapsed Levels)																				
I-4	27	1.14	71	52	1.92	69	51	2.85	70	54	2.32	70	49	2.18	67	31	37.26	68	35	69
I-5	42	1.18	41	39	2.27	41	55	3.34	42	38	2.72	42	59	2.39	41	33	33.12	42	31	42
	Tau$_b$ = .15**			Tau$_b$ = .13*			Mult. R = .24**			Tau$_b$ = .16**										
				Mult. R = .35***						Mult. R = .27***										
I-level (Collapsed Personality Subtypes)																				
Situational	25	1.14	40	31	3.34	39	39	3.54	41	37	2.72	41	54	2.28	39	20	29.86	41	39	41
Neurotic Anxious	43	1.24	30	52	2.05	29	67	2.94	30	52	2.50	29	66	2.08	29	41	40.38	29	38	28
Neurotic Acting-out	29	1.11	31	52	2.03	31	50	2.92	30	55	2.51	31	48	2.29	29	38	36.34	29	30	30
Cultural Identifier	36	1.15	11	82	1.78	11	72	2.77	11	64	2.20	11	27	2.41	11	36	35.54	11	9	11
				Mult. R = .38***			Mult. R = .30**			Tau$_c$ = -.20**						Tau$_c$ = .17**			Tau$_c$ = -.16**	

[a] Percent scoring above 1.00, indicating relatively high fear.

[b] Percent scoring 2.00 or below, indicating inability or reluctance to seek help from others.

[c] Percent scoring 3.00 or below, indicating few tendencies to form friendships with other inmates.

[d] Percent scoring 2.40 or below, indicating limited communication with staff.

[e] Percent scoring 2.25 or below, indicating limited participation in prison activities *as a coping strategy.*

[f] Percent scoring 40 or higher on the CESD Stress Scale, indicating relatively high stress.

[g] Percent reporting stress ranging from excessive worrying to stress that interferes with living.

( ) Results must be viewed with caution because of limited cell frequencies.

* $p \leq .10$

** $p \leq .05$

*** $p \leq .01$

scores were lower for Situational inmates in the camp than for Situational inmates in the penitentiary.

Although we are generalizing from only 6 inmates, prison camp inmates classified as How on the **Megargee MMPI-based system** were significantly more likely than others to report difficulties in coping with stress in prison (tau$_c$ = .17, p ≤ .05). Again they had the highest mean stress scores (CESD), but differences were not significant. Tests of the relationship between the Megargee collapsed types and the communications measure found that significantly more of the inmates classified as How or as one of the neurotic types expressed a reluctance to communicate with staff (χ^2 = 8.20, p ≤ .10).[12]

Results of the tests of **Conceptual Level** found that significantly more CL-3 inmates than others experienced difficulties with fear (tau$_c$ = .11, p ≤ .10). In addition, CL-3 inmates indicated less propensity to participate in prison activities as a means of coping with prison life (tau$_c$ = –.13, p ≤ .10). They also were less likely to perceive that others in the institution were willing to help them. These interpretations are based on the CL3 measure of Conceptual Level, because the CL5 measure was distributed unevenly. On the CL$_5$ variable, most of the inmates were diagnosed as CL-2.

Only three inmates were classified as I$_2$ on the tests of the **Jesness I-level** system. It appears that these inmates had a much more difficult time with fear and stress, and were more isolated than, the other inmates. Statistical tests for the I$_2$ inmates were not possible, however, because of these limited cell sizes. I$_4$Nx inmates evidenced atypically high proportions for stress and fear and a greater tendency to participate in programs. When the personality types were collapsed, the neurotic types combined showed a significantly greater likelihood of receiving high stress scores (tau$_c$ = –.19, p ≤ .05) or of stating that participating helped them to cope with prison life (tau$_c$ = –.14, p ≤ .05).

Similar findings were observed for Neurotic Anxious inmates as classified by the **I-level interview** measure. Neurotic Anxious inmates (I$_4$ and I$_5$ combined) were significantly more likely than others to receive high CESD stress scores (tau$_c$ = .17, p ≤ .05). Along with the Situational inmates, they also were more likely to report difficulty with stress in prison (tau$_c$ = –.16, p ≤ .05). On interaction measures, several tests were observed to be significant, but in these cases the differences were mostly attributable to the responses of the Cultural Identifiers and the Situational inmates. These results find Situational inmates significantly more likely to seek help from others (multiple r = .38, p ≤ .01), to form friendships (multiple r = .30, p ≤ .05), and to communicate with staff (tau$_c$ = –.20, p ≤ .05). Results were the opposite for the 11 Cultural Identifiers, suggesting a more isolated pattern.[13]

The Effects of the Classification Types on Staff Ratings

The final section of this analysis examines classification correlates of staff ratings for the prison camp inmates. The staff ratings on the measures "Loner" and "Follows Crowd" are not analyzed here because of insufficient variability.

Results are shown in table 8-9. **Quay AIMS** classifications differentiated inmates on two of the four measures. A significant relationship between the Quay types and emotional control for the collapsed types revealed that the combined Asocial Aggressive and Manipulative inmates were less likely[14] to receive favorable ratings than others (tau$_c$ = .29, p ≤ .01; multiple r = .43, p ≤ .01). Similarly, staff ratings of maturity increased monotonically for the combined Immature Dependent and Neurotic Anxious inmates and then for the Situational inmates (multiple r = .35, p ≤ .01). Clearly, Situational inmates received the highest ratings by far on the measures for emotional control and for maturity. Results for the collapsed classification measures are given greater credence because of the limited number of cases diagnosed as Asocial Aggressive, Immature Dependent or Neurotic Anxious. The Quay AIMS system failed to differentiate inmates on the measures pertinent to work performance, initiative, and learning ability.

Further examination of these data showed that in 20 cases, the CAC portion of the Quay assessment and the Megargee Prison Adjustment were rated by the same person. In response, we examined the data a second time without the 20 questionable cases. Results and patterns observed for the cross-tabular analyses were nearly identical to those shown in table 8-9. Multiple regression results, however, were somewhat attenuated—approximately .11 points lower than those shown in Table 8-9—but they remained significant and showed similar patterns across the respective types.[15]

Inmates classified as Able, Delta, Foxtrot, George, How, and Jupiter on the **Megargee MMPI-based** system were less likely to receive favorable ratings of emotional control. Small cell sizes for the uncollapsed types, however, place findings for some of these types in question—for example, for Baker, Charlie, Delta, Foxtrot,

Table 8-9: Effects of Classification Types on Staff Ratings, Prison Camp Sample

	Staff Ratings											
	Emotional Control			Maturity			Initiative			Learning Ability		
Classification System	%[a]	X̄	Nc	%[a]	X̄	Nc	%[a]	X̄	Nc	%[a]	X̄	Nc
Quay AIMS												
Asocial Aggressive	11	3.06	9	11	3.04	9	100	3.75	8	88	3.58	8
Immature Dependent	60	3.29	5	80	3.38	5	100	4.29	4	100	4.21	4
Neurotic Anxious	33	3.16	3	33	3.17	3	100	4.22	3	100	4.00	3
Manipulator	24	2.84	21	43	3.09	21	67	3.74	15	80	3.90	15
Situational	56	3.51	78	59	3.59	78	85	3.98	65	92	4.06	65
	$(\chi^2 = 12.53^{**})$			$(\chi^2 = 10.24^{**})$								
	Mult. R = .43***			Mult. R = .35**								
Quay AIMS (Collapsed Categories)												
Aa/Mp	20	2.92	30	33	3.07	30	78	3.75	23	83	3.79	23
Id/Na	50	3.24	8	63	3.29	8	100	4.37	7	100	4.12	7
Situational	56	3.51	78	59	3.59	78	85	3.98	65	92	4.06	65
	$\chi^2 = 11.59^{***}$			$\chi^2 = 6.05^{**}$								
	$Tau_c = .29^{***}$			$Tau_c = .19^{**}$								
	Mult. R = .43***			Mult. R = .35***								
Megargee MMPI-Based Taxonomy												
Able	41	3.52	22	55	3.72	22	86	3.83	21	86	3.94	21
Baker	100	3.63	5	100	3.83	5	100	3.63	5	100	3.71	5
Charlie	50	3.17	6	33	3.33	6	67	3.66	6	83	3.73	6
Delta	0	2.84	7	17	3.00	6	100	3.75	3	100	3.50	3
Easy	50	3.29	12	50	3.38	12	91	4.12	11	100	4.27	11

Foxtrot	25	2.88	4	25	2.87	4	50	3.54	4	75	3.71	4
George	38	3.13	16	44	3.24	16	92	3.96	13	92	4.01	13
How	47	3.44	15	47	3.44	15	100	4.12	8	88	4.08	8
Item	55	3.43	62	63	3.58	62	76	3.87	50	82	3.91	50
Jupiter	33	3.34	3	33	3.50	3	100	4.05	3	67	3.89	3

Megargee MMPI-Based Taxonomy (Collapsed Categories)

Charlie/Foxtrot (Committed Criminal)	40	3.04	10	30	3.13	10	60	3.61	10	80	3.72	10
Able/Delta (Character Disorder)	31	3.46	29	46	3.65	28	88	3.83	24	88	3.90	24
How (Most Disturbed)	47	3.44	15	47	3.44	15	100	4.13	8	88	4.08	8
Baker/George/Jupiter (Neurotic)	50	3.28	24	54	3.42	24	95	3.90	21	91	3.92	21
Item/Easy (Least Disturbed)	54	3.40	74	61	3.55	74	79	3.93	61	85	3.97	61
	$Tau_c = .17^{**}$			$Tau_c = .18^{**}$			$(\chi^2 = 8.79^*)$					

Conceptual Level - CL3

CL-1	29	3.22	24	42	3.40	24	83	3.96	18	100	3.92	18
CL-2	49	3.40	112	53	3.51	112	83	3.84	94	84	4.03	94
CL-3	55	3.33	22	67	3.50	21	87	4.04	16	94	4.19	16
	$Tau_c = .13^{**}$			$Tau_c = .12^{**}$								

Conceptual Level - CL5

CL-1	20	3.15	15	33	3.41	15	73	3.75	11	91	3.71	11
CL-2	47	3.36	131	53	3.48	131	84	3.94	109	87	3.98	109
CL-3	73	3.67	11	70	3.78	10	86	3.83	7	86	4.11	7
	$\chi^2 = 7.31^{**}$			$Tau_c = .11^{**}$								
	$Tau_c = .16^{***}$											

Table 8-9: *(continued)*

	Staff Ratings											
	Emotional Control			Maturity			Initiative			Learning Ability		
Classification System	%[a]	X̄	N[b]	%[a]	X̄	N[c]	%[a]	X̄	N[c]	%[a]	X̄	N[c]
Jesness Inventory I-level												
I-2 Aa	0	—	1	0	—	1	—	—	—	—	—	—
I-2 Ap	60	3.33	5	40	3.62	5	75	3.84	4	100	4.02	4
I-3 Cfm	52	3.45	25	64	3.60	25	86	4.14	22	86	4.05	22
I-3 Mp	55	3.38	33	64	3.53	33	84	3.88	32	94	4.09	32
I-3 Cfc	37	3.33	30	37	3.40	30	74	3.79	27	82	3.73	27
I-4 Se	39	3.21	28	52	3.44	27	88	3.92	16	94	4.01	16
I-4 Na	31	3.33	16	38	3.36	16	92	3.73	12	92	3.83	12
I-4 Nx	73	3.54	15	73	3.59	15	91	4.11	11	82	4.03	11
I-4 Ci	50	3.33	4	50	3.33	4	50	4.00	2	50	4.00	2
Jesness Inventory (Collapsed Levels)												
I-2	50	3.33	6	33	3.63	6	75	3.83	4	100	4.00	4
I-3	48	3.38	88	55	3.51	88	82	3.91	81	88	3.96	81
I-4	46	3.35	63	53	3.46	62	88	3.91	41	88	3.96	41
Jesness Inventory (Collapsed Personality Subtypes)												
Aggressives (Aa, Cfc, Mp)	45	3.35	64	50	3.47	64	80	3.84	59	88	3.93	59
Neurotics (Na, Nx)	52	3.43	31	55	3.47	31	91	3.91	23	87	3.93	23
Dependents (Ap, Cfm)	53	3.43	30	61	3.61	30	85	4.09	26	89	4.04	26
Situationals (Se, Ci)	41	3.22	32	52	3.43	31	83	3.93	18	89	4.01	18

I-level (Interview Method)

	%[a]	Mean[b]	N[c]	%[a]	Mean[b]	N[c]	%[a]	Mean[b]	N[c]	%[a]	Mean[b]	N[c]
I-4 Na	41	3.25	44	48	3.69	44	81	3.75	36	86	3.78	36
I-4 Nx	25	3.00	16	31	3.10	16	92	3.94	12	83	3.92	12
I-4 Se	56	3.41	32	56	3.56	32	86	3.97	29	93	4.01	29
I-4 Ci	50	3.34	16	63	3.55	16	62	3.66	13	62	3.62	13
I-5 Na	44	3.65	9	44	3.38	9	71	3.69	7	71	3.81	7
I-5 Nx	54	3.44	24	57	3.47	23	89	4.16	18	94	4.16	18
I-5 Se	54	3.77	22	68	3.92	22	100	4.26	17	100	4.43	17
I-5 Ci	50	3.34	2	100	3.50	2	100	4.34	2	100	4.33	2
	(Mult. R = .33**)			(Mult. R = .31*)						(Mult R = .35**)		
				$(Tau_c = .17**)$						$(\chi^2 = 14.07**)$		

I-level (Collapsed Sublevels)

	%[a]	Mean[b]	N[c]	%[a]	Mean[b]	N[c]	%[a]	Mean[b]	N[c]	%[a]	Mean[b]	N[c]
I-4	44	3.26	108	50	3.40	108	81	3.75	90	84	3.78	90
I-5	53	3.50	57	61	3.62	56	91	4.10	44	93	4.10	44
	Mult. R - .20**			$Tau_b = .10*$			$Tau_b = .09*$			$Tau_b = .08*$		
				Mult. R = .17*			Mult. R = .25***			Mult. R = .29***		

I-level (Collapsed Personality Subtypes)

	%[a]	Mean[b]	N[c]	%[a]	Mean[b]	N[c]	%[a]	Mean[b]	N[c]	%[a]	Mean[b]	N[c]
Situational	56	3.53	54	61	3.69	54	91	4.07	46	96	4.17	46
Neurotic Anxious	43	3.27	40	46	3.32	39	90	4.07	30	90	4.08	30
Neurotic Acting-out	42	3.31	53	47	3.43	53	79	3.74	43	84	3.79	43
Cultural Identifier	50	3.34	18	67	3.55	18	67	3.75	15	67	3.73	15
				$Tau_c = -.17***$			$Tau_c = -.17***$			$Tau_c = -.18***$		
				Mult. R = .24*			Mult. R = .27**					

[a] Percent rated above average (3.00) on this scale.
[b] Scales range from negatiave behavior (1 and 2) to average (3.00) to positive behavior (4 and 5).
[c] N in the category.
( ) Results must be viewed with caution because of limited cell frequencies.
* $p \leq .10$ ** $p \leq .05$ *** $p \leq .01$

and Jupiter. Upon collapsing types, we find that two combined groups (Charlie/Foxtrot and Able/Delta) were rated less favorably than the neurotic and the least disturbed types (tau$_c$ = .17, p ≤ .05). We obtained similar results for the test of the relationship to the maturity index. Neurotic and least disturbed inmates were significantly more likely to be rated favorably (tau$_c$ = .18, p ≤ .05). On the work performance measures of initiative and ability to learn, differences were not significant. Limiting the analysis to only the most valid cases did not change the resulting statistics.

Tests of **Conceptual Level** showed a pattern similar to that observed for the penitentiary inmates. Inmates classified into the higher levels, CL-2 and CL-3 (especially CL-3 inmates), out-performed others. Significant relationships existed between both CL measures and the two prison adjustment measures, emotional control (tau$_c$ for CL$_3$ measure = .13, p ≤ .05; tau$_c$ for CL$_5$ measure = .16, p ≤ .01) and maturity (tau$_c$ for CL$_3$ measure =.12, p ≤ .05; tau$_c$ for CL$_5$ measure = .11, p ≤ .05). Ratings also were higher for the CL-2 and CL-3 inmates on the work-adjustment ratings of initiative and ability to learn, but they were not significant.

Surprisingly, neither the level nor the personality dimensions of the **Jesness Inventory** differentiated adequately among camp inmates on the prison adjustment or work performance measures. In fact, table 8-9 shows that none of the groups obtained mean ratings of average or less than average.

This was not the case with the **I-level interview** types. Significant relationships were observed across all four criterion measures. Tests of the relationship between the uncollapsed types and emotional control revealed I$_4$Se, I$_5$Na, and I$_5$Se groups to have the highest mean ratings (multiple r = .33, p ≤ .05). Means and proportions also were high for these groups and for I$_4$Cis on the maturity measure (tau$_c$ = .17, p ≤ .05; multiple r = .31, p ≤ .10). When the personality types were collapsed, however, relationships were not significant; this finding suggested instances where effects for similar types at different levels were canceled out (e.g., I$_4$Nx and I$_5$Nx, I$_4$Na and I$_5$Na, I$_4$Se and I$_5$Se).

With this latter finding in mind, it is not surprising that level was correlated with all of the staff ratings. As shown in table 8-9, inmates classified as I$_5$ were significantly more likely than others to receive favorable staff ratings.

Collapsing of the personality types for the interview I-level ratings revealed that the Situational and the Neurotic Anxious inmates were most likely to receive favorable ratings for initiative (tau$_c$ = –.17, p ≤ .01; multiple r = .24, p ≤ .10) and for ability to learn (tau$_c$ = –.18, p ≤ .01; multiple r = .27, p ≤ .05). The latter finding was also significant for the uncollapsed types (multiple r = .35, p ≤ .05).

DISCUSSION

Two generalizations emerge from an overview of the findings presented in this chapter. The first was anticipated: We observed slightly more significant findings in this portion of the research than in the discipline-related correlates that we examined in the previous chapter. This is not to minimize the findings reported in chapter 7. We did, in fact, observe *more* disciplinary correlates than we expected to find, but in comparing the two chapters, it ought to be obvious that the implications of psychological classification systems are primarily for treatment and secondarily for security.

The second observation concerns the differences across settings. The findings were more likely to support the hypotheses generated by specific type descriptions in our analysis of the penitentiary data than of the camp data. Clearly the two institutional environments were very different, housed different types of inmates, and produced dramatically different prison experiences. More specifically, most of the findings observed for camp inmates pertained to their performance, their initiative, and their willingness to work and participate in prison programs. These were also factors for the penitentiary inmates, but so were correlates pertaining to safety, fear, and a tendency to isolate oneself. Maturity, emotional control, privacy, and stress were treatment-related outcomes that affected specific personality and developmental types in both settings.

The differences across institutions suggest caution regarding the claims to be made for psychological classification. Type descriptions are likely to vary across settings; the classic type descriptions and predictors are most observable in more traditional maximum-security settings. Moreover, this technology should be developed further with the establishment of institutional norms in mind.

To this point we have presented a compelling picture of differences among inmates; clearly some types of inmates have a much harder time with the prison experience than others. In the following chapter, we integrate these findings with those set forth in earlier chapters in order to formulate a more comprehensive profile of each classification type.

CHAPTER 9

SUMMARY AND DISCUSSION OF RESEARCH GOALS

As is evident from the preceding four chapters, this research has amassed numerous findings pertinent to specific psychological classification systems, classification technology, and correctional research. This chapter highlights those findings in the context of research questions put forward in chapter 1. Overall, these questions were addressed constructively; the research produced valuable information about the viability of psychological classification. Moreover, our firsthand experiences in using each of the systems in these adult prison settings provided additional important information, which we furnish at various points throughout this and the following chapter.

We begin by discussing the limitations of the study and then address each of the research goals in turn. A large section of this chapter integrates the findings into a profile of each of the types studied and addresses additional research issues as they pertain to each type.

LIMITATIONS OF THE STUDY

In this research we encountered four areas of concern; some were attributable to the study and others to the limitations of the specific classification systems. These areas are (a) reliability of the classification measures, (b) independence of a few of the classification measures from the criterion measures, (c) data-collection difficulties for measures that were obtained by the prison staff, and (d) limited numbers of subjects for some of the tests. The effects of these problems have been addressed extensively throughout the book and are only summarized here. At several points throughout the study we conducted separate analyses in order to determine whether any of these problems were biasing research outcomes. Overall we discovered no indication that any problem had seriously affected the findings which we ultimately presented, but we review each issue in turn.

Reliability

It is somewhat difficult to separate the limitations of this research from the limitations of the classification systems that we studied. In order to address fully the aims of this research, it was necessary to employ each classification system in its current state of technology. Thus, we considered the administration directives and assumptions of each system as given and made no attempts to redesign the system to reflect the needs of a different population. Our purpose instead was to use our experience and our results to recommend directions for future use of the systems with adult male inmates, even though three of these systems had seldom been used with these populations and the remaining two were considered to be in a developmental stage at the outset of this research.

Our analysis of the reliability of the diagnostic systems found interrater reliability measures of the Quay and I-level systems that ranged from 55% to 75%.[1] These figures are somewhat low but are higher than clinical psychological diagnoses, which are notoriously lower. Moreover, results for the I-level measures are similar to the reliability found in other research (Harris 1988). With respect to the Quay AIMS classifications, our reliability analysis appears to be the first available.

In all likelihood, these reliability problems relate to the technology of the classification systems. Most correctional classification systems (with the exception of the Megargee MMPI-based system and perhaps the Jesness Inventory system) have not been refined to an optimal level. Thus we note several areas where additional structure may prove useful. For the I-level and the Quay AIMS, not the least of these problems is the need for a manual, for more detailed decision-making rules, and for clearer definition of test items shown on the Quay AIMS staff rating forms.

In spite of these reliability issues, the analysis produced numerous correlations that occurred in expected directions, showing that inmate types offered predictions that were in keeping with their type description. Thus, if reliability affected the results, it is likely to have operated so as to underestimate the research findings.

Independence of Some Measures

Questions concerning the independence of classification measures from criterion measures arose in two types of analyses: (1) at the prison camp, the interviewer who diagnosed I-level also rated the interview content items analyzed in chapter 8; and (2) a number of the Megargee Prison Adjustment Rating Forms were completed by the same staff member who completed a portion of the Quay AIMS assessment (72 at the penitentiary and 20 at the prison camp).

We did not explore the first problem in depth, because, as shown in chapter 8, I-level was not correlated significantly with the interview content ratings constructed for the prison camp sample. This finding allayed any concerns that a lack of independence might have resulted in spurious correlations between I-level and the items. Furthermore, the matter had been assessed in previous research, where Heide's comparisons of blind ratings with ratings conducted by I-level interviewers showed that content rating items were not affected by the rater's knowledge of I-level (Heide 1982).

The second problem required two analyses of all tests of the relationship of Quay AIMS to measures extracted from the Megargee Prison Adjustment Rating Form. The first analysis was conducted for all cases; the second only for those adjustment measures known to be independent of the Quay AIMS classification. The results were nearly identical in the two sets of tests. This result is not surprising, because some precautions were built into the research design: (a) The AIMS classification was formulated by separate assessments by two individuals, and (b) the adjustment forms were completed approximately 3 months after the AIMS forms were administered.

Data Collection Difficulties for Staff
Assessment Measures

As discussed in chapter 4, the research staff found that some prison staff members initially were reluctant to complete the Quay AIMS Correctional Adjustment Checklist and the Megargee Work and Prison Adjustment Forms. These matters were addressed (a) by hiring a prison case manager to serve as a liaison between the research staff and the institutional case managers, counselors, and work supervisors; (b) by conducting a meeting to address staff concerns; and (c) by readministering forms known to be invalid. These measures appeared to correct our problem for in the final analysis, staff ratings proved to be extremely valuable data. One problem that could not be corrected, however, was the data attrition caused by the initial difficulties in securing staff cooperation. Attrition is discussed in the following section.

Limited Number of Subjects

For reasons explained in detail in chapter 4, data attrition occurred for two of the data collection instruments, namely the Quay AIMS forms and the inmate follow-up survey. This situation, combined with the fact that some classification types were rare in these settings, prevented us from learning much about the rare types. We also encountered problems with degrees of freedom: In some instances, tests resulted in expected differences that did not reach statistical significance.

As a result, we analyzed data once for the uncollapsed types and then again after collapsing similar types. The first analysis was sometimes plagued by limited cell sizes for the rare types, whereas the second analysis improved cell sizes and provided a better situation with respect to degrees of freedom. The second analysis, however, was conducted at the expense of losing some information pertinent to the specific types.

The point of this discussion is that in this study we cannot draw definitive conclusions regarding types observed to be infrequent in the two research settings. To do so would require a much larger study. It is also likely that a larger study could furnish richer type profiles than those presented below.

By research design, we anticipated this situation at the outset and could have averted it only by using a larger sample.[2] In this study, however, the cost of doing so would have been exorbitant, because the cross-classification aspects of the design and the research issues required extensive, time-consuming, collection of data on each subject.

RESEARCH ISSUES

The questions put forward at the outset of this research and listed in chapter 1 are addressed in this section. We begin with findings that affect the technical concerns of psychological classification in general. Then we discuss other matters that pertain to the specifics of each system or to specific types within a system.

Three issues speak to the psychological classification issues of adult male inmates, regardless of what specific system may be chosen. These concern (1) the number of types that are optimally needed for this population, (2) the correctional agency's need for a system with efficient procedures of administration, and (3) differences between institutional settings.

What does the comparison among systems show us about the number of types that are needed to classify these populations in an optimal manner according to psychological criteria?

The first question emerges from a construct validity analysis presented in chapter 6. This analysis examined the extent to which a total of 32 types (across systems) converged or were reduced into personality clusters that were most common and most clearly identified in these institutional settings. We found four such clusters for the penitentiary and three for the prison camp. These do not exhaust all possible types, but merely identify the most common and those most likely to have been identified across systems. Indeed, the systems themselves provided from five to ten types, depending on the system.

In the penitentiary four types appeared common across most of the systems: (1) a committed criminal type, as exemplified by Quay's Asocial Aggressive, Megargee's Charlie and Foxtrot, Jesness's Cultural Conformist (Cfc), and the I-level (interview) I_4 Cultural Identifier; (2) a situational type, as exemplified by Quay's Situational, Megargee's Easy and Item, Jesness's Situational and Ci (adaptive), and the I-level (interview) I_4 and I_5 Situational; (3) a neurotic anxious/high-anxiety type (e.g., Quay's Na, Megargee's George and Jupiter, Jesness's Neurotic Anxious, and the I-level Neurotic Anxious types), a construct which also was observed to converge with type How (disturbed) and immature types; (4) a character-disordered type as shown in Megargee's Able and Delta, and in all of the I-level neurotic acting-out types. These groupings were similar for the prison camp except that the neurotic/high-anxiety convergences were stronger than those for the penitentiary; also, no committed criminal cluster was present in this minimum-security setting.

The systems provide for other personality dimensions, such as immaturity/dependency and manipulative tendencies. These did not converge well, however, and our understanding of these inmates is less clear. These types were more likely to converge with other dimensions (e.g., with the neurotic and the disturbed for the immature dependent types or with committed criminal types for the manipulative types) than with similarly defined types on other systems. Yet immature types and manipulative measures sometimes were correlated with disciplinary and treatment behaviors. Because these types help us to differentiate inmates, it would be misleading to suggest that they are unimportant. Types conveying dependency and immaturity, for example, often identified an institutionalized inmate.

Another important type, Megargee's How, describes a mentally disturbed inmate who is taken into account on the Megargee system but on none of the others. That How is correlated with neurotic and dependent types on other systems suggests that systems that do not account for mental disturbance will find the disturbed inmate in the neurotic and immature classifications. In some ways, this situation becomes problematic, because the needs of a disturbed inmate can be quite different from those of a dependent or a neurotic inmate as defined by these type descriptions.

In sum, if we were to integrate the findings of the predictive analyses with those of the construct validity analysis, we would recommend provision for the following in medium- to maximum-security settings: committed criminal, immature dependent (though further development is needed in this area), character disordered, situational, neurotic, and disturbed. In minimum-security settings, all but the committed criminal type should be important considerations. This is not to recommend omission of committed criminal types in minimum-security settings, but fewer of these types exist in those settings, and both the convergent and the predictive findings are less consistent with hypotheses that one might form on the basis of descriptions of these types.

Cognitive developmental types also converged strongly. While they were most likely to differentiate inmates according to treatment issues, they also identified aggressive inmates

What types of test assessment procedures are most efficient and most useful in these settings?

At the current stage in the technology of correctional classification, we do not find long, inefficient procedures to be superior to the shorter assessments in terms of reliability or construct and predictive validity. This situation might change with the formulation of manuals or more structured testing procedures, but currently little is gained by a longer test or interview and assessment process. In this study, for example, we invested a great deal of time in a rather lengthy I-level interview. Although correctional practitioners might regard an interview as an important first step in a treatment process and although the I-level interview would be ideal in certain settings, choice of this method should not reflect desire for an optimal predictor. It was adequate but not necessarily better than other systems.

This observation should not be taken to an extreme, because brevity, too, can pose problems. We anticipated, for example, that the staff behavioral checklists for the Quay AIMS test would be easy to obtain, given the structure of the checklist format. It *is* easily obtainable, but this fact in itself warrants some caution. The structure of staff observations built into the AIMS test forms may not be the best option for an overcrowded facility, where staff members do not have the opportunity to know inmates well enough to offer a valid assessment of their behavior. Yet, in view of our difficulties with an overburdened staff, we were not expecting the AIMS classification to show the clear predictive correlates that it showed. Thus, we are far from recommending against its continued use.

On the basis of our experience, the following precautions should enhance the validity and reliability of the resulting AIMS classifications: (*a*) Consider completing checklist forms in smaller diagnostic and classification units rather than upon an inmate's admission to a larger population; (*b*) anticipate and prepare for resistance among staff members; (*c*) encourage staff members to return the lists if they do not know the inmate well, and ask another staff member (possibly a work supervisor) to complete the forms; (*d*) check completed test forms for response biases (e.g., checking identical options throughout); and (*e*) anticipate staff members' reluctance to record negative ratings about an inmate.[3] Stated simply, practitioners should not be misled by the apparent efficiency of this system. The need for a well-prepared and well-trained staff is obvious.

For our purposes, the Jesness Inventory was the easiest to administer. It afforded procedures that are amenable to overcrowded facilities, because it obtains the diagnoses through direct input from the inmate in the form of a short test rather than through assessment by staff. Moreover, assessment of the results does not require a clinical assessment or reading of the results, but is obtained from a computerized scoring service. The Jesness Inventory and the Quay AIMS instruments, in fact, are the only systems that would not require a clinical service or unit to score results or evaluate transitional or dual diagnoses.

Are there important differences between institutional
settings that must be considered in using
psychological classification systems?

The findings consistently point to a need to consider institutional conditions and needs in the choice of a psychological classification system. The most obvious difference occurs in the observed distribution of inmates in the two settings. Not surprisingly, proportionately more prison camp inmates than penitentiary inmates were classified as situational or as least disturbed according to the I-level interview, the Megargee MMPI-based typology, and the Quay AIMS typology. These systems also identified more committed-criminal types in the penitentiary than in the prison camp. Distributions for the developmental types were similar across settings except for the Conceptual Level tests, which identified proportionately more high-CL inmates at the prison camp than at the penitentiary.

The fact that most (67%) of the inmates in the prison camp were classified Situational by the Quay AIMS tests may call into question the applicability of this system for use in a minimum-security setting. Ideally, a classification model should divide an inmate population into manageable subgroups that have implications for differences in the management or treatment of each group. This does not occur if most of the inmates fall into a single category on the system.

A less obvious difference across institutional settings may support a need for norming the systems to specific types of facilities. As the following type profiles will show, a situational type in a minimum-security setting is different from a situational type in a maximum-security setting; in most cases, the differences were so important that we generated institution-specific profiles. In addition, types that show poor adjustment to some settings adjust very well in other types of settings, thus rendering institution-specific any predictions we might make for that type. In this study, for example, this occurred for situationals and Jesness Cfms, among others. Unfortunately, the field of corrrections has ignored the notion of norming or validating classifications and tests to specific populations. This neglect strongly affects the validity of our measures and, in all likelihood, the correctness of our case management decisions (Wright, Clear, and Dickson 1984; Van Voorhis 1987).

CLASSIFICATION PROFILES

The remaining research questions are addressed as they pertain to each system. In the following sections, we present an overview of each system, discussing its efficiency, utility, reliability, and predictive merits. This discussion is followed by profiles of each type, which also incorporate the findings of the study.

Quay Adult Internal Management System (AIMS)

Development of the Quay AIMS system was completed in the early 1980s after an extensive validation study in the federal prison system (Quay 1984). The test promised to offer one of the more efficient systems for classifying adult male inmates. Our initial experience, however, taught us that the efficiency of the system certainly did not promise staff compliance.[4] Nevertheless, when we addressed the staff's initial reluctance and when we omitted test results known to be invalid, we were able to assess this system fairly comprehensively.

Our analysis of the system's interrater reliability produced results that were similar to those for I-level but nevertheless were somewhat low (67%). It is quite possible, however, that these figures would be higher in situations where the test was administered in smaller prison classification/observation units rather than in overcrowded situations where staff members do not have sufficient opportunity to know the inmates. In addition, this system might benefit from the development of a manual that defined the terminology of the checklist items.

We also found that the system was more meaningful in the penitentiary setting. As noted earlier, the distribution of prison camp inmates across categories was highly uneven: most of the inmates were classified as Situational. One of the criteria that we and others (e.g., Megargee & Bohn 1979) had established for determining the utility of a system is its ability to differentiate the inmate population into meaningful subgroups. This criterion requires (among other things) that there be several groups of some sufficient size. In the prison camp, we were close to having one large group and three small groups, each classifying 7% or less of the sample. One could argue that this was the case because in fact there were more situational inmates in the prison camp than in the penitentiary. Other classification systems also found more situational inmates in the prison camp; Those systems, however, were more likely than the AIMS system to detect neurotic, dependent, and immature types. Thus, it is likely that staff observation methods may be less sensitive to personality distinctions than methods that involve direct input by inmates in the form of an interview or an inventory.

Notwithstanding these concerns, the system correlated with similarly defined types, disciplinary behaviors, prison experiences, and prison adjustment measures. These findings are integrated into the type profiles shown in table 9-1.

Megargee's MMPI-Based Typology

This system was developed and validated among youthful-offender populations in the federal prison system; ours, however, is not the first application of the system to adult inmates. Overall, we observed somewhat fewer correlates with adjustment behaviors and treatment-related experiences for this system than for the others. One could entertain a number of explanations for this outcome, including (*a*) flawed administrative procedures, which in turn produced invalid classifications; (*b*) small sample size; and (*c*) weak predictive validity in these populations.

The latter two explanations appear to make the most sense, because we did in fact observe expected differences among types that simply did not reach significance. It is likely that in a larger sample, these differences would have proved significant. In support of this idea, a recent review of tests of several classification systems observed that positive findings tend to be limited to the studies using larger samples (Andrews, Zinger, Hoge, Bonta, Gendreau, and Cullen 1990). Still, we found *more* positive correlates for the other systems studied in this research, *in spite of our less-than-ideal number of subjects*. In these populations, differences among the MMPI-based types on many outcome behaviors simply were not strong (nor had they been strong in the pilot study).

The first explanation offered above is ruled out for several reasons. The first is that many of these results were similar to those

Table 9-1: Profiles of Quay AIMS Types

Asocial Aggressive

Penitentiary   Construct validity was supported by convergent correlations with other committed criminal types. Asocial aggressives self-reported more aggressive behaviors than other inmates. They were rated by staff as *(a)* more aggressive than other inmates, *(b)* having difficulties in their relationships with other inmates, *(c)* needing more supervision, and *(d)* having poor emotional control. Raters considered their interviews more likely to show institutionalized traits than the interviews of others, except Immature Dependent inmates. Self-report measures reflected relatively high levels of participation in programs.

Prison Camp   As with the penitentiary inmates, this type correlated with other types defined as committed criminals on other systems. Asocial aggressives were rare in this minimum-security setting and were more likely to be identified by other systems than by staff observation. Nevertheless, minimum-security Asocial Aggressive inmates, along with Manipulative and Immature Dependent inmates, were more likely than others to receive citations for insubordination. As a group, staff tended to rate them as *(a)* having difficulties in their relationships with other inmates, *(b)* uncooperative, *(c)* needing supervision, *(d)* immature, and *(e)* having poor emotional control. Many of these findings are similar to those observed for the penitentiary inmates; we did not observe correlates with measures of aggression, however.

Immature Dependent

Penitentiary   This type was not validated by consistent convergent correlations with other immature types. Moreover, the Immature Dependent type tended to correlate with high-anxiety and disturbed types on other systems. Either this type appears to be rare and difficult to establish empirically among adult male inmates, or its validity is questionable. Nevertheless, unstable correlates identified these inmates as more likely than others to become involved in drug and alcohol infractions. Staff rated them as having difficulties in their relationships with other men and being likely to follow a crowd. Their self-report indexes and interviews found them more likely than others to *(a)* be institutionalized, *(b)* have few friends, *(c)* evidence high stress, *(d)* participate in programs, and *(e)* need social stimulation. Again, these conclusions are tentative because cell sizes were small.

Prison Camp   Only six inmates were classified Immature Dependent in the prison camp. Somewhat unstable construct validity tests suggest conclusions similar to those reported for the penitentiary. Immature dependent measures correlated positively with official measures of insubordination and with staff reports of poor emotional control and difficulties in responding to supervision. Unlike Immature Dependent types in the penitentiary, these inmates evidenced *limited* levels of program parlticipation. They also showed a limited need for institutional programmatic support.

Neurotic Anxious

Penitentiary

This type converged with other neurotic measures, both neurotic anxious and Neurotic Acting-out. The fact that the Na measure also correlated with Megargee Able and I_4Ci suggests character-disordered dimensions. Neurotic anxious inmates self-reported more aggressive tendencies, a finding that may reflect greater levels of anger among these inmates (particularly when we consider the lack of relationship to any of the official or staff measures of aggression). Staff rated these inmates as needing more intense supervision than inmates diagnosed as Situational or Immature Dependent. Staff measures for the group also evidenced problems with immaturity, emotional control, and some tendencies to "follow the crowd." Their interviews showed a need for programmatic support, and surveys taken later in their prison terms showed that they participated in in programs more than some of the other groups. Surveys also showed that these inmates formed few friendships with other inmates.

Prison Camp

Findings that conflict strongly with the penitentiary data may be attributable to the instability of the tests. Surprisingly, only three prison-camp inmates were classified Neurotic Anxious. On construct validity tests, the type converged with only one other neurotic anxious measure (I_4Nx), but correlated with Megargee's How and Jesness's Cfm, suggesting a somewhat troubled group of inmates. Few additional correlations were observed, except that the prison camp inmates, along with the Immature Dependent group, showed a limited need for programmatic support and limited participation in programs, These findings must be viewed with caution.

Manipulative

Penitentiary

This type failed to converge with any manipulative types on the other systems. At the same time, its correlation with How, Jesness Ci, and I_5Ci makes this interpretation difficult because these correlations show few patterns. Yet Manipulative inmates, as identified by this system, were more likely than others to be cited for insubordination. They were noted by staff as having difficult relationships with other men and as needing supervision. Their surveys suggested limited participation in programs and limited communication with staff.

Prison Camp   This measure converged with only one other manipulative measure, Megargee's Delta. Still, manipulative inmates evidenced relatively high rates of insubordination. Staff rated them as *(a)* having poor relationships with other men and with authority, *(b)* uncooperative, *(c)* needing more supervision, *(d)* responding relatively poorly to supervision, and *(e)* showing poor emotional control. Thus, although this type appears to have some behavioral problems in the prison setting, the personality dimensions represented by "manipulative" are unclear.

Situational

Penitentiary   The situational construct was one of the strongest in the study. Quay Situational converges with less mature situational types on other systems (e.g., I_4Se), suggesting a naïve inmate. Although they displayed no criminal value system, neurotic traits, or mental disturbance, these inmates had a difficult time during the period monitored by our study. Their self-reports indicated victimizing and threatening experiences, high stress, limited participation and communication with staff, and a need for programmatic support, but revealed a belief that others were willing to help. Interviews expressed a need for safety and privacy. At the same time, these inmates looked good to staff and tended, as a group, to receive the highest ratings. We anticipate that most difficulties stem from Situationals' relatively limited prison experience. A longer follow-up period might have shown some improvement in their adjustment.

Prison Camp   Results of tests of construct validity produced results similar to those found for the AIMS Situationals in the penitentiary, but these inmates had an easier time adjusting to the minimum-security environment. Staff ratings were consistently favorable; as a group, these inmates showed no difficulties with stress, victimization or other negative experiences. This environment does not require the same degree and type of experience as the penitentiary environment.

---

observed in previous studies. The distributions of types, for example, were remarkably similar to those found in other studies. Similarly, the proportions of cases that could be scored by computer or ultimately could be rated clinically were also consistent with previous research. Moreover, construct validity findings (reported in chapter 6) showed strong results for several of the types as they correlated with similarly defined types on other systems. Finally, we painstakingly conducted these analyses several times, controlling for the validity of the protocols and collapsing types (among other methods) in order to check against the effects of design and measurement problems. These additional analyses seldom changed the results.

This finding is unfortunate because the system is efficient to administer. The test is longer than others (566 questions), but securing inmates' cooperation was not unduly difficult. Results were scored by computer. This procedure required us to send results to a service at Florida State University, but programs have been developed for use with personal computers. Agencies using the system must provide for the fact that a portion of the test results (approximately 33%) cannot be scored mechanically and requires clinical assistance. A staff clinician experienced in the use of the MMPI, however, should be able to perform this task.

Although our results were not ideal, we observed some valuable findings for some of the Megargee types. As with the other systems, our most conclusive findings are for types that classified a number sufficient to permit meaningful statistical analyses. Observations are summarized in table 9-2.

Conceptual Level

To our knowledge, this study was the first application of Conceptual Level to adult inmates. The study did not conduct a reliability assessment, but we sent the results to a scoring service that had established strong reliability. The sentence-completion test proved efficient to administer and was completed within 15 to 18 minutes by most inmates. The rater reported no difficulties with the results furnished by these inmates.

As with the two I-level developmental measures, construct validity tests were conducted for the system as a whole rather than type by type, as with the personality constructs. Results were strong: All of the cognitive developmental measures correlated with each other.

Table 9-2: Profiles of Megargee MMPI-Based Types

Able

Penitentiary

This type did not converge well with the matches that were hypothesized to correlate with Able. Other correlates, however, formed a valuable pattern. In construct validity tests, Able correlated most strongly with neurotic acting-out types and less strongly with committed criminal types. These findings portray Able as a character-disordered type with neurotic, defended characteristics. The type diverged from situational, dependent, and neurotic anxious types. Ables were among the types receiving relatively high overall citations for disciplinary infractions, particularly for insubordination. Self-report measures supported the official-record data, indicating high incidence of nonaggressive infractions. There were no correlates, favorable, or unfavorable, to prison needs, participation, formation of friendships, stress, or other adjustment factors.

Prison Camp

Results for the construct validity tests reveal a description similar to that reported for the penitentiary inmates. In this setting, however, Ables appeared to report relatively frequent aggressive behaviors, as well as experience with the the threatening behaviors of other inmates. There were no correlates to staff ratings, but self-report stress measures found that Ables were experiencing less stress than other types.

Baker

Penitentiary and Prison Camp

Few inmates were classified as Baker. As a result, most tests were unstable, and the research offers few conclusions for either the penitentiary or the prison camp inmates. The only correlates found Bakers in the penitentiary indicating a high need for programmatic support. In the prison, they reported limited communication with staff.

Charlie

Penitentiary

Type Charlie converged strongly with other committed criminal types. Moreover, correlates with official and self-report disciplinary measures were observed. Charlies correlated with overall disciplinary rates, insubordination, and self-report nonaggressive incidents. The only treatment-related correlate found Charlies more likely to be "institutionalized," reflecting long criminal careers and extensive prison experience.

Prison Camp

In contrast to findings for the penitentiary, Charlie *did not* correlate with other committed criminal types in this setting. Instead, correlates with neurotic types were observed. Correlates to self-report measures of aggression *and* victimization experiences were noted. Charlies in the prison camp, however, were also found to be oriented to rehabilitation goals and saw others as willing to help. Staff rated them as relatively immature. Overall, the findings suggest that inmates classfied as Charlie were not adjusting and behaving according to descriptions set forth for this type.

Delta

Penitentiary

Delta did not correlate with other manipulative types and, unlike Able, did not correlate with neurotic acting-out types. Deltas had relatively high rates of disciplinary infractions and self-reported high rates of nonaggressive behaviors. There were no correlates to treatment-related measures.

Prison Camp

Findings were similar to those observed for type Able. This type was more likely to correlate with neurotic types than with manipulative types. They reported relatively high rates of aggression and threatening experiences. Staff rated them as immature and as evidencing poor emotional control.

Easy

Penitentiary

The description of Easy as a well-adjusted, benign type was validated in this study. The type correlated strongly with other situational measures, particularly less mature types. Easy also correlated with Jesness Cfm in both samples, suggesting that these inmates, although not evidencing a criminal value system or high-anxiety patterns, nevertheless may be quite naïve. There were no correlates to official, self-report, or staff ratings of disciplinary behaviors, nor were there any adjustment difficulties noted.

Prison Camp

Construct validity tests produced the same results for the prison camp as for the penitentiary sample. Although there were no correlations with disciplinary measures, inmates classified as Easy were more likely to report experiencing threats from other inmates. In contrast to Ables, Charlies, Foxtrots, and Hows, these threats were not likely to have been provoked. These inmates' only treatment-related distinction was a significantly greater need for privacy than expressed by other types.

Foxtrot

Penitentiary

This measure converged with other committed-criminal types, but not as strongly as for Charlie. There were also some anomalous correlations to situational and neurotic types. The latter finding is not surprising, in view of the high Sc and Ma scale scores needed to classify an inmate as Foxtrot. Unlike type Charlie, Foxtrots did not evidence high rates of disciplinary infractions, but self-report indexes tapping nonaggressive infractions were high. On adjustment measures, these inmates reported having few friends. Staff gave them low ratings for motivation.

Prison Camp   In terms of construct validity, tests in the prison camp correlates did not converge or form any patterns leading to meaningful interpretations. Foxtrots evidenced high self-reported aggressive tendencies and more threats from other inmates. Staff rated them as significantly more likely to have poor relationships with other men, to need supervision, and to respond poorly to supervision.

George

Penitentiary   This type correlated with Quay Immature dependent but with few of the other neurotic types. No correlates with record, self-report, or staff ratings of disciplinary behaviors were observed. Correlations with treatment-related prison-adjustment ratings were favorable: these inmates indicated a need for program support, formed friendships, saw others as willing to help, and showed high initiative.

Prison Camp   In contrast to the penitentiary findings, type George converged with other neurotic types in the prison camp. There were no correlates to any official or self-report disciplinary measures, or to unfavorable staff ratings. Adjustment measures indicated that these inmates might be somewhat isolated (e.g., limited communication with staff and few friends).

How

Penitentiary   Because How is described as psychologically disturbed rather than by personality traits per se, no matches were hypothesized. Type How correlated with neurotic and dependent types, however. Hows were among the groups with higher disciplinary infractions. They had relatively high ratings on self-reports of nonaggressive behaviors. They had by far the highest stress scores of all the Megargee types, and also evidenced a good deal of fear of others and limited communication with staff. Surprisingly, their surveys suggested that they had more friends in the prison setting than all other groups except Item.

Prison Camp   Again, type How correlated with neurotic and dependent types. Self-report measures indicated aggressive tendencies and threats from other inmates. The surveys also showed adjustment difficulties such as high stress, need for privacy, limited communication with staff, and a belief that they could not get help from others.

	Item
Penitentiary	Type Item converged with other situational types, particularly mature I_5Ses. There were correlates to official citations for disciplinary infractions, but correlations with self-report infractions or with unfavorable staff ratings were not significant. Adjustment appeared to be favorable. Items reported supportive friendships, and staff rated them as motivated.
Prison Camp	Converged with situational types but also (anomalously) with criminal and neurotic acting-out measures. No correlates to official or self-reported disciplinary behaviors were found, but Items reported problems with threats from other inmates.

	Jupiter
Penitentiary	Converged with neurotic types, but few cases were identified, and tests are limited. No correlations with disciplinary infractions or unfavorable staff ratings were found. Adjustment appeared favorable; the only correlate was to a tendency to see others as willing to help.
Prison Camp	Converged with only one other neurotic type, but (as in the penitentiary) very few cases were identified in this setting. No correlates to disciplinary problems, unfavorable staff ratings, or adjustment difficulties were found.

In addition, we observed a number of correlates with disciplinary and adjustment measures. Most important, the lowest CL types correlated either directly with a measure tapping the individual's need for structure or with other measures relevant to such a need. Such findings validated one of the central tenets of Conceptual Level theory (Reitsma-Street and Leschied 1988). Type descriptions are summarized in the profiles presented in table 9-3.

Jesness Inventory (I-level)

The Jesness Inventory was another one of the systems that was developed for juvenile populations but was tested in this study with adults, presumably for the first time. Because the system was developed for juveniles, we were somewhat surprised by the construct and predictive validity of some of the types. Moreover, the Jesness Inventory was practical to administer. Test sessions were brief, and the results were sent to Consulting Psychologists Press for scoring.

At present, no clinical assessment procedures are required in order to use this system. In developing the system for use with adults, however, refinements to the I_2 types should be considered. These will warrant a thorough understanding of *who* the I_2 inmate is (an assessment that we are reluctant to make with so few I_2 inmates) and the formation of assessment and treatment procedures. With the Jesness Inventory, as with other systems, rare types warrant further research and development. These developments may ultimately result in a recommendation for more intense clinical attention to these rare but apparently troubled types.

We did not conduct a reliability assessment of the Jesness I-level types. Jesness and his colleagues have devoted considerable attention to reliability of the instrument; we relied upon their figures in the interests of efficiency. Nevertheless, because adult populations differ considerably from those used in most of Jesness's research, further developments of this system should examine psychometric qualities.

As with the Conceptual Level, tests of the construct validity of cognitive-development measures are conducted for the system rather than for each type. The Jesness Inventory I-level measures converged strongly with other developmental constructs. This is an important finding: Cognitive development, as a measure of social cognition that taps thought patterns and world views, is typically obtained through observation of those thought processes. Such

Table 9-3: Profiles of Conceptual Level Types[a]

Conceptual Level 1 (CL-1)

Penitentiary   Although no correlates to official disciplinary infractions were noted, inmates classified as CL-1 reported relatively few instances of aggressive behaviors and less tendency to be victimized by the threatening behaviors of other inmates. Staff, however, rated these inmates unfavorably on several measures, including *(a)* relations with other men, *(b)* relations with authority, *(c)* cooperation, *(d)* need for supervision, and *(e)* response to supervision. Their adjustment difficulties were numerous. They evidenced high stress and high fear, and raters reported that many expressed concern for their safety. On a number of measures, they appeared to be amenable to treatment, indicating *(a)* a need for programmatic support, *(b)* an orientation to correctional rehabilitation goals, and *(c)* a tendency to participate in programs. Even so, staff rated them as unmotivated.

Prison Camp   Weak relationships were observed between the CL measure and official disciplinary measures: CL-1 inmates were found *less* likely than the other inmates to be cited for acts of insubordination. Staff rated them as having difficulties with authority, as immature, and as evidencing poor emotional control. At the same time, they evidenced a need for structure and appeared to favor correctional rehabilitation intentions.

Conceptual Level 2 (CL-2)

Penitentiary   CL-2 inmates reported more frequent aggressive behavior and more frequent threats from other inmates than did CL-1 inmates. Staff ratings showed that CL-2 inmates also evidenced some difficulties in their relationships with other inmates. They also rated the CL-2 inmates as needing supervision. CL-2 inmates showed a greater need for privacy than the CL-1 inmates and a greater need for safety than inmates classified as CL-3. Even though they appeared oriented to notions of rehabilitation at intake, the subsequent follow-up survey showed minimal participation in prison programs.

Prison Camp   CL-2 inmates at the prison camp showed a slightly greater tendency than CL-1 inmates to be cited for acts of insubordination. Staff ratings of problem behaviors showed no conclusive results. The interview indicated a need for structure and an orientation to rehabilitation.

Conceptual Level 3 (CL-3)

Penitentiary   CL-3 inmates reported relatively frequent instances of aggressive behaviors and experience with victimizing, threatening behavior from other inmates. Yet staff rated them favorably as mature, motivated, and having good emotional control. At intake they showed needs for privacy, social stimulation, and programmatic support, but the follow-up survey showed limited participation in programs.

Prison Camp   CL-3 and CL-2 inmates showed somewhat more acts of insubordination than did CL-1 inmates. Staff rated these inmates as mature, and generally viewed them favorably on other measures. In their interviews they did not appear oriented to notions of rehabilitation and were not likely to seek help from others. Their participation in programs was limited. Surprisingly, they expressed some fear of the prison environment.

---

[a] This table combines results of CL3 and CL5 tests

observation usually involves administering open-ended questions for either verbal or written responses. Simply stated, we must observe thought processes in order to classify thought processes; sources have expressed skepticism about the possibility of classifying cognitive development through a series of objective questions requiring yes-or-no answers. Thus, it is notable that the objective paper-and-pencil format of the Jesness Inventory formulated developmental measures that correlated with observational open-ended measures.

The profiles for the personality types are shown in table 9-4; I-level profiles are shown in table 9-5.

I-level (Interview Method)

When Marguerite Warren and her associates at the California Community Treatment Project designed the I-level assessment and treatment package, the promotion of intensive treatment-related interactions with offenders was a desired and presumably a workable intent. Indeed, intake interviews are a commendable first step for treatment that endeavors to work through therapeutic relationships. Moreover, the notion of getting to know a client *and* obtaining a psychological assessment that will guide the treatment of the client has sound foundations in mental-health practice. In a different type of correctional setting, the I-level interview would make good sense. Interviewers for this study felt that the I-level intake interview was a valuable tool for understanding prison inmates. Moreover, the construct and predictive validity of the system was reasonably strong.

Interrater reliability, however, was 74% for level and 51% for subtype. On the basis of our experience in using the system, we identified several sources of difficulty in arriving at a reliable assessment. Most important, the system needs greater standardization, particularly rules for dealing with multiple classifications. Raters in our study, for example, often were able to recognize the same levels and subtypes in the subjects' statements, but could not reach a final classification when more than one type had been heard. The system also could benefit from an updated manual of prototypical statements for each type and level.

In spite of the inefficiency and the difficulties with reliability, this system offered valuable predictions to disciplinary and adjustment-related behaviors. We would not recommend its use in large, crowded facilities. Our experience with the system was time-consuming and expensive, and practitioners for large correctional

Table 9-4: Profiles of Jesness Inventory I-level Personality Types

I_2Aa (Asocial Aggressive)

Penitentiary   Because only five inmates were identified, our conclusions about this type are quite tentative. Construct validity tests found correlates with troubled, immature, and high-anxiety types (eg.g., How, Quay Id, and I_4Nx). I_2 inmates as a group evidenced higher self-report nonaggressive incidents than I_3 inmates. Most of their behavioral problems, however, appeared on staff ratings. Staff rated these inmates as *(a)* having poor relationships with other inmates *and* with authority figures, *(b)* aggressive, *(c)* uncooperative, *(d)* in need of supervision, *(e)* showing poor response to supervision, and *(f)* immature. Prison adjustment measures suggested that these inmates were institutionalized and evidenced a need for programmatic support. Again, these results must be viewed with caution.

Prison Camp   Only two inmates were classified I_2Aa in this setting. As a result, statistical tests for this type could not be conducted.

I_2Ap (Asocial Passive)

Penitentiary   Only three inmates were identified. Construct validity tests were not meaningful. These three inmates were not evident as behavioral problems on official, self-report, or staff measures, but they showed some need for programmatic support and evidenced some difficulty with stress. Staff ratings, however, appeared favorable.

Prison Camp   Five inmates were classified Asocial Passive. This type correlates with How, suggesting a troubled group of inmates. These inmates also were cited for more disciplinary infractions than others. They scored very high on stress measures but evidenced limited use of prison programs as a coping strategy. At intake, however, interviewers rated these inmates as oriented to rehabilitation, as seeing others as willing to help, and as having a high need for structure and programmatic support.

I_3Cfm (Immature Conformist)

Penitentiary   Immature types did not converge well in either setting. The Jesness Cfm type, nevertheless, correlated strongly with How and situational types in the penitentiary. Divergent correlations were observed with committed-criminal types. These findings render Cfms somewhat difficult to describe. They do not appear to evidence a criminal value system, and would appear somewhat benign on the basis of correlations with situational types; yet the correlation with How suggests a somewhat troubled, but not troublesome, inmate. Subsequent tests confirm this description: There were no correlates to official or self-report disciplinary behaviors. Staff believed, however, that these inmates were having difficulties in their relationships with other inmates. Prison adjustment measures showed that these men had few friends and rather high stress scores, but the relationship was not statistically significant. They evidenced a strong need for safety and programmatic support and viewed others as willing to help.

Prison Camp   Correlates were found with situational and neurotic measures but not with other immature or dependent types. Cfms showed higher rates of official disciplinary citations than others, but staff reports and self-report measures were favorable. No adjustment difficulties were observed. Cfms evidenced only a need for programmatic support at intake, but on follow-up, actually evidenced limited participation.

I_3Cfc (Cultural Conformist)

Penitentiary   This type converged strongly with other committed criminal types and diverged from situational and high-anxiety measures. We also noted a correlation with neurotic acting-out types. Cfcs showed no correlates to official disciplinary reports, but they were more likely than others to self-report nonaggressive behavioral problems. Staff ratings were unfavorable, finding that Cfcs *(a)* showed poor relationships with other inmates, *(b)* were aggressive, *(c)* were uncooperative, *(d)* needed supervision, and *(e)* responded poorly to supervision. Adjustment measures were favorable; these inmates were not loners (according to staff) and formed friendships (according to their surveys). They also expressed a need for safety early in their prison terms and showed few tendencies to participate in prison programs.

Prison Camp   Committed criminal types did not converge well in the prison camp setting, but the Cfc type was correlated with Quay's Asocial Aggressive and with Able. Cfcs were observed to show relatively high rates of official disciplinary citations and self-reported aggressive behaviors. Staff ratings and adjustment measures were favorable.

I_3Mp (Manipulator)

Penitentiary   This was the only manipulative measure to converge with others and to show no stronger anomalous correlations with unrelated types. The type is divergent from (negatively related to) situational, committed criminal (Charlie), and disturbed types. Mps scored relatively high on self-report nonaggressive infractions and poorly on some of the staff ratings. Staff observed them as *(a)* having poor relationships with other inmates, *(b)* aggressive, *(c)* uncooperative, *(d)* in need of supervision, *(e)* responding poorly to supervision, *(f)* unmotivated, and *(g)* having poor emotional control. In their interviews they showed a need for safety. Their survey disclosed limited program participation but revealed an ability to form supportive friendships.

Prison Camp   Mp measures for this group converged with one other manipulative measure (Able) and diverged from disturbed, committed criminal, and neurotic anxious types. These inmates showed relatively high rates of official disciplinary infractions and insubordination. Self-report measures of aggressive behaviors were also high. Staff reports and adjustment ratings were favorable.

I_4Na (Neurotic Acting-out)

Penitentiary   This type does not converge with other neurotic types in this setting; instead it correlates with committed criminal and character disordered types. Nevertheless, neurotic dimensions were apparent in the high stress scores detected for this group. These results are not surprising in view of the defended aspects of neurotic acting-out behavior. Self-reports of nonaggressive infractions were relatively high. Staff rated these inmates as aggressive but favorably on other measures. Nas expressed a need for programmatic support and did not form supportive friendships.

Prison Camp   In contrast to findings for the penitentiary, we found correlates to other neurotic types, such as George and I_4Na (interview method). Nas showed significantly higher disciplinary citations and citations for insubordination. They also scored high on self-report measures of aggression. Staff ratings were favorable. As among the penitentiary inmates, however, stress scores were high.

I_4Nx (Neurotic Anxious)

Penitentiary   This type converged with MMPI neurotic types but not with Quay or I-level (interview) types. Self-report measures of nonaggressive infractions were high. Staff rated these inmates has having difficulties with authority. On other measures, however, their ratings were favorable, including ability to learn and motivation. Adjustment difficulties were noted in high stress scores, which the type description would predict. Finally, these inmates expressed needs for safety and for programmatic support.

Prison Camp   This type converged weakly with other neurotic types but strongly with How, a sign of disturbed qualities which also were shown in high stress scores. These inmates scored high on self-report aggression but did not receive unfavorable staff ratings or atypically high rates of official citations.

I_4Ci (Adaptive)

Penitentiary   Only three inmates were classified Ci on this system; therefore, results are tentative. In contrast to the I-level Ci described by the interview system, the Jesness Ci is described as a type comparable to situational offenders. In the penitentiary, this type converged with other situational measures and no correlates to disciplinary infractions were observed. Most staff ratings were favorable; correlates were observed to good emotional control, high initiative, and high ability to learn. Their participation in programs, however, appeared limited.

Prison Camp   Only one correlate to another situational measure was observed, but this type diverged from committed-criminal and neurotic acting-out measures. No disciplinary or adjustment correlates were noted. These inmates expressed a need for programmatic support at the beginning of their stay, but the follow-up survey found their participation in prison programs to be limited.

I_4Se (Situational)

Penitentiary   The type converged strongly with other situational types, but seems to identify perhaps a less sophisticated inmate than the Ci type. Ses also diverged clearly from committed criminal, neurotic acting-out, and disturbed types. The type correlated with self-report nonaggressive infractions, but not with official citations. Staff ratings and adjustment were favorable. These inmates showed low stress scores, and staff found them to evidence maturity, good emotional control, initiative, and a high ability to learn. They were rated as loners, however, and showed limited participation in programs.

Prison Camp   Construct validity test results were similar to those observed for the penitentiary inmates. We observed no correlates to adjustment or disciplinary problems, but, like the Cis, these inmates showed a need for programmatic support at the beginning of their stay, but evidenced little actual participation upon follow-up.

Table 9-5: Profiles of Jesness Inventory I-level Types

I_2

Penitentiary   Only eight inmates were classified I_2 in the penitentiary. Although, as a result, we can offer few generalizations about this group, we suggest that their adjustments to prison life may have been difficult. Staff ratings showed that they were uncooperative and needed to be supervised. There were no correlates to official disciplinary infractions, but self-reports indicated high infractions. Most of the correlations were to adjustment difficulties. These inmates were more likely than others to be rated as "institutionalized." They displayed tendencies toward high stress, limited participation, and few friends. Yet at intake, these inmates also tended to view others as willing to help.

Prison Camp   Seven inmates were classified I_2. These inmates were more likely to incur disciplinary citations, but we observed no unfavorable staff ratings. Interviews suggested that these inmates needed structure, program-matic support, and emotional feedback. They saw others as willing to help, and were oriented to the notion of rehabilitation. The survey also indicated that fear and stress were high.

I_3

Penitentiary I_3 inmates showed significantly fewer self-report disciplinary infractions than either the I_2 inmates or the I_4 inmates. Staff, however, rated them as more aggressive than other inmates and as uncooperative, more likely than others to have difficult relationships with others, needing supervision, and likely to respond unfavorably to supervision. No adjust-ment difficulties were observed.

Prison Camp I_3 and I_2 inmates showed higher rates of official citations for disciplinary infractions than I_4 inmates in the prison camp. Staff ratings and adjust-ment measures were favorable, however.

I_4

Penitentiary   These inmates indicated relatively high rates of self-report nonaggressive infractions. Staff ratings were favorable, showing good emotional con-trol, high motivation, maturity, and ability to learn. Upon intake, inter-views with I_4s indicated a need for emotional feedback.

Prison Camp I_4 inmates in the prison camp received favorable ratings on all adjust-ment and disciplinary measures.

facilities do not have the time that was afforded our research staff to formulate the I-level classifications. Small, treatment-intensive correctional facilities, however, would be well served by the system, particularly if the assessment process could be refined. No other system provided interviewers with a richer understanding of the inmate than that afforded by the interview. Type profiles are shown in table 9-6; the profiles for the two I-levels I_4 and I_5 are shown in table 9-7.

Table 9-6: Profiles of I-level Personality Types (Interview Method)

I_4Na (Neurotic Acting-out)

Penitentiary   We found convergent correlations with committed criminal types and with Ables, but no correlations with other neurotic types. Also, we did not observe high stress scores. I_4Nas were high on self-report aggressive behaviors, but the relationship was not significant. Staff ratings of relations with authority, emotional control, ability to learn, and need for supervision were unfavorable.

Prison Camp   Na measures converged better for prison camp inmates than for the penitentiary inmates. This type was correlated with Megargee George and Jesness Na, as well as with the committed criminal types. I_4Nas did not evidence stress-related problems, but self-report measures of aggression were high.

I_4Nx (Neurotic Anxious)

Penitentiary   This type did not converge well with other neurotic types in the penitentiary. Instead, the measure correlated with measures of immature types. These inmates, however, showed some adjustment difficulties (e.g., high stress and poor emotional control). Their interviews showed a need for emotional feedback; their surveys showed that they were participating in prison programs. They scored relatively low on staff ratings of their need for supervision.

Prison Camp I_4Nx measures converged much better in the prison camp than in the penitentiary, with at least one other neurotic type on each of the other systems. Nx inmates showed high stress scores and appeared unlikely to form supportive friendships. They evidenced a need for programmatic support, and staff considered them motivated. Staff also rated these inmates as aggressive, but this was not reflected in self-report aggression measures.

I_4Se (Situational)

Penitentiary I_4Ses converged with Quay Si and anomalously with Jesness Cfm, suggesting a relatively immature, naïve individual. This type also diverged from neurotic and committed criminal types. These inmates appear to be inexperienced in coping with prison life. At intake they indicated a need for safety and emotional feedback, and felt that others would be willing to help. Upon follow-up their surveys indicated high scores on fear and stress measures and a reluctance to participate. They showed the highest rates of official citations for insubordination; yet staff ratings were favorable. In chapters 6 and 7 we speculated that these inmates simply do not know how to do time (i.e., to stay out of trouble and to cope with prison life). If this is the case, we would expect to find improved adjustment over time in subsequent follow-ups.

Prison Camp   Convergent validity (correlations with other situational types) was strong. Construct validity tests also showed correlations with Jesness Cfm and divergent correlations with neurotic and committed criminal types. Like the penitentiary I_4Se inmates, these inmates appear to be immature, but they do not experience the same disciplinary-related difficulties. We note that their stress scores were high, but in this setting they were also found *(a)* to seek help from others, *(b)* to form friendships, and *(c)* to communicate with staff.

I_4Ci (Cultural Identifier)

Penitentiary   This type converged strongly with other committed criminal measures, but we also found anomalous correlations to situational and neurotic measures. Cis had high overall disciplinary rates and significantly more citations for insubordination than other inmates. Staff reported that this group needed more supervision than other inmates. They showed high stress and fear scores and communicated with staff, but also showed a greater tendency to be institutionalized than other types. The latter finding was not significant, however.

Prison Camp   Committed-criminal types did not converge as strongly in the prison camp as in the penitentiary, and there was an anomalous correlation with Able. No disciplinary-related problems were observed, and staff ratings were favorable. Staff rated these inmates as highly motivated, for example. Stress measures were low. If there were any adjustment difficulties, they showed consistently on measures tapping the inmates' level of interaction with others. I_4Ci inmates, for example, did not seek help from others, had few friends, and showed limited communication with staff.

I_5Na (Neurotic Acting-out)

Penitentiary   As with the I_4Nas, this type converged with Able but not with other neurotic types. I_5Na inmates showed high overall rates of insubordination. Self-report measures of aggression also were higher than for other I_5 types but not as high as for their I_4 counterparts. Staff ratings for these inmates generally were unfavorable. As a group, they received lower scores on *(a)* relations with authority, *(b)* aggressiveness, and *(c)* need for supervision. Adjustment measures showed high fear scores and some learning difficulties, but revealed a willingness to communicate with staff.

Prison Camp	Construct validity tests were similar to those observed for the penitentiary. I₅Nas showed high aggression scores, and staff rated them as aggressive. No additional adjustment difficulties were observed for these inmates, although they appeared to form few frindships.

I₅Nx (Neurotic Anxious)

Penitentiary	This type converged with Quay and MMPI neurotic types. Staff and disciplinary measures were favorable. Nevertheless, these inmates showed adjustment difficulties in the form of stress, fear, and needs for emotional feedback and programmatic support. Follow-up surveys showed that they were participating in programs.
Priosn Camp	The measure did not converge well in this setting. Self-report aggression results were high, as were stress scores. Nevertheless, the group indicated a need for programmatic support, and staff rated them as motivated and adept at learning.

I₅Se (Situational)

Penitentiary	This type converged with situational measures of more highly functioning types. Difficulties were not observed on disciplinary-related measures; staff rated these inmates quite favorably, as motivated and demonstrating good emotional control and an ability to learn. Nevertheless, these inmates experienced some difficulties, such as high stress, limited participation in programs, and needs for safety and emotional feedback.
Prison Camp	Measures converged with other high-functioning situational types. No correlates to disciplinary behaviors were observed; staff rated them favorably, as motivated and able to learn. Their intake interviews generally indicated a need for programmatic support and a willingness to seek help from others. Follow-up surveys showed that these inmates had formed friendships and were willing to communicate with staff.

I₅Ci (Cultural Identifier)

Penitentiary	This measure failed to converge with other committed criminal measures, and correlated only with type Able. These inmates incurred a high number of disciplinary citations and significantly higher rates of self-report, nonaggressive infractions. Staff reported a relatively high need for supervision as well as good emotional control and a high ability to learn.
Prison Camp	Only two inmates were diagnosed I₅Ci in the prison camp. Thus, the results cannot be interpreted.

Table 9-7: Profiles of I-level Types (Interview Method)

I_4

Penitentiary I_4 inmates evidenced significantly more self-report aggressive infractions than their I_5 counterparts. Staff also rated them significantly more aggressive than the I_5 inmates and found them to be less cooperative and more likely to have poor relationships with their fellow inmates. Not surprisingly, I_4s made difficult adjustments to prison. They were more likely to evidence "institutionalized" patterns and showed high fear and stress and poor emotional control.

Prison Camp   These inmates were no more likely than I_5 inmates to incur disciplinary infractions, but staff reported that they were slightly more likely to need supervision. They also showed poor emotional control and a tendency to form few friendships.

I_5

Penitentiary I_5 inmates evidenced more self-reported nonaggressive infractions, but showed favorable adjustments on other measures. They indicated a need for programmatic support and appeared to be oriented to rehabilitation. Staff reported that these inmates were motivated and showed a high ability to learn new skills.

Prison Camp   In spite of favorable staff reports, these inmates indicated high fear and a tendency to report more instances of being threatened by other inmates. Yet they were also found to be *(a)* willing to seek help from others, *(b)* willing to communicate with staff, *(c)* mature, *(d)* motivated, and *(e)* to evidence strong learning skills.

CHAPTER 10

POLICY AND RESEARCH IMPLICATIONS

The policy and research implications put forward in this chapter emerge from the singularly most important observation made throughout the preceding four chapters: that there are compelling psychological differences among inmates with regard to their experiences of the prison environment. These differences influence most of the important aspects of prison life, including communication and interactions with others, participation in prison programs, stress, fear, and vulnerability, as well as the difficulties that these inmates pose to others. Most important, these differences can be identified systematically.

When this conclusion is considered in the larger picture of correctional policy, one might assume that individual differences, particularly as they pertain to treatment recommendations, are of little concern to practitioners, administrators, and policy makers. After all, we are still operating in a restrictive political and fiscal climate, in which policy makers are endeavoring to cut most public expenditures and maintaining that prisons are for little more than punishment. With the advent of the Justice Model and more stringent, more determinate sentencing models, many jurisdictions have abandoned treatment-focused sanctions and government-mandated therapy (von Hirsch 1985). Moreover, it is well known that policy makers and some correctional scholars have questioned the effectiveness of correctional treatment (e.g., Martinson 1974). From these perspectives, individualized treatment would seem to be of limited importance, and psychological classification, for all intents and purposes, is a tool for individualized treatment.

Although psychological classification of adult inmates for treatment may seem to have no place in current policy deliberations, the two components—treatment and classification separately—have made significant strides. Indeed, against a history of pessimism and perhaps poor research (Petersilia 1991), a number of scholars have produced results from more recent treatment-evaluation literature that successfully challenge the ineffectiveness argument (e.g., Garrett 1985; Gendreau and Ross 1987; Greenwood and Zimring 1985; Hubbard, Marden, Rachal, Harwood, Cavanaugh, and Ginzburg 1989; Van Voorhis 1987). Further, despite uncongenial funding agendas, public support for constructive treatment interventions with offenders is strong (see Cullen, Skovron Scott, and Burton 1990; Public Agenda Foundation, 1987). Finally, interest in classification has grown, as shown by the emergence of several reviews of the technology (e.g., Andrews, Bonta, and Hoge 1990; Farrington and Tarling 1985; Gottfredson and Tonry 1987; Posey 1988; Sechrest 1987; Van Voorhis 1991), by the ongoing development of new systems (e.g., Andrews 1982; Megargee and Bohn 1979; Quay 1984), and by legal mandates.

Yet integration of these two trends, in the form of support for psychological classification as an aid to treatment, is not an obvious recent direction of correctional policy, at least for adults. Indeed, much of the technology of predicting and classifying adult-offender populations has supported the development and implementation of risk-assessment instruments (e.g., Baird, Heinz, and Bemus 1979; Kane and Saylor 1983; NIC 1982). As discussed in chapters 1 and 3, psychological classification of adult populations appears to be an area in which practice has not caught up with a growing body of research suggesting its use.

TREATMENT AND MANAGEMENT IMPLICATIONS

The present study contributes to that body of research. The five systems studied in this research differentiated inmates clearly on both adjustment-related measures and disciplinary/management-related measures. At the beginning of this research, we assumed that these systems would correlate with their more proximate outcome measures, those related to treatment and prison-adjustment considerations and not to prison infractions. We found instead that the psychological systems correlated with both disciplinary and adjustment (treatment-related) follow-up measures.

This observation should help to dispel previously formulated (albeit neat) compartmentalizations of the classification technology into systems that speak to risk or management and those that speak to treatment (e.g., Farrington and Tarling 1985; MacKenzie, Posey, and Rapaport 1988; Van Voorhis 1991). Indeed, our results tend to support Andrews's assertion that the two may be more interchangeable than was previously assumed[1] (Andrews, Bonta and Hoge 1990). Differences probably have been overstated. In fact, in another analysis of these data, we compared the effects of one of the psychological systems to traditional institutional risk measures on outcome measures such as overall disciplinary infractions, self-reported infractions, staff ratings of aggressiveness, and inmates' needs for supervision. We found that, depending on the criterion measure, the psychological measure (in this case the Jesness Inventory I-level) accounted for as much variation as the risk measure and sometimes more (Van Voorhis 1990). Comparisons similar to this will be addressed in future analyses of these data.

Although this study generally supports the viability of psychological classification, showing that the systems differentiate among inmates in important and sound ways, it does not take us to the next step: that of identifying ways to incorporate the differences identified by the systems. The study clearly supports this direction, however. That is, one of our clearest research and policy implications is in favor of differential treatment, or incorporating identified psychological differences into the ways in which agencies plan treatments and the ways in which staff members interact with inmates.

Unfortunately, as policy recommendations go, systematic differential treatment is far from innovative. We have known, with convincing stability across studies, that the success of given treatment modalities is highly dependent on clients' amenability to that option (Andrews, Zinger, Hoge, Bonta, Gendreau, and Cullen 1990; Gendreau and Ross 1987; Palmer 1978; Van Voorhis 1987; Warren 1971). The studies themselves found that important factors (e.g., personality and developmental characteristics, program conditions, supervisors' characteristics, treatment modality, or treatment environment and conditions) interact in ways that influence the success or failure of both clients and programs (for foundations see Andrews and Kiessling 1980; Palmer 1974; Warren 1969). For the most part, however, this body of research is limited to: (*a*) experimental efforts that seldom are adopted as systemwide correctional policy, and (*b*) juveniles. Among adults, the notion of differential treatment has received little attention.

From a policy and programmatic standpoint, the alternative is to treat all offenders as if they were alike. Innovative programs are administered to agencies or to categories of need, with no concern for psychological differences among clients. According to one of the most dedicated adherents to the policy of differentiation, researchers and practitioners routinely mask the treatment effect (Palmer 1978). In other words, the success of clients assigned to treatments that match their individual needs and characteristics is likely to be canceled out by the failure of those who were assigned to options that aggravated individual problems.

As for possible implications of the present study, the next step would be to pose questions relevant to findings observed for specific types, such as the following: What types of strategies might be used to confront antisocial values espoused by committed criminal types? Can these direct approaches be used with clients whose acting-out behaviors are triggered by confrontation or by direct reminders of personal difficulties? How can we help inmates such as situational types to make adjustments to prison environments? Do all inmates need similar assistance? Will interventions designed to deal with anxiety prompted by adjustment difficulties help those inmates whose anxiety is far more integral to their psychological makeup? Which inmates need help with issues of self-esteem and self-image? Who will benefit from, who will be hurt by, and who will exploit the various treatment options that have been proposed or will be proposed?

The next steps in treatment policy research also should include tests of the differential effects of specific treatment strategies (e.g., cognitive or behavioral) and program conditions. Most of the recent studies of differential practice, however, have taken place in Canadian correctional systems (see Andrews, Bonta, and Hoge 1990) and in the California Youth Authority during the 1960s and 1970s (Jesness 1971; Palmer 1974; Warren 1983). Among adults, differential treatment and management prescriptions have received little attention, with the exception of Warren's early work with military offenders (Grant and Grant 1959) and with prison inmates (Grant 1961) and, to some extent, the writings of Quay (1983, 1984) and Megargee and Bohn (1979). We can be more confident that assignment to living units on the basis of psychological characteristics has been found to reduce infractions among adult male inmates (Austin, Holien, Chan, and Baird, 1989; Bohn 1979, 1980; Levinson

1988; Quay 1984), but this finding appears to support a management and a custody function, once again ignoring treatment issues.

If a well-controlled evaluation study of differential treatment effects seems to be beyond the resources of most correctional agencies, an alternative but still valuable question could be addressed more easily: What is the effect of case managers' and counselors' awareness of psychological typologies on correctional outcomes? In such a situation, the only treatment effect being tested would be the treaters' trained awareness of the psychological differences among clients. We would ask only whether we can improve treaters' understanding of their clients; if so, would the improvement help?

In view of the current state of staffing for correctional treatment, the outcomes of such a study could be fairly dramatic. The typical adult correctional facility, for example, employs few full-time psychologists. Even those services are so heavily overwhelmed by inmates' crisis management needs that few resources are left for treatment (Schrink 1991). In addition, some observers have asserted that the field of "psychology has been at best neutral if not adverse to the notion of training clinical and social psychologists in the criminal justice area" (Andrews, Zinger, Hoge, Bonta, Gendreau, and Cullen 1990). Finally, case managers and counselors in most adult correctional facilities are not trained clinicians. In some systems, such positions are steps on a hierarchy from custodial to administrative careers. In most systems, however, trained clinicians are neither affordable nor available to correctional facilities in adequate numbers (Lester, Braswell, and Van Voorhis 1991). Therein lies a clear value of psychological classification systems: they may serve as a means of teaching nonclinically trained treatment staff members constructive ways of thinking about important personality and developmental differences among their clients.[2] Such training, for example, could alert the staff to think in terms of inmates who are likely to make the most difficult adjustments, to those who experience more stress than others, to those who might be more vulnerable or who might instigate their own vulnerability. The possibilities are numerous.

These systems may be valuable for helping practitioners to engage in certain types of problem-centered approaches, particularly with stress, anxiety, vulnerability, and a tendency to isolate oneself. In these cases, psychological classification systems may be more valuable than others, because they identify key problem areas for clients, especially where an interview or a central file may fail to help identify potential sources of difficulty. To this point, we have discussed psychological systems that perhaps serve both treatment and risk needs; in this situation, however, a risk-related problem is addressed more effectively than might be possible through a risk instrument, simply because the psychological systems can identify vulnerabilities prior to the onset of a problem behavior. Certainly the neurotic inmates are only one example of a group who may not show especially high risk on the risk-based instruments but who nevertheless possess certain personality characteristics that suggest propensity for aggressive behavior.

Another important program and treatment implication of this study concerns implementation, staff training, and monitoring procedures. Our experience in administering these systems has caused us to look askance at any promises for easy implementation of *any* classification system, whether risk assessment or psychological. Unfortunately, many systems were developed and touted as easy and efficient to administer. Although efficiency is important, it must be viewed in proper perspective. Indeed, it is doubtful that any system handed down from top administration, with limited attention to training, use, retraining, and monitoring, would prove very effective with populations similar to ours.

Adequate attention to a system's appropriateness to certain organizational characteristics is also important. For optimum effectiveness, facilities should plan to integrate classification clearly into the treatment and management functions of the facility. That is, classification must be linked to important case-management decisions throughout the correctional term in order to receive proper attention from prison staff. This procedure may involve (for example) citation of classification measures in report preparation and team meetings. To do otherwise invites the familiar situation in which assessments are filed and are not used.

Assessment and classification procedures themselves also must fit the organizational and environmental structure of a facility. Overcrowded situations, for example, which do not afford contained observation periods are not ideal settings in which to require staff members with high caseloads to complete behavioral observation forms, inmate by inmate. Finally, even easy systems generate more mistakes (e.g., Austin 1986), and higher staff estimates of the use of overrides (Schneider 1990) than one might expect. These potential problems perhaps are addressed most effectively by formulating a classification unit with responsibility for training, retraining, and monitoring for accuracy, response bias, excessive use of overrides, and noncompliance. Such a unit also could check for reliability by conducting periodic empirical tests of the consistency of the classification assessments.

DIRECTIONS FOR FUTURE RESEARCH

This research appears to have contributed substantially to showing the viability of psychological classification of adult male prison inmates, but our main finding is that the inmates are differentiated on the basis of psychological criteria. The next step—identifying treatment options most suitable for each group and testing the differential effectiveness of those options—poses an important agenda for future research, but one that should result in clearer treatment plans for inmate types.

Although a central rationale for the present study was that psychological classification was better understood among juvenile populations than among adult populations, we could also maintain that even some of the systems for juveniles, though used much more widely, stopped short of full development of the treatment packages. This study and the work of others only begins to tap the treatment potential of this technology.

Greater attention to the psychometric considerations must also be considered vital to the prospects of using these systems in a sound manner. If we were using these tests and measurement procedures in another field, such as education, mental health, or medicine, we would seldom utilize an instrument that (a) had not been normed to our population, unless we chose, out of our own ignorance, to use an inappropriate assessment; (b) had not published adequate assurances regarding construct and predictive validity; and (c) had not published results of various reliability tests. We would also be entitled to expect that the preliminary tests of the psychometric qualities of the systems had led to refinements, which in turn had improved the construct and predictive validity of the systems. With few exceptions, correctional diagnosis, assessment, and classification have not reached this point. This problem is compounded by the fact that most systems were developed with government funds and remain in the public domain. Thus, no mechanism is available for preventing widespread misapplication of systems that still need refinement.

Our finding regarding the construct validity of the more common neurotic, committed criminal, situational, character disordered, and developmental constructs is no small contribution to the confidence that can be placed in these systems. In addition, however, we have identified new issues. Most important, our findings point to a need to norm these systems to different institutional settings. Although this observation would appear to uncover more issues than we resolve, norming is hardly new to psychological, medical, and educational measurement. Further, our recommendations are not unlike those put forward by Wright, Clear, and Dickson (1984) with regard to risk-assessment measures, which typically are not validated to specific jurisdictions. Quite likely, failures to norm and validate instruments to specific types of populations contribute greatly to problems of overprediction and to setting inappropriate cutoff points for assignment to correctional options (Clear 1988). Such mistakes place tremendous strains on existing resources.[3]

Another area of concern regards procedures for describing and planning for rare, tied, and transitional types. At the outset of this research, we asserted that we would assess each system according to whether it classified the majority of inmates into a unique category on the typology created by the system. In hindsight, the question itself appears to reflect inadequate understanding of the personality constructs. A more accurate response might be that, overall, approximately four personality types will classify a major portion of the prison population. Beyond those four categories are rare types, transitional types, and types with multiple classifications. The research in this regard should not aim for a system that does not incur these problems, but should aim to accept that the rare and multiple types are important in themselves and to plan for them. Larger studies should endeavor to understand the characteristics of these individuals more fully and to discover the correctional treatment settings and options that make the most sense for them.

Thus, for each of the systems, we appear to understand some types very well but not others. A more thorough understanding of the types that do not fit the typology closely might, for example, direct clinical attention to these inmates and perhaps to the development of a more individualized assessment and treatment process. Alternatively, subsequent research might lead either to a questioning of the validity of the type as described originally or to a reformulation of the type descriptions.

IMPLICATIONS FOR CORRECTIONAL RESEARCH

A number of correctional and prediction scholars have warned that prediction is more than a function of sound independent (classification/predictor) measures. Criterion or dependent measures are also crucial to the prediction problem (Gottfredson, 1987b). In response, some sources advocate multiple measures of outcome (see Farrington 1987). This study incorporates that suggestion. Even so, we were surprised at the extent of the differences in results across official, self-report, and staff-based criterion measures. Most notably, if official measures of prison infractions had been our only criterion measure, they would have left us with a very misleading picture of the importance of psychological classification. Unfortunately, much of the literature on prison inmates limits analysis to official citations for disciplinary infractions (Light 1990).

Regardless of the measure employed, interpretations of findings should reflect knowledge of the data source. Official-record data (such as official crime-arrest data, for example) reflect the biases of selective reporting and citation patterns. Official prison data specifically may reflect the discretionary decision-making practices of line-level correctional staff members. Thus, measures can be marred by organizational pressures in favor of handling infractions informally, by administrative practices, by difficulty in detecting certain inmate behaviors, and by staff members' perceptions (Light 1990). In any event, official prison-record data tend to underestimate the prevalence of certain inmate behaviors and experiences (Poole and Regoli 1980).

In chapter 7, we speculated that in a number of situations our self-report data were affected by inmates' perceptions of attribution and differential concepts of acceptable and unacceptable behavior. Thus (although the matter must be subject to further research), some individuals may report more infractions in some instances because they are more introspective than other people about their own behavior. This point is particularly pertinent to offender populations where such defenses as "thinking errors" (Samenow 1984) and "techniques of neutralization" (Matza 1964) abound.

Finally, although staff data generally are adequate to our research needs, the staff members showed a tendency to rate most inmates at the norm and to underrate behaviors that inmates might need to hide, such as anxiety. The former tendency, a reluctance to issue negative evaluations unless they are extremely negative, reflects (as some employees told us) heightened concern about inmates' litigation against staff members. The latter tendency is understandable in view of inmates' well-founded concerns about the types of behaviors that are likely to place them in a vulnerable position with respect to other inmates (see Bowker 1980).

We will explore these criterion-measurement issues in future research, perhaps examining some approaches based on multiple indicators (Sullivan and Feldman 1979). For purposes of this report, however, a first step—exploring the relationship of classification types to varied indicators—seemed preferable. Indeed, construction of composite measures appeared to show limited promise, in light of the disparity of outcomes across criterion measures.

Our final observation concerns another direction for future research, which diverges somewhat from the applied focus of this study. We have placed this study in the context of serving as a test of practitioner-oriented psychological classification systems of behaviors relevant to prison management and treatment. In another sense, however, every test we conducted also assessed the importance of personality and cognitive psychological constructs in the adjustment and prisonization of prison inmates; this notion also fits a less applied, more basic, and theoretical approach. That part of the research also was successful and should recommend a more differential focus to the prisonization literature. Unfortunately, with the exception of the work of Hans Toch (e.g., Toch 1977; Toch, Adams, and Grant 1989), such differential patterns of prisonization and prison adjustment are seldom proposed.

In part, psychological considerations—particularly those regarding personality—have been undervalued in recent years as a means of understanding criminal behavior and prison experiences. Early research on the role of personality in crime causation was quite equivocal, but much of the early work endeavored to identify personality differences between offenders and nonoffenders, and concluded that personality was not an important crime correlate (Vold 1980). Consideration of the personality distinctions *among* criminals, however, has received little attention. One recent observer of this trend asserted that the "psychology of criminal conduct has been discounted for years within major sectors of mainstream criminology" (Andrews and Wormith 1989). Instead of reflecting concern for variations among individuals, research has focused on understanding aggregate crime rates, assessing the impact of structural inequality, and overstating the ineffectiveness of clinical interventions with individuals alone or in their family and peer groups. The result has been destruction of knowledge, with the implication that an understanding of variation in individual traits has little bearing on much-needed understandings of offending behaviors (Andrews and Wormith 1989; Hirschi and Hindelang 1977). The findings presented in this research appear to support the assertions of these authors.

APPENDIX A

Background Data Collection Form (PSR)

CROSS CLASSIFICATION STUDY - Background (PSR) Data

I. Social and Demographic Data

1. Inmate ID _ _ _

2. Month and year of entry into THFP
   _ _ / _ _
   98/99 = unknown
   99/99 = missing

3. Date of birth
   _ _ / _ _ / _ _
   98/98/98 = unknown
   99/99/99 = missing

4. Age at intake into THFP
   _ _ = actual age in years
   98 = unknown
   99 = missing

5. Race
   1 = white
   2 = black
   3 = American Indian
   4 = Spanish surname
   5 = Asian
   6 = other (specify)
   8 = unknown
   9 = missing

6. Marital status at intake into THPF _
   1 = married
   2 = single, never married
   3 = divorced
   4 = separated
   5 = widower
   6 = common law marriage
   7 = other (specify)
   8 = unknown
   9 = missing

7. Total number of dependents (exclusive
   of the inmate)
   1 - 5 = actual number
   6 = six or more
   7 = dependents/number unknown
   8 = unknown
   9 = missing

8. Education level of inmate/highest grade
   completed
   00 - 15 = actual number of years
             completed
   16 = college graduate
   17 = some graduate work completed
   18 = GED
   97 = other (specify)
   98 = unknown
   99 = missing

9. Evidence of school failure (e.g.,
   dropout, repeated grades, etc.) _
   1 = yes
   2 = no
   3 = NA, inmate did not attend school
   4 = unknown
   5 = missing

10. IQ

    Shipley _ _ _
             998 = unknown
             999 = missing

    WISC/WAIS _ _ _ (from files)
              998 = unknown
              999 = missing

275

11. Evidence of an urban background __
    1 = yes
    2 = mixed
    3 = no
    4 = unknown
    5 = missing

12. Psychological diagnosis (specify) __ __

13. Primary occupation of inmate __ __ (code regardless of whether or not inmate was employed in his main line of work prior to his arrest)
    00 = no occupation
    01 = professional, technical
    02 = owner, manager, or administrator excluding farmer
    03 = sales worker
    04 = clerical
    05 = craftsman
    06 = operative, except transport
    07 = transport
    08 = laborer, excluding farmer
    09 = farmer or farm manager
    10 = service worker except private household
    11 = private household worker
    12 = armed forces
    13 = student
    14 = housewife
    15 = criminal occupation/professional crime
    97 = other (specify)
    98 = unknown
    99 = missing

14. Inmate's work status at time of arrest for the present offense(s). __
    1 = not working
    2 = working, full-time
    3 = working, occasionally
    4 = working, status unknown
    8 = unknown
    9 = missing

15. Has the inmate served in the military __
    1 = yes
    2 = no
    3 = unknown
    4 = missing

16. Evidence of problems in military service __
    1 = yes (specify)
    2 = no
    3 = no military service
    4 = unknown
    5 = missing

17. Evidence of adult gang membership __
    1 = yes
    2 = no
    3 = unknown
    4 = missing

18. Evidence of inability to hold a job __
    1 = yes
    2 = no
    3 = unknown
    4 = missing

WRAP SHEET – Enter Contents of Wrap Sheet/NCIC Data

Arrest Date	Offense	Location	Disposition/Date	Time Served (MO)	Revocation (Y/N)

Append additional forms as needed.

277

19. Inmate's socioecomonic status at time of arrest ___
    1 = poverty
    2 = less than adequate
    3 = adequate
    4 = more than adequate
    5 = unknown
    6 = missing

II. Prior Record

20. Prior adult or juvenile record ___
    1 = yes
    2 = no
    3 = unknown
    4 = missing

A. Adult Record

21. Prior adult arrests ___
    1 = yes
    2 = no
    3 = unknown
    4 = missing

22. Prior convictions ___
    1 = yes
    2 = no
    3 = unknown
    4 = missing

23. Wrap Sheet (fill out the next page prior to completing items 24-46.)

24. Age at first non-traffic arrest (compute from wrap sheets) __ __ age (years)

25. Total number of prior misdemeanors __ __
    00 - 96=actual number
    97 = misdemeanors on record, total number unknown
    98 = unknown
    99 = missing

26. Total number of prior felonies __ __
    00 - 96 = actual number
    97 = felonies on record, actual number is unknown
    98 = unknown
    99 = missing

27. Does inmate's prior record show evidence of dealing in drugs?
    0 = no prior record
    1 = yes
    2 = no
    3 = unknown
    4 = missing

28. Does inmate's prior record show evidence of professional criminal activity? ___
    0 = no record
    1 = yes
    2 = no
    3 = unknown
    4 = missing

29. Does inmate's prior record show evidence of violence against persons? (inflicted violence)?
    0 = no prior record
    1 = yes
    2 = no
    3 = unknown
    4 = missing

30. Prior prison sentence___
    0 = no prior record
    1 = yes
    2 = no
    3 = unknown
    4 = missing

31. Prior Jail Sentence. (Note: Do not include pretrial detention for current or prior offenses.)
    0 = no prior record
    1 = yes
    2 = no
    3 = unknown
    4 = missing

32. Excluding the present offense, how many months has the inmate spent in a prison setting as an adult?

000-995 = actual months
996 = no time
997 = time spent in prison, actual amount of time is unknown.
998 = unknown
999 = missing

33. Prior prison escapes ___
0 = no prior record
1 = yes
2 = no
3 = no prior prison record
4 = unknown
5 = missing

34. Prior probation revocation ___
0 = no prior record
1 = yes
2 = inmate was on probation but was not revoked
3 = inmate was not on probation
4 = unknown
5 = missing

35. Prior parole revocation ___
0 = no prior record
1 = yes
2 = inmate was on parole but was not revoked
3 = inmate was not on parole
4 = unknown
5 = missing

36. Does the inmate's prior record or current offense indicate any relationship between the use of alcohol and his criminal behavior? ___
1 = yes/prison record
2 = yes/immediate offense
3 = yes/both prior record and immediate offense
4 = no
8 = unknown
9 = missing

37. Does inmate's prior record or current offense indicate a relationship between the use of drugs and his criminal behavior? ___
1 = yes/prior record
2 = yes/immediate offense
3 = yes/both prior record and immediate offense
4 = no
8 = unknown
9 = missing

38. Has the inmate ever been convicted for the same offense as the present conviction offense? ___
0 = no prior record
1 = yes
2 = no
3 = unknown
4 = missing

39. Was the inmate ever convicted for a sex offense? ___
0 = no prior record
1 = yes
2 = no
3 = unknown
4 = missing

B. Juvenile Record

40. Prior arrests as a juvenile ___
0 = no prior record
1 = yes
2 = no
3 = unknown
4 = missing

41. Prior adjudications for delinquent activity ___
0 = no prior record
1 = yes
2 = no
3 = unknown
4 = missing

42. Prior status offense declarations ___
0 = no prior record
1 = yes
2 = no
3 = unknown
4 = missing

43. Does the juvenile record show evidence of violent behavior against persons? (Inflicted violence?) ___
   0 = no record
   1 = yes
   2 = no
   3 = unknown
   4 = missing

44. Was the inmate institutionalized as a juvenile? ___
   0 = no record
   1 = yes
   2 = no
   3 = unknown
   4 = missing

45. Does the juvenile record show any relationship between the use of drugs and his delinquent behavior? ___
   0 = no record
   1 = yes
   2 = no
   3 = unknown
   4 = missing

46. Does the juvenile record show any relationship between the use of alcohol and his delinquent behavior? ___
   0 = no record
   1 = yes
   2 = no
   3 = unknown
   4 = missing

III. Current Offense

47. Total number of charges for the inmate ___
   01 - 96 = actual number
   97 = more than one, actual number unknown
   98 = unknown
   99 = missing

Specify Charge

Most serious

48. First Charge _____
49. Second Charge _____
50. Third Charge _____
51. Fourth Charge _____
52. Fifth Charge _____
53. Sixth Charge _____
54. Seventh Charge _____
55. Eighth Charge _____
56. Ninth Charge _____
57. Tenth Charge _____
58. Eleventh Charge _____
59. Twelfth Charge _____
60. Thirteenth Charge _____
61. Fourteenth Charge _____
62. Fifteenth Charge _____ Least serious

63. Type of weapon involved (carried or used) ___
   1 = knife/sharp instrument
   2 = gun
   3 = blunt instrument
   4 = no weapon
   5 = other (specify)
   7 = weapon involved, type unknown
   8 = unknown
   9 = missing

64. Co-offender involvement ___
   1 = yes, not organized or conspiracy
   2 = yes, organized/conspiracy
   3 = no
   4 = unknown
   5 = missing

65. Victim-offender relationship(s) __ __
    00 = no victim
    01 = family/relative/paramour
    02 = private employer
    03 = government employer
    04 = neighbor
    05 = other acquaintance
    06 = stranger
    07 = government
    08 = a collective (other than government)
    95 = combination of two or more of the
        above (specify)
    96 = other (specify)
    97 = victim, relationship unknown
    98 = unknown
    99 = missing

66. Type of victim __ __
    00 = no victim
    01 = personal victim
    02 = business victim
    03 = government victim
    04 = collective victim
    95 = combination of two or more of the above (specify)
    96 = other (specify)
    97 = victim types unknown

67. Evidence of victim precipitation __
    0 = no victim
    1 = yes
    2 = no
    3 = unknown
    4 = missing

68. Evidence of professional criminal activity (e.g. repeated embezzlement/racketeer, bank robberies, etc.)
    1 = yes
    2 = no
    3 = unknown
    4 = missing

69. Evidence of criminal activity requiring complex skills of persuasion, organization, computer expertise, etc. (e.g. some forms of fraud, embezzlement computor fraud, etc.)
    1 = yes
    2 = no
    3 = unknown
    4 = missing

IV. System Processing

70. Date of arrest
    __ __ / __ __ / __ __
    98/98/98 = unknown
    99/99/99 = missing

71. Date of conviction
    __ __ / __ __ / __ __
    98/98/98 = unknown
    99/99/99 = missing

72. Type of conviction __
    1 = plea of guilty, no trial
    2 = plea of nolo, no trial
    3 = convicted by trial, bench
    4 = convicted by trial, jury
    7 = other (specify)
    8 = unknown
    9 = missing

73. Date of sentencing
    __ __ / __ __ / __ __
    98/98/98 = unknown
    99/99/99 = missing

281

74. Mode of intake into Terre Haute Federal
    Penitentiary _____
       1 = First institutional
           assignment on present term
       2 = Transfer
       3 = Federal part of a state/federal
           concurrent
       4 = Parole violation
       5 = Probation violation
       6 = other (specify)

75. Sentence length for current
    offense (months)
    _____ _____ (actual months)
    9999 unknown

282

APPENDIX B

I-level Interview

CROSS CLASSIFICATION STUDY

I-Level Interview

I. EXPECTATIONS OF THE PRISON SENTENCE

Intent: This section is intended to provide content information pertaining to the following: (1) interactions within the prison, (2) an indication of inmates salient concerns about prison life, (3) primary difficulties and strategies for coping with them, and (4) placement of self within the various intents of corrections. In addition, descriptions of staff and other inmates often provides initial I-level diagnoses, primarily level material. But remember that level is most evident in people that the inmate is close to.

1. Have you ever done time before?

2. What have you heard about Terre Haute?

3. How long do you expect to be here?

4. Do you think that they'll do anything for you here?

> 4a. Will anything good come out of this?
>
> 4b. Is that something that will help you?
>
> 4c. Why? / Why not?

5. What do you think it is going to be like here?

> 5a. Do you expect any difficulties?
>
> 5b. Like what?
>
> 5c. How will you handle them?

6. How about the other people in here?

> 6a. Will you spend any time with the other guys in here—get to know any of them?
>
> 6b. **If no:** Why not?
>
> 6c. **If Yes:** What kinds of guys will you spend time with?
>
> 6d. Do you feel that there's anyone you can trust here?

7. **OPTIONAL:** Are there any guys that you'll stay away from?

> 7a. What kind of guys will you stay away from? 7b. Why?

8. Do you have a work assignment yet?

       8a. Is that the assignment of your choice?

       8b. Is there something that you'd rather do?

       8c. How about the no. of work hours? Are they about right for you?

       8d. Do you have enough free time? Why?

       8e. Do you feel a need to be kept busier? Why?

9. How about the staff?

       9a. Do you think that they're concerned about you as a person, or are you just another inmate to them?

       9b. How do you feel about that?

10. Do you think that any of them will try to help you out?

11. What do you think makes a good staff member? Why?

       11a. **OPTIONAL:** What's your idea of a bad staff member? Why?

12. What do you think it's like to be a staff member here?

13. How wuld you handle being a staff member?

14. What would you say is the purpose of your stay here in Terre Haute? Why are you here?

15. What should be the purpose of prisons?

16. Do you belong here? Why? / Why not?

II. OFFENSE

Intent: This section is important for both level and subtype. Content items include: (1) evidence of guilt or empathy, (2) orientation to the criminal label, and (3) dynamics of the offense.

17. What were you convicted of?

18. Can you tell me about the incidents that led up to your arrest?

19. What led up to [describe the behavior] your arrest?

20. Did you spend much time planning it?

21. Was it just you or were others involved?

   If others were involved:

       21a. Who else was involved?

       21b. Were you in charge of things?

       21c. Did the others do what they were supposed to do?

       21d. Do you work with these people often?

22. Have you ever done this before?

23. Thinking about it now, how do you feel about this offense?   Why is that?   How about your behavior?

24. How important was [the behavior] at the time that you did that?

25. Do you think that [the behavior] was serious or not?   Why? / Why not?

26. If I were to draw a line from zero to 100, with zero meaning not serious and 100 meaning very serious, where would you place your offense?

       26a. Why there?

27. If we could go back in time to just before you [behavior], would you do anything differently?   What?   Why?

III. VICTIM(S)

Intent: This section obtains level information (e.g. What do you think it would be like to be a victim?). We are also obtaining information pertinent to the inmate's guilt about the offense and his empathy for the victim.

28. Was anyone affected by this offense?

       28+. **Optional:** Was there a victim?

If a personal victim:

       28a. What was s/he like?

       28b. How do you feel about him/her?

      28a. Can you tell me what the business that you hit was like?

      28b. Why did you hit this place and not some place else?

      28c. Do you think that anyone there was affected by the offense?

29. What do you think it would be like to be a victim?

V. PRIOR CRIMINAL INVOLVEMENTS

Intent: This section obtains important subtype material.

30. Have you ever been arrested for anything before?

      30a. After all of that was over, did you ever think you'd get involved
             again?   Why / Why not?

      30b. Do you have any idea why this happened again?

48. This happens to others (they get arrested again—sometimes over and over
again). Do you have any thoughts about why this might happen?

49. How are the reasons that others repeatedly get into the criminal justice
system different from yours?

VII. FAMILY

Intent: This section is one of the most important sections for obtaining
level material. In addition, neurotic and situational information also is
given as inmate discusses how he hanles difficulties with others and his
feelings about how he was raised.

33. Are you married?

    If Yes or if invloved in a relationship:

        33a. How did your wife [friend] take this [inmate's incarceration]?

        33b. Does she hold it against you?

        33c. How do you feel about that?

        33d. What is your wife [or friend] like?

        33e. Do you think that you have a good marriage?

If **divorced** or **separated**:

33a. What was your wife like (probe for reasons for the separation or divorce)?

33b. Do you think that you'll ever get married again—once you get out of here?

If **currently married, involved, or formerly married**:

34. What would a good marriage be like?

35. What kind of a woman would make a good wife for you?

36. How do/did you and your wife handle disagreements?

37. What would you disagree about?

38. Do you think that you handled these disagreements well?

40. Did you ever get really mad at her?

40. Do you have any Children?

If **Yes**:

40a. How many?

40b. Did you see them very often?

40c. Did they live with you?

40d. Did you do things with them?   What sort of things?

40e. Do you have a favorite child?

40f. What is s/he like?

40g. Does s/he take after you?   How? How do you feel about that?

40h. How is s/he different from you? How do you feel about that?

40i. What is it like for you, being a father?

40j. Do you think that you're a good parent?   Why / Why not?

40k. What would make a good parent?

401. Have you been raising your children pretty much the way you were raised or are there some differences?

40a. Do you think that you'd make a good parent?   Why? / Why not?

40b. Would you raise your kids the way you were raised of would there be some differences?

For all inmates:

41. Who did you live with while you were growing up?

42. How about your parents?

43. What kind of woman was your mother (or your mother figure) while you were growing up?

If inmate talks about mother in only positive or negative terms:

What things about your mother would you have changed if you could have? (Pull for positive if only negative is given and vice versa).

43a. Why was / is she like that?

43b. How do you think she got that way?

43c. Did others see her that way?

43d. How would others describe her?

43e. How did the two of you get along while you were growing up?

43f. What is she like now?

45. How about your father (or father figure)?   What was he like while you were growing up?   (Pull for negative if all comments are positive and vice versa).

45a. Why was he like that?

45b. How do you think he got that way?

45c. Did others see him that way?

45d. How would others describe him?

45e. What do other people think about him?

45f. Did you and he spend much time together?

45g. Did you and he get along?

45h. How would you describe him now?

290

46. Are you more like your mother or father?

47. In what ways are you similar to your [whomever Mo or Fa]?

       47a. How do you feel about the similarity to your [M or F]?

48. Did either your mother or father discipline you a lot?

       48a. What sorts of things would they punish you for?

       48b. How would they punish you?

       48c. How did you feel about the times they punished you?

49. Did your family have enough money while you were growing up?

50. How did your family handle disagreements?

       50a. At the time, did you think that that was a good way?

       50b. What do you think about it looking back now?

51. What were you like as a child? (If inmate cannot answer: "What kinds of things would you like to do?")

       51a. Would you say your childhood was happy?

52. What was the neighborhood1 that you grew up in like? (probe for rural, urban, inner-city background).

53. How about the kids that you used to hang around with?

       53a. What were they like?

       53b. What sorts of things would you do?

54. Do you have any brothers or sisters?

       54a. Where do you fall in the group (oldest, youngest, middle, etc.?)

       54b. Were you close to any of them while you were growing up?

       54c. What was that brother / sister like?

55. Has anyone in your family, besides yourself, been involved with the law?

56. Have things with your parents changed over the years?

57. How do your parents feel about all of this?

58. Is your family going to be all right while your're here?

59. Do you want your family (e.g. parents, wife, kids, and siblings) to visit your here?   Why? / Why not?

60. Do you think that they will?

61. How often do you communicate with your parents now?

62. How often do you communicate with your children now?

63. How often do you communicate with your Wife / paramour / girlfriend?

64. How often do you communicate with your (closest) brother / sister?

VIII. FRIENDS

Intent: These questions offer primarily level information and, to a lesser extent, subtype data.

65. Are friends important to you?   Why? / Why not?

66. Do you have many friends?

67. What sort of person makes a good friend?   Why?

Optional: 68. When you meet someone for the first time, what things about him/her would make you want him/her for a friend?

69. Do you have any especially close friends?

70. What is the difference between a close friend or just an average friend?

71. Have any of you friends been involved with the law?

        72. Did you work with them?

        73. Are these most of your friends or just some of them?

        74. **if inmate was involved with co-offenders:** How did you meet the people you worked with?

IX. SELF

Intent: This section obtains level and subtype information as well as content information of self esteem.

75. Can you tell ne what you're like?

76. What sort of a person are you?

77. Do you think that others see you that way?

X. HANDLING PROBLEMS AND AFFECTIVITY

Intent: This section obtains subtype information and information on difficulties in prison and coping strategies.

78. Are you the sort of person who gets strong feelings about things, or would you say that you're more easy going?

79. How do you handle anger?

      79a. What sorts of things make you feel that way?

      87c. Do you handle anger differently in here?

80. Do you ever feel kind of down or depressed?

      81a. What sorts of things make you feel sad like that?

      81b. How do you handle these feelings?

      81c. Do you handle these feelings of sadness differently in here?

82. Do you ever find yourself thinking things over a lot, kind of mulling them over in your head?

      82a. What is that like for you?

      82b. Do you do more of that in here?

83. Do you worry about things a lot?

      83a. What sorts of things do you worry about?

      [83b. How about in here?]

      83c. If you were really worried about something in here, would you ask for help?

      83d. How about the staff, would you go to them if you had a problem?

84. Have you ever been attacked or threatened in a prison?

      84a. How did you handle that?

      84b. Was that a good way to deal with it?

85. Have you ever been really happy about something?

      85a. When was that?

      85b. How do you express it?

      85c. Is there **anything** in here that can make you happy?   What?

293

XI. ALCOHOL

Intent: This section and the next section provide both content, and I-level information. We are looking for information pertinent to drinking patterns, and the extent to which alcohol and drugs may be involved in the inmate's pattern of behavior. In addition, reasons for drinking may also provide some subtype information with respect to the neurotic subtypes.

86. Before you came here, did you drink?

87. How much?

88. How often?

89. There are many reasons why people drink. Do you have any thoughts about why you drink?

90. How do you act when you've had a lot to drink?

91. Had you been drinking when (offense)?

92. Has drinking ever been a problem for you?

XII. DRUGS

93. How about drugs?   Were you into that at all?

       93a. What kind of drugs did you use?

       93b. How often did you take them?

       93c. When did you start?

       93d. How long have/had you been using them?

       93e. What do drugs do for you?

       93f. Were you using drugs when you committed this offense?

       93g. Would you say that you have a problem with drugs?

94. Have you ever used drugs?

   If YES:

   94a. What kind?

   94b. How often did you use them?

   94c. Why did you stop?

   94d. When would you use them?

   If NO:
   94e. Why not? What stopped you?

XII. WORK

Intent: This section and the next section obtain material for content items pertaining to job responsibility, stability, etc. Some I—Level information may be presented.

95. Were you working before your arrest?

   95a. **If NO:** When was the last time that you worked?

96. What were you doing?

97. How long were you at that job?

98. What did you do before that?

99. Did you get along with your boss?

100. How about other bosses that you've had?

101. Did they respond to you as a person or were you just another worker to them?

102. How much time did you miss from work?   Why couldn't you go to work?

103. Did you ever quit a job?

   103a. Why?

   103b. Did you ever feel like quitting?

   103c. Why didn't you quit?

If not employed:

104. How did you make a living?

295

XIII. SCHOOL

106. How did things go for you in school?

107. Did you finish up?   When did you leave?

108. Can you get any schooling here?   Will you take any classes?

109. Do you have any plans for the remainder of your prison term?

XIV. ADVICE TO NEW INMATES

Intent: This section collects content information only.

110. If you were to advise a new inmate about how to best handle prison life, what would you tell him?

111. What advice would you give to him about communicating with other inmates?

XV. FUTURE ORIENTATION

112. Do you have any plans for when you get out of here?

113. What sorts of things will help you stay out of future trouble?

114. What will you be doing with your life then?

APPENDIX C
Follow-up Survey

Research ID_____

CROSS CLASSIFICATION STUDY

FOLLOW-UP INTERVIEW

DIRECTIONS: Please do not put your name on either the questionnaire or the answer sheet. In order to keep your answers confidential, you will be given a number to place on both forms.

If there is any question that you do not wish to answer, you may skip it and go on to the next one.

As we explained to you earlier, we are being careful to make sure that no one will ever know how you personally responded to this or to other parts of our study. Therefore, we hope that you will answer these questions honestly and carefully.

PART I

The first part of the survey asks about some of your experiences since you were admitted to this institution. Please indicate the number of times you have had these experiences since you wereadmitted. The questions are answered by darkening in the appropriate letter on the computerized answer sheet and by answering questions on this sheet when you are asked to do so. Please use a number 2 pencil.

REMEMBER YOUR ANSWERS ARE PRIVATE.

1. I have been helped by other inmates.

   a. never
   b. once
   c. more than once

2. I have been helped by my case manager or counselor.

   a. never
   b. once
   c. more than once

3. I have been helped by people in the chapel.

    a. never
    b. once
    c. more than once

4. I have been helped by my work supervisor.

    a. never
    b. once
    c. more than once

5. I have been helped by a correctional officer.

    a. never
    b. once
    c. more than once

6. I have been helped by one of the prison medical doctors

    a. never
    b. once
    c. more than once

7. I have been helped by a prison psychologist.

    a. never
    b. once
    c. more than once

8. I participate in educational programs.

    a. no
    b. I started a program but stopped attending
    c. yes

    Please list the programs that you have fully participated
    in. Do not include programs that you tried but stopped
    attending on a regular basis:
    _____   _____

    _____   _____

9. I participate in selfimprovement and selfhelp groups. For
   example: Alcoholics Anonymous, Vietnam Veterans, etc.

    a. no
    b. I started a program but stopped attending
    c. yes

Please list the programs that you have fully participated in. Do not include programs that you tried but stopped attending on a regular basis:

_____   _____

_____   _____

10. I have missed work on days that I was not sick.

    a. never
    b. once
    c. more than once

11. I have been written up for missing work.

    a. never
    b. once
    c. more than once

12. I have been threatened by other inmates.

    a. never
    b. once
    c. more than once

13. I have been pressured for sex by other inmates.

    a. never
    b. once
    c. more than once

14. I have been physically attacked by other inmates (do not include a sexual attack).

    a. never
    b. once
    c. more than once

15. I have been sexually attacked by other inmates.

    a. never
    b. once
    c. more than once

16. I have had money or possessions stolen from me.

    a. never
    b. once
    c. more than once

17. I have been insulted by other inmates.

    a. never
    b. once
    c. more than once

18. I have received a certificate or other reward while in this institution. For example: clean cell, completing a school or other program.

    a. never
    b. once
    c. more than once

    List the certificates or rewards that you have received:

    _____

    _____

    _____

    _____

19. I have verbally threatened another inmate.

    a. never
    b. once
    c. more than once

20. I have physically attacked another inmate.

    a. never
    b. once
    c. more than once

21. I use drugs in here.

    a. never
    b. once
    c. more than once

22. I drink in here

    a. never
    b. once
    c. more than once

302

23. I have stolen money or possessions from other inmates.

    a. never
    b. once
    c. more than once

24. I gamble.

    a. never
    b. once
    c. more than once

25. I have verbally insulted another inmate.

    a. never
    b. once
    c. more than once

26. I have reported another inmate to institutional officials.

    a. never
    b. once
    c. more than once

27. I have trouble sleeping.

    a. never
    b. once a week
    c. more than once a week

28. I have had visits from family members (not including a wife or girlfriend).

    a. never
    b. once
    c. more than once

29. I have had visits from my wife or girlfriend.

    a. never
    b. once
    c. more than once

30. I have had medical problems.

    a. never
    b. once
    c. more than once

List the medical problems that you have experienced since
you were admitted:

_____   _____

_____   _____

_____   _____

_____   _____

31. I have formed friendships with the other inmates.

    a. no, none
    b. one
    c. more than one

32. I have formed close friendships with other inmates.

    a. no, none
    b. one
    c. more than one

33. I talk to correctional officers.

    a. never
    b. seldom
    c. regularly (at least every other day)

34. I talk to chapel staff.

    a. never
    b. seldom
    c. regularly (at least once a week)

35. I talk to my case manager.

    a. never
    b. seldom
    c. regularly (at least once a week)

36. I talk to my counselor.

    a. never
    b. seldom
    c. regularly (at least once a week)

37. I talk to my work supervisor.

   a. never
   b. seldom
   c. regularly (at least every other day)

38. I talk to one of the psychologists.

   a. never
   b. seldom
   c. regularly (at least once a week)

39. I call family or friends on the outside.

   a. never
   b. seldom
   c. regularly (at least once a week)

40. I am working in the job of my choice.

   a. yes
   b. no

   Please list the work assignments that you have had:

   _____

   _____

   _____

41. I have had trouble with my cell mate.

   a. never
   b. once
   c. more than once

   If you have had trouble with your cell mate, specify the nature of the difficulties.

   _____

   _____

42. I have changed cellmates due to difficulties between us.

   a. never
   b. once
   c. more than once

PART II

The purpose of this part of the interview is to determine the extent and nature of any stress that you may be experiencing while in this institution. In response to the situations listed below, please indicate whether it is: a) not at all stressful, b) somewhat stressful, c) very stressful, or d) extremely stressful.

SAMPLE ITEM:

Holidays.

A = Not at all stressful
B = Somewhat stressful
C = Very stressful
D = Extremely stressful

If you feel that holidays are very stressful for you, you would darken circle "C" on your answer sheet. Your answer sheet would look like this:

A	B	C	D
1	2	3	4

43. Having nothing to do.

44. Thinking about my family.

45. Loud inmates.

46. Having to share a cell with another inmate.

47. The noise level in this institution.

48. Lack of privacy.

49. Feeling guilty about my arrest and the events that led up to it.

50. Thinking about meetings with the parole board.

51. Thinking about what my wife or girlfriend is doing.

52. Concern about whether or not I will be sexually attacked by another inmate.

53. Inmates who are not of the same race as me.

54. Concern for my physical safety.

55. Not being able to have sex.

56. The staff.

57. My health.

58. Thinking about what I will do with my life after my release.

59. Not being able to understand the rules and regulations here.

60. Not being able to find anyone to talk my problems over with.

61. Not knowing where to go for help.

62. Not having anyone who cares about me.

Response Categories

   A) Not at all stressful
   B) Somewhat stressful
   C) Very stressful
   D) Extremely stressful

63. Thinking that I am not a good person.

64. Trying to get into programs that would benefit me.

65. Not having time to myself.

66. Having rules.

67. Not knowing many of the people here.

68. Tough people.

69. Not having visits.

70. Not knowing when I will get out of here.

Please list the three things that have caused you the most stress since you were admitted.

1. _____

2. _____

3. _____

71. Select the one statement that best describes you since you began your sentence.

   A. I have not experienced stress. I usually don't worry about things.

   B. I sometimes worry about things, but I feel that I can keep it under control. I have learned to cope with the things that worry me.

   C. I worry a lot about things, but usually I can find someway to feel better after a while.

   D. I worry a lot and have difficulty finding something that will help me feel better.

   E. I worry so much that I sometimes feel sick, can't sleep, or experience some other difficulty as a result of my worrying. I have difficulty finding something that will help me feel better.

PART III

After the first few weeks in prison, many inmates learn ways that help to make their day to day life easier. This part of the questionnaire is designed to help us learn about some of the things that you find helpful.

We have listed several activities below. Please respond to each item by indicating on the answer sheet whether you find the activity:

    A) Not at all helpful
    B) Somewhat helpful
    C) Very helpful
    D) Extremely helpful

Please remember that we are not asking you to tell us whether you <u>do</u> the activity, but whether or not you find it helpful in coping with your prison time.

72. Working out in the gym or outside recreation facilities.

73. Preparing a daily schedule of activities.

74. Working at my assigned job.

75. Talking to another inmate about my problems.

76. Working extra hours.

77. Talking to my case manager about my problems.

78. Talking to my counselor about my problems.

79. Talking to the chapel staff about my problems.

80. Talking to the prison psychologists about my problems.

81. Talking to a correctional officer about my problems.

82. Talking to my work supervisor about my problems.

83. Socializing with other inmates.

84. Talking to a family member on the outside about my problems.

85. Thinking things over.

310

Response Categories

A) Not at all helpful
B) Somewhat helpful
C) Very helpful
D) Extremely helpful

86. Staying away from tough inmates.

87. Participating in some of the school activities.

88. Writing letters.

89. Gambling.

90. Participating in a program that may help me to improve myself.

91. Contact with my family and my friends on the outside.

92. Letting other inmates and staff know where I stand.

93. Forming friendships with other inmates.

94. Helping others.

95. Getting physically aggressive when I need to be.

96. Telling prison officials when they're not doing their job.

97. Finding someone who will keep me out of trouble.

98. Gambling.

99. Receiving encouragement from other inmates.

100. Letting others know that I can be violent if they cause me any trouble.

101. Making plans for my futurewhen I get out of here.

102. Helping my family out.

103. Finding someone who will tell me how to handle my problems.

104. Drinking.

105. Doing something to get my mind of of my problems.

106. Praying

Response Categories

    A) Not at all helpful
    B) Somewhat helpful
    C) Very helpful
    D) Extremely helpful

107. Telling someone off.

108. Watching TV.

109. Saving money.

110. Keeping to myself.

111. Gambling

112. Playing cards.

113. Participating in activities that will improve my chances for being released.

114. Facing my problems head on.

115. Going to my cell when I am scared.

116. Meditating.

117. Doing something creative.

118. Being reminded by others to keep myself out of trouble.

119. Helping other inmates.

120. Receiving words of encouragement from prison staff.

121. Knowing people who will help me out.

122. Practicing my religion.

123. Running.

124. Being alone.

125. Doing drugs.

126. Finding other inmates who will fight along side me if I need protection.

127. Listening to music.

128. Reporting an inmate who is giving me problems.

PART IV

With your help, we have learned a good deal about the beliefs and attitudes that inmates have toward doing time. This final section asks more questions about these issues. We want to get a sense of your thoughts now that some time has passed since we talked with you.

In response to the statements that follow, please choose one of the following reactions:

    A) Strongly disagree
    B) Disagree
    C) Neutral
    D) Agree
    E) Strongly agree

129. When you're in a place like this you should be careful to mind your own business.

130. Prison time is easier if you make some friends.

131. Don't burden others with your problems.

132. Inmates should make every effort to keep busy.

133. Inmates should look for activities that will show the parole board that they've used their time constructively.

134. Never rat on another inmate.

135. You have to be prepared to use violence if need be.

136. Programs are important if they help people to improve themselves.

137. You can't get through this experience on your own. You need the help of others.

Response categories

A) Strongly disagree
B) Disagree
C) Neutral
D) Agree
E) Strongly agree

138. No purpose can be served by my doing prison time.

139. It is important to help the other inmates out.

140. Don't make trouble for other inmates.

141. It's important to make it known that no one should mess with me.

142. I deserve to do some time.

143. This experience is helping me to grow.

144. Do your own time.

145. Don't talk to the correctional officers unless you absolutely have to.

146. There are some inmates whom I can trust here

147. I was rehabilitated before I came here.

148. People will respect an inmate if he's loud and tough.

149. It's advisable to stay to yourself in here.

150. Doing this time makes me feel like I'm paying back society for my offense.

151. There are staff people who can help me out.

152. It is impossible to experience any feelings of happiness in here.

153. Sometimes I actually feel like I'm accomplishing something here.

154. It is possible to psych the staff out.

155. It ok to find a friend who will protect me.

156. This experience has taught me a lesson. I have sworn off criminal activity forever.

Response categories

A) Strongly disagree
B) Disagree
C) Neutral
D) Agree
E) Strongly agree

157. Sometimes I feel like I cannot succeed on the outside.

158. Society is safer with me in here.

159. Some staff have shown concern for me as a person.

160. The best reason for participating in programs is to make your record look good. In reality, they can't do much to improve me.

161. I am depressed most of the time here.

162. Anyone who rats on another inmate deserves the consequences.

163. If it weren't for some of the other guys in here, I'd never make it.

164. Avoid homosexual inmates.

165. I was sent here to be punished and I deserve it.

166. It's possible to trust some of the inmates here.

167. It's possible to trust some of the staff here.

168. Help is available when I really need it.

169. I deserve to be here in this institution.

APPENDIX D

Items Composing Penitentiary Follow-up Scales

Items Composing Penitentiary
Follow-up Scales

Victimization Scales
---

1. Victimization
About how many times have you been
threatened by other inmates?
physically attacked by other inmates (not a sexual attack)?
insulted by other inmates?
pressured by other inmates?

2. Fear
I am stressed by
thinking about whether or not I will be sexually
attacked by another inmate.
tough inmates.
concern for my physical safety.

Support Networks
---

1. Perceives help
About how many times have you been helped by
other inmates?
your case manager or counselor?
the prison chaplain?
the inmates in the chapel?
your work supervisor?
a correctional officer?
a prison psychologist

2. Has friends/support
About how many
friendships have you formed with other inmates?
close friendships have you formed with other inmates?

3. *Communication*
  About how often do you talk with/to
    correctional officers?
    the chaplain?
    your case manager?
    your counselor?
    your work supervisor?
    one of the psychologists?

Program Utilization

---

1. *Program Participation*
  Have you participated in
    educational programs?
    self-improvement or self-help groups?

  Participating in some of the school programs (as a coping strategy)
  Participating in a program that may help me to improve
    myself (as a coping strategy)

2. *High Activity (for coping)*
  Things that you do in order to cope with prison life:
    Working out
    Preparing a daily schedule of activities
    Working at my assigned job

Stress

---

1. *Nature and Extent of Stress (check one)*
  I have not experienced stress. I usually don't worry about things.
  I sometimes worry about things, but I feel that I can keep it
    under control. I have learned to cope with the things
    that worry me.
  I worry about a lot of things, but usually I can find some way to
    feel better after a while.
  I worry a lot and have difficulty finding something that will help
    me feel better.
  I worry so much that I sometimes feel sick, can't sleep, or
    experience some other difficulty as a result of my worrying.
    I have difficulty finding something that will help me feel
    better.

2. *Center for Epidemiologic Studies Depression Scale (check all that
  apply)*
  During the past four weeks
    you were bothered by things that don't usually bother you.

you did not feel like eating; your appetite was poor.
you felt that you would not shake off the blues even
with help from your family and friends.
you felt that you were just as good as other people.
you had trouble keeping your mind on what you
were doing.
you felt depressed.
you felt that everything you did was too much work.
you felt hopeful about the future.
you thought your life had been a failure.
you felt fearful
your sleep was restless.
you were happy.
you talked less than usual.
you felt lonely.
you enjoyed life.
you had crying spells..
you felt sad.
you felt that people disliked you.
you could not get going.

Self-Report Disciplinary

---

1. *Self-Report Aggression*
   About how many times have you
   verbally threatened other inmates?
   physically attacked another inmate?
   verbally insulted another inmate?

2. *Nonviolent Disciplinary Infraction*
   About how many times have you
   been written up for missing work?
   gambled (money) in this institution?
   drunk alcoholic beverages in here?
   used illegal drugs in here?

APPENDIX E

Items Composing Prison Camp Follow-up Scales

Items Composing Prison Camp
Follow-up Scales

Victimization Scales

---

1. Victimization

About how many times have you been
threatened by other inmates?
physically attacked by other inmates (not a sexual attack)?
insulted by other inmates?
had money or possessions stolen from you?

2. Fear

I am stressed by
thinking about whether or not I will be sexually
attacked by another inmate.
tough inmates.
concern for my physical safety.

Support Networks

---

1. Perceives help

About how many times have you been helped by
other inmates?
your case manager or counselor?
the prison chaplain?
the inmates in the chapel?
your work supervisor?
a correctional officer?
a prison psychologist

2. Has friends/support

About how many
friendships have you formed with other inmates?
close friendships have you formed with other inmates?

3. Communication
About how often do you talk with/to
correctional officers?
the chaplain?
your case manager?
your counselor?
your work supervisor?
one of the psychologists?

Program Utilization

---

1. Program Participation
Have you participated in
educational programs?
self-improvement or self-help groups?

Participating in some of the school programs (as a coping strategy)
Participating in a program that may help me to improve
myself (as a coping strategy)

2. High Activity (for coping)
Things that you do in order to cope with prison life:
Working out
Preparing a daily schedule of activities
Participating in school activities
Participating in a program that may help me to improve myself

Have you participated in education programs?

Have you participated in self-help programs

Stress

---

1. Nature and Extent of Stress (check one)
I have not experienced stress. I usually don't worry about things.
I sometimes worry about things, but I feel that I can keep it
under control. I have learned to cope with the things
that worry me.
I worry about a lot of things, but usually I can find some way to
feel better after a while.
I worry a lot and have difficulty finding something that will help
me feel better.
I worry so much that I sometimes feel sick, can't sleep, or
experience some other difficulty as a result of my worrying.
I have difficulty finding something that will help me feel
better.

2. *Center for Epidemiologic Studies Depression Scale (check all that apply)*

During the past four weeks

you were bothered by things that don't usually bother you.

you did not feel like eating; your appetite was poor.

you felt that you would not shake off the blues even with help from your family and friends.

you felt that you were just as good as other people.

you had trouble keeping your mind on what you were doing.

you felt depressed.

you felt that everything you did was too much work.

you felt hopeful about the future.

you thought your life had been a failure.

you felt fearful.

your sleep was restless.

you were happy.

you talked less than usual.

you felt lonely.

you enjoyed life.

you had crying spells.

you felt sad.

you felt that people disliked you.

you could not get going.

Self-Report Disciplinary

---

1. *Self-Report Aggression*

About how many times have you

verbally threatened other inmates?

physically attacked another inmate?

verbally insulted another inmate?

2. *Nonviolent Disciplinary Infraction*[a]

About how many times have you

been written up for missing work?

gambled (money) in this institution?

drunk alcoholic beverages in here?

used illegal drugs in here?

---

[a] Index was not used because of limited variability. Only seven inmates responded affirmatively to these items.

327

NOTES

CHAPTER 1

1. Systems that focus on treatment-relevant needs, or "needs assessment systems," offered a different approach to internal classification, Yet, although they identify treatment goals, such as education and job development, the needs assessment systems devoted little attention to psychological or personality characteristics (see NIC 1982). Both the needs and the risk/security systems serve important functions, but, in contrast to the psychological systems, they offer little to further our understanding of criminal behavior or to help us understand how we might interact with clients (MacKenzie 1989).

2. Unfortunately, sources sometimes defined the classification process as involving a choice between risk systems and psychological systems (e.g., see Hanson, Moss, Hosford, and Johnson 1983; Motiuk 1984). Implementation of the psychological systems is *not* advocated as an alternative to existing techniques that assign adult male inmates to institutional settings on the basis of security criteria. Instead, the use of psychological systems recognizes that "every institution has a range of inmates—from the predators at one extreme to their prey at the other end of the spectrum" (Levinson 1988, 27), even after these inmates have been assigned to the same institution on the basis of security criteria. Indeed, the two types of systems are distinct in both an applied and a conceptual sense (Van Voorhis 1991).

3. Most notably, the Federal Bureau of Prisons has implemented Quay's AIMS (Quay 1984) in several federal facilities and Megargee's MMPI-Based Criminal Classification System (Megargee and Bohn 1979) at others. State systems, including facilities in South Carolina, Washington, and Wisconsin, also have used both of these systems or a similar system called Prisoner Management Classification (PMC) (see Austin, Holien, Chan, and Baird, 1989; Levinson 1988; Zager 1988).

4. Several comprehensive reviews and discussions of classification and prediction technology have been published. Most notably, Gottfredson and Tonry (1987) compiled a series of papers that span a broad array of methodological and policy issues. In addition, a 1988 edition of *Criminal Justice and Behavior* presents overviews of several psychological classification systems.

5. This question addressed the interrater reliability of the I-level and the Quay systems. The remaining systems were sent to established scorers and raters for assessment. Because the subjects had already agreed to participate in one lengthy interview, two testing sessions, and one follow-up survey, staff determined that any additional test sessions would incur the risk of compromising inmates' willingness to cooperate. The I-level reliability assessment involved a second rating of a recorded I-level interview; the AIMS reliability involved both the correctional staff and the research staff in obtaining a second assessment for a subsample of the cases. Thus, in neither instance were the inmates required to appear for a second interview or test. See chapter 4 for additional details.

6. This assessment was conducted for each of the systems.

7. This question is most relevant to the juvenile systems (e.g., the I-level, the Jesness Inventory, and the Conceptual Level), because they have not been tested widely among adult inmates. Type descriptions for the MMPI and AIMS systems were developed through research with adult populations; thus, one would expect to see fewer findings which would suggest revisions of the type descriptions.

8. In fact, in the course of administering the various tests and interviews, the project staff gained a valuable comparative sense of how the systems work across institutional settings and administrative processes. For some persons, particularly the future consumers of these systems, our field experiences and findings may prove to be as valuable as the results of our statistical tests.

9. For example, the history of boot camps, "scared straight," and other deterrent treatment models has taught us the sad lesson that favorable television coverage, coupled with the effects of a culture turned "tough on crime," can rapidly unravel years of strong empirical evidence of the failures of these measures (see Gendreau and Ross 1987; Morash and Rucker 1990; Palmer 1992).

10. The Federal Bureau of Prisons adheres to a 6-level system of security designation. Levels 5 and 6 are considered maximum. Levels 1 and 2 are minimum-security institutions.

11. Of course, one would expect to see far more I_5 adults than juveniles. As the subsequent analyses will show, 35% of the camp subjects and 42% of the penitentiary subjects were diagnosed at I_5 according to the interview method.

CHAPTER 2

1. This system has also been referred to as the Behavioral Classification System for Adult Offenders.

CHAPTER 3

1. The reader is referred to the following overviews: (1) the Megargee MMPI-Based Criminal Classification System (Megargee and Bohn 1979;

Zager 1988); (2) Quay AIMS (Quay 1984); (3) I-level (Harris 1983, 1988; Warren 1983); (4) the Jesness Inventory (Jesness 1988); and (5) Conceptual Level (Reitsma-Street 1984; Reitsma-Street and Leschied 1988). For several excellent discussions of classification and prediction methodology, see Gottfredson and Tonry 1987.

2. The reader is referred to the following for more in-depth discussions: Brennan 1987; Gottfredson 1987a, Gottfredson 1987b; Loeber and Dishion 1983; Monahan 1981.

3. These sources maintain that psychological classification is more valuable as a tool for assisting prison adjustment and treatment planning than as a predictor of recidivism or offense behaviors (Jesness 1988; Megargee and Bohn 1979). Because samples already had been identified as criminal and delinquent and as having propensities toward future offending behaviors, the types were not expected to differentiate offenders on offense-related behaviors. Nevertheless, research shows some weak to moderate correlations; but the stronger correlates generally are to attitudes, adjustment, and other treatment-related factors. These results are not surprising, because offenders are quite varied on attitudinal and adjustment indices and less so on offense-related measures. Further, attitude and adjustment are theoretically more proximate correlates of psychological types than are offending behaviors.

4. Without much further attention to this issue, this author would have to agree with Andrews and Wormith (1989). At least four well-known criminologists are cited consistently and erroneously for dubious interpretations of extremely carelessly read literature and for questionable understanding of the workings and nature of personality constructs and systems designed to measure them.

5. Although this is a useful example, the answer is not as obvious as it appears, because it may ignore the other human errors that might occur without the prediction instrument. Indeed, research shows that subjective, intuitive, and discretionary decisions are less accurate than actuarial methods of prediction (Carroll, Wiener, Coates, Galegher, and Alibrio 1982; Glaser 1962).

6. But research is currently underway at the University of Washington and the Washington Department of Corrections which endeavors to combine personality, background, and adjustment variables into a prediction format through the use of algorithms that combine numerous relevant indices (86-IJ-CX-0072). Another system that incorporates psychological variables with more traditional predictor variables is the Level of Supervision Inventory (LSI) (Andrews 1982).

7. The MMPI is becoming an exception to this observation (see Zager 1988).

8. Attempts to attain a less broadly defined criminal subtype (e.g., character disorder, psychopathic, manipulative, subcultural), however, did not produce significant results.

9. Types designated as "situational" on the various systems risk being used as "catch-alls" that actually identify individuals who could not be

placed into any of the other types. If this is the case, one would not expect the type to correlate to other measures in a meaningful way.

10. The subtypes, however, were not developed fully at the time of the Camp Elliot study.

11. This point was confirmed in a discussion with Dr. Jesness in August 1989.

12. In contrast to the present study, these tests involve correlations with related but not identical constructs.

13. The existing tests limit "differentiation" to assignment to living units on the basis of a diagnosed type. A valid test of the results of a more comprehensive use of the differential treatment recommendations proposed by each of the systems has yet to be conducted.

CHAPTER 4

1. Shortly after their admission, inmates were asked whether they would be interested in participating in the study. They were informed of the purpose of the study, the level of participation that would be expected of them, and the data needs of the research. They were assured that the information collected (e.g., interviews, tests, surveys, and staff ratings) would be taken from the institutions and considered confidential unless, for their own reasons, they chose to sign a release of information at a later date. They were told that they could withdraw from the study at any time and that there was no obligation to participate. The inmates were informed that no remuneration would be offered in exchange for their participation but that a letter would be placed in their central file, thanking them for their participation. Finally, they were required to agree to these terms in writing by signing a consent form prepared for the project. Research procedures were reviewed and approved at various times by the Human Subjects Committees at Indian State University and the University of Cincinnati and by the Federal Bureau of Prisons.

2. Each interviewer participated in extensive training sessions during the first month of his or her employment. In addition, week-long training sessions were held with I-level trainers in December 1986 and March 1988.

3. "Unavailable" inmates often became ineligible because of early transfers. Thus, it is somewhat misleading to include them in the pool of eligibles.

4. The rate for the penitentiary falls to 72% when "no shows" are included among the refusals, but generally it was not possible to determine why an inmate was not responding to callouts. Thus, an inmate's failure to report to the interview session was not necessarily a refusal; nor do we know that it occurred for any systematic reason. Fortunately, this situation was surprisingly infrequent throughout the course of the research. There were no "no shows" at the camp because of the lower security level and because the interviewer had greater mobility throughout the facility. She could talk to inmates before the scheduled interview, and could locate them if they failed to report to the session. In contrast, the

penitentiary interviewer had more limited access to systems for contacting inmates.

5. The original design for the follow-up data included only official records of disciplinary infractions and the Megargee staff ratings. When the staff began collecting these data four to six months after the start-up of the project, they expressed concerns about difficulties in obtaining staff ratings and about whether there would be sufficient variability on the disciplinary measures. The survey initially was developed as a back-up source of follow-up data in case the original sources proved insufficient. Ultimately, all follow-up data proved sufficient, and the self-report survey proved to be a wise addition in its own right. As will be shown in subsequent chapters, the self-report data greatly expanded the scope of this research.

6. The Shipley scale is used in many settings as an efficient (60-item) method for estimating IQ (WAIS) (Wechsler 1955; Zachary, Paulson, and Gorsuch 1985). This process has been refined in recent years to correct for early difficulties in accounting properly for age and to estimate scores on the revised Wechsler Adult Intelligence Scale (WAIS-R; Wechsler 1981). In converting the Shipley scores to WAIS-R scores, we used estimation tables developed by Zachary, Crumpton, and Spiegel (1985) for the WAIS-R.

7. In addition to the listed variables, however, this form contains a number of variables that could not be obtained reliably, such as psychological diagnoses, religious preference, and evidence of adult gang membership. In this case, the research staff learned fairly early in the project that the PSIs were not reporting this information consistently.

8. One of the sentence stems, "What I think about parents . . . ," is typically omitted from most uses of the PCM because of reliability problems (Reitsma-Street and Leschied 1988).

9. Quay scores did not appear to vary significantly according to the role of the person completing the CAC. Chi-square tests for differences between the counselors', case managers' and work supervisors' assessments were not significant, as shown below.

Percentage Distribution of Inmates across AIMS Classification, by CAC Rater

Quay Type	Counselor	Case Manager	Work Supervisor
Aa/Id/Na[a]	11	14	18
Manipulator	33	16	9
Situational	56	70	73
Total	100	100	100

Chi-square = 5.78, p = .22

[a]Asocial Aggressive, Immature Dependent, and Neurotic Anxious categories were collapsed because of insufficient numbers for the chi-square test.

10. Some prison camp inmates served actual sentences of four months or less. In fact, 31% of the sample were sentenced to terms of twelve

months or less. We do not have data pertaining to the actual time served by these inmates before their release, but according to federal policy allowing for good time, many could have been eligible for release after serving only one-third of their sentence (i.e., a four-month term).

11. Some of the CALHs, however, were rated by the project interviewer at the camp. Because this interviewer also conducted the I-level assessments for the camp, it was necessary to entertain the possibility that her knowledge of I-level could have influenced her ratings on the CALH. A number of factors act as a check against this possibility. Most important is the fact that the resulting AIMS classification is a synthesis of the assessments by two individuals, the person completing the CAC and the person completing the CALH. Moreover, the CALH often was completed after the interview, but it is entirely possible that the interviewer also was considering I-level dimensions. To test this possibility, we conducted a difference-of-proportions test in order to ascertain whether substantial differences existed between the AIMS results in which the CALH was completed by the interviewer and those in which the CALH was completed by graduate assistants in Cincinnati. The result of the chi-square test (5.22, df = 4, p = .26) was not significant, an indication that the interviewer's knowledge of the I-level diagnosis probably did not affect the final AIMS results.

12. This is not to question the validity of these diagnoses at this point, because one would expect a far grater proportion of situational offenders in a minimum-security facility than in a maximum-security institution.

13. Sentences of less than four months occurred occasionally at the prison camp but not at the penitentiary.

14. Although these constitute a relatively small number of cases, they were important to follow because the transfer may have been prompted by a serious infraction or victimization experience.

15. An attempt to code the severity level for each offense was unsuccessful because the Bureau's severity code was not entered consistently onto the disciplinary reports.

16. Data availability for the two evaluations at the prison camp is as follows:

Adjustment Forms
      Inmates with one evaluation = 55 (33%)
      Inmates with two evaluations = 43 (26%)
      Inmates with three evaluations = 69 (41%)
Work Performance Forms
      Inmates with one evaluation = 0
      Inmates with two evaluations = 40 (30%)
      Inmates with three evaluations = 95 (74%)

CHAPTER 5

1. On the average, the penitentiary inmates had completed 10.2 years of school and the camp inmates had complete 11.3 years.

2. Age at first recorded arrest ranged from 7 to 40 for the penitentiary

inmates (mean = 18.2, median = 18.0). Among prison camp inmates, the ages at first arrest ranged from 12 to 46 (mean = 23.1, median = 22.0). These figures, however, cannot account for those whose records as juveniles were expunged; therefore, data pertaining to age at first arrest may not describe each sample accurately.

3. Firearms-related convictions among the penitentiary inmates occasionally were somewhat misleading because the interviews often revealed that federal agents were investigating these offenders on other charges. For a variety of reasons, however—usually expedience—they decided to arrest them on the weapons charge.

4. As discussed in chapter 3, it was not clear initially whether the camp results for the AIMS system were biased by problems incurred in administering the AIMS instruments, because research staff members had discovered that some of the prison personnel were returning CAC forms in which all responses were checked as zero (not pertaining to the inmate). These results suggest that our corrective measures were effective. Our concerns are allayed by two considerations: (1) the diagnosis of "Situational" on this system is the type we would expect to be the modal type in a minimum-security facility, and (2) the manipulative rather than the situational type would be overrepresented in a case of response bias similar to the one we corrected.

5. In fact, in comparison to Heide (1982), we observed no I_3 inmates and a much higher proportion of inmates diagnosed at I_5. This finding could be attributable either to the differences in samples or to problems with the reliability of I-level across raters (Harris 1988).

6. Specifically, the criteria were more generous for moving to I_4 inmates who also demonstrated I_3 traits and for moving to I_5 inmates who also demonstrated I_4 traits.

CHAPTER 6

1. In this sense, an "anomaly" is a correlation with a theoretically unrelated variable. Sometimes that finding makes sense, as when an immature dependent type correlates with a neurotic type, because both types evidence high levels of anxiety. In such a case, we have chosen to *suggest* that the finding may be furthering our understanding of the type, and that perhaps the flaw lies in our original hypothesis or in an overly simplified type description rather than in the variable. Alternatively, when the relationship exists with an unrelated variable (e.g., when a situational type correlates with a committed-criminal type), we question the validity of the type or perhaps the reliability of the measure. Use of this bootstrap approach most certainly will necessitate further testing of these findings in later research.

2. Because results for the statistical test (phi) range from 0 to 1.0, no negative correlations are observed. However, unless otherwise indicated, the divergent findings can be interpreted as significant disagreements even though they are not presented as negative.

3. In spite of the similarity in names, the Jesness Ci is described quite differently from the I-level interview Ci. In the interview system, Cis are described as subcultural offenders who have a criminal value system and usually a criminal network (Warren et al. 1966). Jesness (1988), however, describes Cis (also called "adaptive") as "high verbal aptitude; highly motivated for school; positive attitudes toward authority, school, parents, and self; confident; good interpersonal relationships; nondelinquent orientation; and low self-reported and official delinquency (p. 82)."

4. Because we recognize that I_3 inmates would be unlikely to be found in this population, all interviews for inmates classified as I_3 by the research staff were sent out for second ratings to the I-level consultants hired to assist with this research. In every case, the consultants changed the classifications to I_4. In previous chapters we discussed reliability problems with the I-level system, different rating conventions across raters, and the need for a more structured rating system. One area of disagreement clearly concerns criteria for establishing level. Some raters employ "threshold" criteria, classifying an inmate into the highest level heard in the interview regardless of the extent of use. Other raters require an integrated use of the diagnosed cognitive characteristics. Such raters, for example, classify an inmate according to the predominant level of use. Our use of the former approach may explain why we have inflated our level diagnoses over what we would have observed using the latter criteria. Weak correlations with outside measures of immaturity would seem to support this suggestion.

5. The I-level interview method identifies a manipulative type I_3Mp, but our research identified no I_3 inmates.

6. This is not to say that the Jesness Inventory I-level classifications map directly onto the I-level classifications obtained through the interview process. Both theoretically and empirically, the Jesness Inventory I-level classifications are lower than the interview classifications for the same individual.

7. This issue is a familiar one to psychology, corrections, and education. In corrections, it is perhaps most analogous to the argument for validating risk-assessment systems on a jurisdiction-by-jurisdiction basis, with admonitions that the systems otherwise will not be as accurate or as predictive (Wright, Clear, and Dickson 1984).

CHAPTER 7

1. Results of the probit analysis are not presented in the tables because the maximum-likelihood probit coefficients for the probit models are less readily interpretable than the parameters for the cross-tabular and OLS models. Instead, results for the probit analyses are presented in the text.

2. In this case, use of the multiple-correlation figure is preferred to the R^2 value, because the independent factors in each multiple regression equation together represent one underlying variable. Thus, the multiple r coefficient might be viewed as comparable to a bivariate Pearson's r coefficient.

3. Because the Quay system is already a highly structured process, difficulties may be corrected through an effort to construct a manual that defines clearly the terms used in the two checklists. The I-level interview method, however, is a semistructured clinical process that would require, at a minimum, the development of a structured manual detailing rules for making decisions about transitional cases.

4. Another analysis of the Jesness Inventory and of the MMPI data correlated only the types with an N greater than 5 on the official data. Although this procedure improved the degrees of freedom and removed types that were likely to be unstable, the results were not noticeably different from those reported in table 7-2.

5. As stated earlier, we analyzed the MMPI data a second time, using only the 123 most valid profiles. "Most valid" in this sense referred to cases in which none of the validity scores were noted to be problematic and to those scales in which the F-K index was greater than 13. The latter identify the test taker's attempt to "fake bad" or to feign psychopathology. Some sources, however, have questioned the ability of the F-K scale to make such a distinction (see Greene 1980). Moreover, our checks for "faking good" and "faking bad" included an alternative choice: that of excluding cases with F scores surpassing 79T and cases flagged by the scoring process as "faking good." These exclusions are made only for the purpose of conforming to this second, conservative view of the MMPI data; they are not necessarily recommended by the system's designers. In fact, according to Megargee and Bohn (1979), fake good and fake bad responses are, to some extent, reflective of the nature of a criminal population.

The results of the regression tests were not significant, but some patterns regarding results for specific types are noteworthy. Among the most valid tests, for example, average scores for Hows were higher than those reported in table 7-2. Mean scores were 5.8 on all disciplinaries, 3.5 on drug offenses, and 4.3 on offenses involving insubordination. Table 7-2 shows the comparable scores as 4.2, .7, and 2.8, respectively. Similarly, scores were lower on the disciplinary variable (5.5) and the subordination variable (1.1) for inmates classified as Item. Thus, although the differences between the types do not reach significance, the most valid tests produce results that conform somewhat more closely to the type descriptions. It is not surprising that validity problems would be most likely to affect the results pertaining to type How. They typical profile for the inmate who responds randomly to items on the MMPI is quite similar to the profile for How. Moreover, the mental disorganization noted to characterize How is often reflected in the validity scores of the MMPI (Megargee and Bohn 1979). As a result, controlling for validity problems removes a substantial proportion of the Hows from the analysis.

6. We analyzed the MMPI data a second time using only the 85 cases that were considered to be most valid. We observed similar results: None of the multiple regression or cross-tabular tests produced significant findings. The only exception occurred in the regression of the Megargee MMPI types on self-reported disciplinary infractions for the inmates classified as

How. As in the official data (see 5, above), their mean scale score was more pronounced (mean = 1.6) in this second test.

7. Conversation with Dr. Marge Reitsma-Street, August 1989, Albuquerque.

8. Cross-tabular analysis of the relationship between the *uncollapsed* types and nonaggressive incidents was also significant when the types with fewer than five inmates were removed from the analysis(χ^2 = 8.50, p ≤ .10).

9. At Dr. Jesness's suggestion, we removed those inmates whose score on the Repression Scale of the Jesness Inventory surpassed 70, and we ran these analyses again.

10. None of the goodness-of-fit, chi-square values for the probit analyses were observed to be significant.

11. Examining these data a second time by removing the 25 cases with questionable scores on the MMPI validity scales failed to change these results from those reported in table 7-5.

12. Cross-tabular and multiple regression analysis produced similar results when the types with few cases were excluded from the analysis in order to improve cell frequencies and degrees of freedom.

13. In addition, results were significant for cross-tabular and multiple regression analysis of the uncollapsed types when I_2Aa and I_4Ci inmates were removed in another analysis, which also was conducted to improve cell frequencies (χ^2 = 17.32, p ≤ .01; multiple R = .44, p≤ .01).

14. Analysis of the collapsed types among the most valid cases did not change these findings.

15. When the I_2 types and the I_4Ci inmates were removed, multiple regression analysis revealed a significant relationship between the uncollapsed Jesness Inventory types and the cooperation measure.

16. This is not to say that official, self-report, and staff rating measures were always comparable across similar constructs. In several instances, a measure (e.g., aggression) would be available for one method and not another. For example, data pertaining to officially recorded acts of aggression and victimizations were collected by the research staff, but these occurrences were too infrequent to support subsequent analysis. Instead, measures of aggressive tendencies were obtained through self-report and staff ratings.

17. We found few such correlates of staff ratings of the prison camp inmates, however (table 7-7). This result is likely to be attributable to poor variability on the prison camp staff ratings. As shown in table 7-7, very few inmates were rated as problematic on any of these items. In fact, staff members often rated inmates in the middle of the scale, as average.

18. For purposes of this report, we decided that it would be premature to consider the possibility of creating composite indexes using official, self-report, and staff measures of a single construct. A more comprehensive examination of the comparison across follow-up measures is the subject of another study (Van Voorhis, forthcoming).

CHAPTER 8

1. We should note, however, that the participation variable may be tapping either an inmate's reluctance to participate *or* limited opportunities for participating. Thus, if an inmate felt that there were few programmatic options, he probably indicated limited participation. For another inmate, limited participation might have indicated limited initiative, as he neglected to take advantage of programs that were available to him.

2. The excluded rating items include: *(a)* need for activity, because of limited variability; *(b)* need for freedom, because of poor interrater reliability; and *(c)* most salient need, because of poor interrater reliability. In addition, we excluded need for safety from the analysis of the prison camp data, because variability was limited; few minimum-security inmates are concerned about their safety.

3. We analyzed the MMPI data a second time, excluding cases that evidenced problems on the validity scales of the MMPI (see chapter 7, note 5). Our discussion is limited to the collapsed types because of insufficient cell sizes. Statistical results were unchanged; all of the tests proved to be nonsignificant. For three of the tests, however, the distribution of types across categories of prison needs changed for group How and the combined Charlie and Foxtrot group. When we controlled for potential validity problems, proportionately more How inmates (38%) than others indicated a need for privacy. Fewer inmates in the combined Charlie and Foxtrot group (14%) and more inmates classified as How (25%) showed a need for programmatic support.

4. It is important to note that the prior prison experience is much longer for the Asocial Aggressive and the Immature Dependent penitentiary inmates than for the inmates classified into the other Quay groups. In fact, more than 50% of the Asocial Aggressive and Immature Dependent inmates had served more than five years in prior prison sentences. As expected, the Situational inmates had the least prior experience; only 27% of those inmates had more than five years of prison experience, and 39% had less that four months. The relationship between the Quay AIMS types and the amount of prior time served was significant ($\chi^2 = 20.42$, $p \leq .05$).

5. As with the Quay AIMS types (see above), inmates diagnosed as Charlie and Foxtrot on the Megargee MMPI-based system were significantly more likely to have more extensive prior prison experience than those diagnosed as Item or Easy ($\chi^2 = 45.10$, $p \leq .01$).

6. When the tests were conducted a second time, using only the most valid MMPI profiles, the results did not change. All significant tests remained significant. Means and proportions for group How on tests of its relationship to fear, friendships, CESD stress, and stress, however, are considerably higher.

7. The data were run a second time, using only the cases known to be independent of the adjustment data. As stated in chapter 4, 71 (48%) of the Megargee Adjustment Forms had been completed by the same counselor

or case manager who completed the CAC portion of the Quay assessment. Although we addressed this issue in chapter 4, we ran these data a second time to determine whether findings had been inflated by the potential lack of independence. The results of the second analysis were nearly identical to those shown in table 8-5 for the cross-tabular analyses; measures of association remained significant.

8. Once again, the findings do not change when only the most valid MMPI results are analyzed, except that the scores for group How are somewhat higher.

9. The results for the Megargee MMPI-based types do not differ greatly when only the most valid cases are analyzed, except that the one weak relationship was no longer significant.

10. One certainly could question the independence of the I-level data from the interview rating items, because in most cases the two were rated by the same rater, even though she was asked to rate I-level and interview measures at different times. We do not correct for possible biases here, because concern for independence of measures is obviously reserved for situations where findings may be inflated as a result of lack of independence. Because the tests for I-level and the interview items did not produce significant results, we did not pursue the question further.

11. When we conducted the analysis a second time without the MMPI profiles that showed questionable validity, the significant relationships held. In the test of the relationship between the MMPI types and whether the inmate saw others as willing to help, none of the (now) 10 How inmates stated that others would help.

12. Once again, we analyzed these data a second time, excluding 18 cases that scored poorly on the validity scales. Some differences were noted: Multiple regression tests of the relationship between the MMPI types and "has friends" and between the MMPI types and communication were now significant (multiple $r = .39$, $p \leq .10$ and multiple $r = .39$, $p \leq .10$, respectively). In both instances, average scores for inmates diagnosed as How were considerably lower than those for the full sample. The average scores for Hows on the "Sees Help" scale and the "Participates" scale were also lower. This finding repeats a pattern for other tests of this nature: Exclusion of the potentially invalid profiles has the effect of making the How inmates appear even more dysfunctional and more consistent with their type descriptions.

13. In chapter 4, we noted that self-report scores on the fear and friendship indexes were related significantly to the variable measuring the number of months served between intake and inmates' completion of the survey. As a result, we conducted these tests a second time controlling for this time factor. In all of the tests, entering the time variable changed R^2 values; R^2 change values ranged from .03 to .09 and were significant for all but one test. Controlling for the time variable, however, did not change the relative effects of the psychological factors over those observed in table 8-8. Other self-report indexes were not affected by the amount of time served and thus were not subjected to these controls.

14. Proportions obtained for the cross-tabular analysis and shown in table 8-9 represent the proportion of inmates scoring above the mean for each scale. This table differs from the presentation of the penitentiary-staff data, in which the proportion represented the inmates who received negative ratings (below the mean). As might be expected, the camp inmates as a group received more favorable staff ratings than the penitentiary inmates. Hence distributions and decisions regarding collapsed categories were different for each sample, and thus allowed us to obtain collapsed distributions most favorable to the analyses and assumptions of the statistical tests.

15. This second analysis was performed only for the relationships shown to be significant in table 8-9. One would not expect the removal of the 20 cases to improve the results for tests of the relationship between the Quay types and the measures of initiative and learning ability, because the issue of independence pertains to findings that may have been inflated rather than to nonsignificant relationships.

CHAPTER 9

1. Other diagnoses (Conceptual Level, Megargee's MMPI-based taxonomy, and the Jesness Inventory I-level classifications) were obtained through their respective scoring services. The reliability figures for these systems are those published for the systems and presented in chapter 4.

2. Other studies, particularly the research that served as the basis for designing the classification systems, correct this problem with large sample sizes, approaching 2,000 in some case. These studies typically require the administration of only one classification instrument and do not include lengthy interviews.

3. This point refers to an emerging concern about litigation against staff members, brought by inmates who disagree with negative ratings or unfavorable classifications.

4. This conclusion is emerging from other studies of classification instruments designed to be administered quickly. Risk-assessment instruments, for example, are observed to evidence surprisingly high error rates and a substantial number of estimated overrides (Schneider 1990). A related concern is whether the instruments require *enough* thought from practitioners to receive the attention they need in order to be completed validly (Van Voorhis 1990).

CHAPTER 10

1. Andrews's research shows that risk assessment systems often have treatment-related implications, even though they were created ostensibly to reduce prison infractions. His study compares the Wisconsin Risk Assessment Instruments (Baird, Heinz, and Bemus 1979), which does not include psychological factors, with his Level of Supervision Inventory

(LSI), which incorporates psychological, sociological, and environmental factors as well as traditional risk factors such as prior record, age at first arrest, and addiction patterns (Andrews, Bonta, and Hoge 1990). Our study finds that psychological systems, although created primarily for treatment and adjustment, also have implications for management and custody.

2. Throughout the course of this research, several psychologists questioned whether the systems were "rich enough" to provide them with the information needed to treat problem clients. From the standpoint of a clinician, particularly one who is trained in the use of a variety of assessment and clinical techniques, this question is probably important. It is less relevant, however, when we consider the users and the purposes of these systems. Indeed, the systems make more sense for nonclinically trained treatment personnel and for decision making for large numbers.

3. Our critique here is relevant to Quay AIMS systems, which has been studied among several inmate populations but has not received the necessary additional attention and development in recent years, and to both of the I-level systems and the Conceptual Level, which only now are being applied to adults. The Megargee MMPI system is currently being revised to examine the applicability of the MMPI-2. The validation research for this revision is being conducted in several inmate populations, including a sample of female inmates. All systems could benefit from more centralized reporting of psychometric values for adult populations, as well as from more careful attention to administrative procedures.

REFERENCES

Allen, H. and C. Simonsen. 1986. *Corrections in America*. New York: Macmillan.

Andrews, D. 1982. *The Level of Supervision Inventory (LSI)*. Toronto: Ontario Ministry of Correctional Services.

Andrews, D., J. Bonta and R. Hoge. 1990. Classification for effective rehabilitation: Rediscovering psychology. *Criminal Justice and Behavior* 17(1): 19–52.

Andrews, D., and J. Kiessling. 1990. Program structure and effective correctional practices: A summary of CaVIC research. In *Effective correctional treatment*, ed. R. Ross and P. Gendreau, pp. 441–63. Toronto: Butterworth.

Andrews, D., and J. Wormith. 1989. Personality and crime: Knowledge destruction and construction in criminology. *Justice Quarterly* 6(3): 289–310.

Andrews, D., I. Zinger, R. Hoge, J. Bonta, P. Gendreau, and F. Cullen. 1990. Does correctional treatment work? A clinically relevant and psychologically informed meta-analysis. *Criminology*. 28(3): 369–404.

Austin, J. 1983. Assessing the new generation of prison classication models. *Crime and Delinquency* 29(3): 561–576.

————. 1986. Evaluating how well your classification system is operating: A practical approach. *Crime and Delinquency* 32(3): 302–22.

Austin, J., D. Holien, L. Chan, and C. Baird. 1989. *Reducing prison violence by more effective inmate management: An experimental field test of the Prisoner Management Classification (PMC)*. San Francisco, CA: National Council on Crime and Delinquency.

Babbie, E. 1986. *The practice of social research*. 1983. Belmont, CA: Wadsworth.

Baird, C., R. Heinz, and B. Bemus. 1979. *Project report 14: A two-year follow-up*. Milwaukee: Department of Health and Social Services.

Baum, M., R. Hosford, and C. Moss. 1983. Predicting violent behavior within a medium security correctional setting. Unpublished manuscript. Santa Barbara: University of California.

Beker, J., and D. Hyman. 1972. A critical appraisal of the California Differential Treatment typology of adolescent offenders. *Criminology* 10(1): 1–59.

Berkson, J. 1947. Cost utility as a measure of efficiency of a test. *American Statistical Association Journal* 42: 246–55.

Bohn, M. 1979. Classification of offenders in an institution for young adults. *FCI Research Reports* 9: 1–31.

———. 1980. Inmate classification and the reduction of institution violence. *Corrections Today* 42(4): 8ff.

Bonta, J., and L. Motiuk. 1985. Utilization of an interview-based classification instrument: A study of correctional halfway houses. *Criminal Justice and Behavior* 12(3): 333–52.

Booth, R., and R. Howell. 1980. Classification of prison inmates with the MMPI: An extension and validation of the Megargee typology. *Criminal Justice and Behavior* 7(4): 407–22.

Bowker, L. 1980. *Prison victimization.* New York: Elsevier.

Brennan, T. 1987. Classification: An overview of selected methodological issues. In *Prediction and classification: Criminal justice decision-making,* ed. D. Gottfredson and M. Tonry, 323–366. Chicago: University of Chicago Press.

Bukstel, L., and P. Kilmann. 1980. Psychological effects of imprisonment on confined individuals. *Psychological Bulletin* 88(3): 469–93.

Bureau of Justice Statistics. 1985. Prisoners in 1984, U.S.Washington, DC: Department of Justice.

Campbell, D., and D. Fiske. 1959. Convergent and discriminant validity by the multitrait-multimethod matrix. *Psychological Bulletin* 56(2): 81–105.

Carbonnel, J. 1983. Inmate classification systems: A cross-tabulation of two methods. *Criminal Justice and Behavior* 10(3): 285–92.

Carey, R., J. Garske and J. Ginsberg. 1986. The prediction of adjustment to prison by means of an MMPI-based classification. *Criminal Justice and Behavior* 3(4): 347–65.

Carmines, E., and R. Zeller. 1985. *Reliability and validity assessment.* Beverly Hills: Sage.

Carroll, J., R. Wiener, D. Coates, J. Galegher, and J. Alibrio. 1982. Evaluation, diagnosis, and prediction in parole decision-making. *Law and Society Review* 17: 199–288.

Clear, T. 1988. Statistical prediction in corrections. *Research in Corrections* 1(1): 1–39.

Clear, T., and G. Cole. 1986. *American corrections.* Monterey, CA: Brooks/Cole.

Clements, C. 1981. The future of offender classification: Some cautions and prospects. *Criminal Justice and Behavior* 8(1): 15–35.

———. 1982. The relationship of offender classification to the problems of prison overcrowding. *Crime and Delinquency* 28(1): 72–81.

Clinard, M., and M. Quinney. 1986. *Criminal behavior systems*. Cincinnati: Anderson.

Cohen, F. 1985. Legal issues and the mentally disordered inmate. In *Sourcebook on the mentally disordered prisoner*, U.S. Department of Justice, part 2, 14–30. Washington, DC: Department of Justice.

Cullen, F., and K. Gilbert. 1982. *Reaffirming rehabilitation*. Cincinnati: Anderson.

Cullen, F., S. Skovron, J. Scott and V. Burton. 1990. Public support for correctional treatment: The tenacity of rehabilitative ideology. *Criminal Justice and Behavior* 17(1): 6–18.

Dahlstrom, W., J. Panton, K. Bain, and L. Dahlstrom. 1986. Utility of the Megargee-Bohn MMPI typological assignments: Study with a sample of death row inmates. *Criminal Justice and Behavior* 13(1): 5–17.

Dunford, F., and D. Elliot. 1984. Identifying career offenders using self-reported data. *Journal of Research in Crime and Delinquency* 21(1): 57–86.

Edinger, J. 1979. Cross validation of the Megargee MMPI Typology for prisoners. *Journal of Consulting and Clinical Psychology* 47(2): 234–42.

Edinger, J., and S. Auerbach. 1978. Development and validation of a multidimensional multivariate model for accounting for infractionary behavior in a correctional setting. *Journal of Personality and Social Psychology* 36(12): 1472–89.

Farrington, D. 1987. Predicting individual crime rates. In *Prediction and classification: Criminal justice decision-making*, ed. D. Gottfredson and M. Tonry, 53–101). Chicago: University of Chicago Press.

Farrington, D., and R. Tarling. 1985. *Prediction in criminology*. Albany, NY: State University of New York Press.

Garrett, C. 1985. Effects of residential treatment on adjudicated delinquents: A meta-analysis. *Journal of Research in Crime and Delinquency* 22(4): 287–308.

Gendreau, P., P. Madden, and M. Leipciger. 1980. Predicting recidivism with social history information and a comparison of their predictive power with psychometric variables. *Canadian Journal of Criminology* 22(1): 3–11.

Gendreau, P., and R. Ross. 1987. Revivification of rehabilitation: Evidence from the 1980s. *Justice Quarterly* 4(3): 349–407.

Gibbons, D. 1975. Offender typologies—two decades later. *British Journal of Criminology* 15(2): 140–56.

Glaser, D. 1962. Prediction tables as accounting devices for judges and parole boards. *Crime and Delinquency* 8(4): 239–58.

Gottfredson, D. 1987a. Prediction and classification in criminal justice decision making. In *Prediction and classification: Criminal justice decision-making*, ed. D. Gottfredson and M. Tonry, 1-20. Chicago: University of Chicago Press.

Gottfredson, D., and M. Tonry, eds. 1987. *Prediction and classification: Criminal justice decision-making.* Chicago: University of Chicago Press.

Gottfredson, D., L. Wilkins, and P. Hoffman. 1978. *Guidelines for parole and sentencing.* Lexington, MA: Lexington Books.

Gottfredson, S. 1987b. Prediction: An overview of selected methodological issues. In *Prediction and classification: Criminal justice decision-making,* ed. D. Gottfredson and M. Tonry, 21–51. Chicago: University of Chicago Press.

Grant, M. 1961. A study of conformity in a nonconformist population. Ph.D. diss. University of California at Berkeley.

Grant, D., and M. Grant. 1959. A group dynamics approach to the treatment of nonconformists in the Navy. *Annals of the American Academy of Political and Social Sciences* 371: 126–35.

Greene, R. 1980. *The MMPI: An interpretive manual.* New York: Grune & Stratton.

Greenwood, P., and F. Zimring. 1985. *One more chance: The pursuit of promising strategies for chronic juvenile offenders.* Santa Monica, CA: Rand Corporation.

Hanson, R., C. Moss, R. Hosford, and M. Johnson. 1983. Predicting inmate penitentiary adjustment: An assessment of four classificatory methods. *Criminal Justice and Behavior* 10(3): 293–309.

Harris, P. 1979. The interpersonal maturity of delinquents and nondelinquents. *Dissertation Abstracts International.* University Microfilms. State University of New York at Albany.

———. 1983. The interpersonal maturity of delinquents and non-delinquents. In *Personality Theory, Moral Development, and Criminal Behavior,* ed. W. S. Laufer and J. M. Day. Lexington, MA: Lexington Books.

——— 1988. The Interpersonal Maturity Level Classification System: I-level. *Criminal Justice and Behavior* 15(1): 58-77.

Harvey, O., D. Hunt, and H. Schroder. 1961. *Conceptual systems and personality organization.* New York: John Wiley.

Heide, K. 1982. Classification of offenders ordered to make restitution by Interpersonal Maturity Level and by specific personality dimensions. *Dissertation Abstracts International,* University Microfilms. State University of New York at Albany.

Hirschi, T., and M. Hindelang. 1977. Intelligence and delinquency: A revisionist review. *American Sociological Review* 42(4): 571–87.

Hoffman, P. and J. Beck. 1985. Recidivism among released federal prisoners: Salient Factor Score and five-year follow-up. *Criminal Justice and Behavior* 12(4): 501-7.

Hoffman, P., and B. Stone-Meierhoefer. 1979. Post-release arrest experiences of federal prisoners. *Journal of Criminal Justice* 7(3): 193–216.

Hubbard, R., M. Marden, J. Rachal, H. Harwood, E. Cavanaugh, and H. Ginzburg. 1989. *Drug abuse treatment: A national study of effectiveness.* Chapel Hill, NC: The University of North Carolina Press.

Hunt, D. 1971. *Matching Models in Education: The Coordination of Teaching Methods with Student Characteristics.* Toronto: Ontario Institute for Studies in Education.

Hunt, D., L. Butler, J. Noy, and M. Rosser. 1978. *Assessing Conceptual Level by the Paragraph Completion Method.* Toronto: Ontario Institute for Studies in Education.

Irwin, J. 1980. *Prisons in turmoil.* Toronto: Little, Brown.

Isaac, S., and W. Michael. 1990. *Handbook in research and evaluation.* San Diego: Edits.

Jesness, C. 1971. The Preston typology study: An experiment with differential treatment in an institution. *Journal of Research in Crime and Delinquency* 8(1): 38–52.

———. 1988. Jesness Inventory Classification System. *Criminal Justice and Behavior* 15(1): 78–91.

Jesness, C., and R. Wedge. 1983. *Classifying offenders: The Jesness Inventory Classification System.* Sacramento: California Youth Authority.

Johnson, D, J. Simmons, and B. Gordon. 1983. Temporal consistency of the Meyer-Megargee inmate typology. *Criminal Justice and Behavior* 10(3): 263–68.

Kane, T., and W. Saylor. 1983. *Security designation/custody classification of inmates.* Unpublished manuscript. Washington, DC: Department of Justice.

Karpman, B. 1947, Passive parasitic psychopathy: Toward the personality structure and psychogenesis of idiopathic psychopathy. *Psychoanalysis Review* 34(1): 102–18.

Keck, G. 1978. A study of correlates of the development of Interpersonal Maturity and the Differential Behavioral Classification System of the Juvenile Offender. *Dissertation Abstracts International.* Union Graduate School.

Kohlberg, L. 1958. The developmental modes of moral thinking and choice in the years ten to sixteen. Ph.D. diss. Chicago: University of Chicago Press.

Kohlberg, L., A. Colby, J. Gibbs, B. Speicher-Dubin, and D. Candee. 1978. *Standard form scoring manual.* Cambridge: Harvard University Press.

Laaman v. Helgemoe, 347 F. Supp. 269,275 (1977).

Lerman, P. 1975. *Community treatment and social control: A critical analysis of juvenile correctional policy.* Chicago: University of Chicago Press.

Lester, D., M. Braswell, and P. Van Voorhis. 1991. *Correctional counseling.* Cincinnati: Anderson.

Levinson, R. 1982. A clarification of classification. *Criminal Justice and Behavior* 9(2): 133–42.

———. 1988. Development in the classification process. *Criminal Justice and Behavior* 15(1): 24–38.

Light, S. 1990. Measurement error in official statistics: Prison rule infraction data. *Federal Probation* 54(4): 63–68.

Loeber, R., and T. Dishion. 1983. Early predictors of male delinquency: A review. *Psychological Bulletin* 94(1): 68-99.

Loevinger, J. 1966.The meaning and measurement of Ego Development. *American Psychologist* 21(3): 195–217.

Louscher, P., R. Hosford, and C. Moss. 1983. Predicting dangerous behavior in a penitentiary using the Megargee typology. *Criminal Justice and Behavior* 10(3): 263–68.

McCarthy, B. 1985. Mentally ill and mentally retarded offenders in corrections. In *Sourcebook on the mentally disordered prisoner*, U. S. Department of Justice, part 2, 14–30. Washington, DC: Department of Justice

MacKenzie, D. 1989. Prison classification: The management and psychological perspectives. In *The American prison: Issues in research and policy*, ed. L. Goodstein and D. MacKenzie, 163–189, New York: Plenum Press.

MacKenzie, D, C. Posey, and K. Rapaport. 1988. A theoretical revolution in corrections: Varied purposes for classification. *Criminal Justice and Behavior* 15(1): 125–36.

Maltz, M. 1984. *Recidivism*. New York: Academic Press.

Martinson, R. 1974. What works?—Questions and answers about prison reform. *Public Interest* 35(1): 22–54.

Matza, D. 1964. *Delinquency and drift*. New York: John Wiley.

Meehl, P. 1954. *Clinical vs. Statistical Prediction*. Minneapolis: University of Minnesota Press.

Megargee, E. 1972. Standardized reports of work performance and inmate adjustment for use in correctional settings. *Correctional Psychologist* 5(1): 48–54.

Megargee, E., and M. Bohn. 1979. *Classifying criminal offenders: A new system based on the MMPI*. Beverly Hills: Sage.

Megargee, E., and J. Carbonnel. 1986. Predicting prison adjustment with the MMPI: A summary of three studies. *Differential View* 14: 8-15.

Monahan, J. 1981. *Predicting violent behavior: An assessment of clinical techniques*. Beverly Hills: Sage.

Morash, M., and L. Rucker. 1990. A critical look at the idea of boot camp as a correctional reform. *Crime and Delinquency* 36(2): 204–222.

Moss, C., M. Johnson, and R. Hosford. 1984. An assessment of the Megargee Typology in lifelong criminal violence. *Criminal Justice and Behavior* 11(2): 225–34.

Motiuk, L. 1984. *Offender classification systems: Psychometric properties*. Ph.D. diss. Carleton University.

Motiuk, L., J. Bonta, and D. Andrews. 1986. Classification in correctional halfway houses: The relative and incremental predictive criterion validities of the Megargee-MMPI and LSI systems, *Criminal Justice and Behavior* 13(1): 33–46.

National Institute of Corrections (NIC). 1982. *Classification: Principles, models, and guidelines*. Washington, DC: Department of Justice.

Palmagiano v. Garrahy, 443 F. Supp. 956 (1977).

Palmer, T. 1974. The Youth Authority's Community Treatment Project. *Federal Probation* 38(1): 3-13.

————. 1978. *Correctional intervention and research: Current issues and future prospects.* Lexington, MA: Lexington Books.

————. 1992. *The reemergence of correctional intervention: Developments through the 1980s and prospects for the future.* Beverly Hills: Sage.

Palmer, T., and E. Werner. 1972. A review of I-level reliability and accuracy in the Community Treatment Project. Unpublished manuscript. Sacramento, CA: California Youth Authority.

Petersilia, J. 1991. The value of corrections research: Learning what works. *Federal Probation* 55(2): 24–26.

Poole, E., and R. Regoli. 1980. Race, institutional rule breaking and disciplinary response: A study of discretionary decision-making in prison. *Law and Society Review* 14(4): 931–46.

Posey, C. 1988. Introduction. *Criminal Justice and Behavior* 15(1): 5-7.

Public Agenda Foundation. 1987. *Crime and punishment: The public's view.* New York: Edna McConnell Clark Foundation.

Pugh v. Locke, 406 F. Supp. 318 (1977).

Quay, H. 1983. *Technical manual for the Behavioral Classifications System for Adult Offenders.* Washington, DC: Department of Justice.

————. 1984. *Managing adult inmates: Classification for housing and program assignments.* College Park, MD: American Correctional Association.

Quay, H., and L. Parsons. 1972. *The differential behavioral classification of the juvenile offender.* Washington, DC: Department of Justice.

Radloff, L. 1977. CESD Scale: A self-report depression scale for research in the general population. *Applied Psychological Measurement* 1: 385–401.

Reitsma-Street, M. 1984. Differential treatment of young offenders: A review of the Conceptual Level Matching Model. *Canadian Journal of Criminology* 26(2): 199–212.

Reitsma-Street, M., and A. Leschied. 1988 The Conceptual Matching Model in corrections. *Criminal Justice and Behavior* 15(1): 92–108.

Rest, J. 1976. New approaches in the assessment of moral development. In *Moral development and behavior: Theory, research, and social issues,* ed. T. Lickona, 198–218. New York: Holt, Rinehart, and Winston.

Rothman, D. 1980. *Conscience and convenience.* Boston: Little, Brown.

Samenow, S. 1984. *Inside the criminal mind.* New York: Times Books.

Sawyer, J. 1966. Measurement and prediction, clinical and statistical. *Psychological Bulletin* 66(3): 178-200.

Schafer, N. 1984. Prisoner behavior, staff response: Using prison discipline records. Paper presented at the annual meeting of the Academy of Criminal Justice Sciences, Chicago.

Schneider, A. 1990. Offender Classification and Prediction of Criminal Behavior Program. Report to the NIJ grantees' meeting, April, Tempe, AZ.

Schrink, J. 1991. Understanding the correctional counselor. In *Correctional counseling*, ed. D. Lester, M. Braswell, and P. Van Voorhis, 41–55. Cincinnati: Anderson.

Schur, E. 1971. *Labeling deviant behavior*. New York: Harper and Row.

Sechrest, L. 1987. Classification for treatment. In *Prediction and classification: Criminal justice decision-making*, ed. D. Gottfredson and M. Tonry, 293–322. Chicago: University of Chicago Press.

Shipley, W. 1940. A self-administering scale for measuring intellectual impairment and deterioration. *Journal of Psychology* 9(2): 371–77.

Solomon, H. 1977. *Crime and delinquency: Typologies*. Washington, DC: University Press of America.

Sullivan, C., M. Q. Grant, and D. Grant. 1957. The development of Interpersonal Maturity: An application to delinquency. *Psychiatry* 20: 373–86.

Sullivan, J., and S. Feldman. 1979. *Multiple indicators: An introduction*. Beverly Hills:

Sykes, G. 1958. *The society of captives*. Princeton: Princeton University Press.

Toch, H. 1977. *Living in prison*. New York: Free Press.

———. 1981. Inmate classification as a transaction. *Criminal Justice and Behavior* 8(1): 3-14.

Toch, H., K. Adams, and D. Grant. 1989. *Coping: Maladaptation in prisons*. New Brunswick: Transaction.

Van Voorhis, P. 1984. Psychological classification of the adult, male, maximum security inmate; Applications of the MMPI, I-Level, Conceptual Level, and Moral Judgment. Paper presented at the annual meeting of the American Society of Criminology, Cincinnati.

———. 1987. Correctional effectiveness: The high cost of ignoring success. *Federal Probation* 51(1): 56-62.

———. 1988. A cross-classification of five offender typologies: Issues of construct and predictive validity. *Criminal Justice and Behavior* 15(1): 24–38.

———. 1990. A comparison of five psychological classification systems among adult, male prison inmates. Paper presented at the annual meeting of the American Society of Criminology, Baltimore.

———. 1991. Offender classification as a tool for effective treatment, decision-making, and supervision. In *Correctional counseling*, ed. D. Lester, M. Braswell, and P. Van Voorhis, 73–92. Cincinnati, Anderson.

———. (forthcoming). A multiple-indicators approach to measuring the prison experience. *Justice Quarterly*.

Vold, G. 1980. *Theoretical criminology* 2d ed. New York: Oxford University Press.

von Hirsch, A. 1985. *Past or future crimes; Deservedness and dangerousness in the sentencing of criminals*. New Brunswick: Rutgers University Press.

Walters, G.,T. Scapansky, and G. Marlow. 1986. The emotionally disturbed military criminal offender: Identification, background, and institutional adjustment. *Criminal Justice and Behavior* 13(3): 261–85.

Warren, M. 1969. The case for differential treatment of delinquents. *Annals of the American Academy of Political and Social Science* 381(1): 47-59.

————. 1971. Classification of offenders as an aid to efficient management and effective treatment. *Journal of Criminal Law, Criminology and Police Science* 62(1): 239–68.

————. 1976. Interventions with juvenile delinquents. In *Pursuing justice for the child*, ed. M. Rosenheim, 176–204. Chicago: University of Chicago Press.

————. 1983. Applications of Interpersonal Maturity Theory to offender populations. In *Personality Theory, Moral Development, and Criminal Behavior*, ed. W. S. Laufer and J. M. Day, 23-50. Lexington, MA: Lexington Books.

Warren, M., and M. Hindelang. 1979. Current explanations of offender behavior. In *Psychology of Crime and Criminal Justice*, ed. H. Toch, 166–182. New York: Holt, Rinehart, and Winston.

Warren, M., and Staff of the Community Treatment Project. 1966. *Interpersonal Maturity Level classification: Diagnosis and treatment of low, middle, and high maturity delinquents*. Sacramento: California Youth Authority.

Wechsler, D. 1955. *Manual for the Wechsler Adult Intelligence Scale*. New York: Psychological Corp.

————. 1981. *Manual for the Wechsler Adult Intelligence Scale*. New York: Psychological Corp.

Werner, E. 1975. Relationships among Interpersonal Maturity, personality configurations, intelligence, and ethnic status. *British Journal of Criminology* 15(1): 51-68.

Wright, K. 1988. The relationship of risk, needs, and personality classification systems and prison adjustment. *Criminal Justice and Behavior* 15(4): 454–71.

Wright, K., T. Clear, and P. Dickson. 1984. Universal application of probation risk-assessment instruments: A critique. *Criminology* 22(1) 113–34.

Wrobel, N., T. Wrobel, and J. McIntosh. 1988. Application of the Megargee MMPI Typology to a forensic psychiatric population. *Criminal Justice and Behavior* 15(2): 247–54.

Zachary, R., E. Crumpton, and D. Spiegel. 1985. Estimating WAIS IQ from the Shipley Institute of Living Scale. *Journal of Clinical Psychology* 41(4): 532-540.

Zachary, R., M. Paulson, and R. Gorsuch. 1985. Estimating WAIS IQ from the Shipley Institute of Living Scale using continuously adjusted age norms. *Journal of Clinical Psychology* 41(6): 832–33.

Zager, L. 1983. Response to Simmons and associates: Conclusions about the MMPI-based classification system's stability are premature. *Criminal Justice and Behavior* 10(3): 310–15.

————. 1988. MMPI-based criminal classification system: A review, current status, and future directions. *Criminal Justice and Behavior* 15(1): 39–57.

NAME INDEX

Page numbers in italics indicate figures; page numbers followed by n indicate notes.

353

SUBJECT INDEX

Page numbers in italics indicate figures; page numbers followed by n indicate notes; page numbers followed by t indicate tables.

9980